Praise for *The Trinity and the Spirit*

"Robert Jenson's contribution to the multi-authored *Christian Dogmatics* in the early 1980s has always been the most under-rated part of his corpus, for the simple reason that few readers ever happened upon it. This stand-alone republication is there-fore a gift to all readers of Jenson, whether seasoned veterans or those new to this great American theologian. The whole work is worthy of one's attention, but the section on the Holy Spirit is alone worth the price of the book. The ongoing reception of Jenson's thought will be bolstered by having his full pneuma-tology ready to hand, and the church will be edified once more by a pastor, scholar, and doctor of the sacred page whose love for the Lord and for his bride suffused all that he said and did, to the very end of his life."

—Brad East, assistant professor of theology,
Abilene Christian University

"Robert Jenson's thinking about the Trinity has been an exceed-ingly potent force in Christian theology for more than a gener-ation, not least for the novel roles he assigns to the Holy Spirit in the Trinity. These two essays present with particular clarity and in all their raw originality the ideas that would later serve as the basis for Jenson's influential *Systematic Theology*. Whether one agrees with him or not—in fact especially if one does not—these essays are a uniquely stimulating provocation to theolog-ical reflection about the most basic matters of Christian faith."

—Bruce D. Marshall, Lehman Professor
of Christian Doctrine, Perkins School of
Theology at Southern Methodist University

The Trinity and the Spirit

The Trinity and the Spirit

TWO ESSAYS FROM CHRISTIAN DOGMATICS

Robert W. Jenson

Fortress Press
Minneapolis

THE TRINITY AND THE SPIRIT
Two Essays from *Christian Dogmatics*

Cover design and illustration: Brad Norr Design

Print ISBN: 978-1-5064-8812-7
eBook ISBN: 978-1-5064-8813-4

Contents

Publisher's Note

Originally published in 1984, the landmark two-volume *Christian Dogmatics* became a touchstone reference volume for generations of seminarians, pastors, and scholars. The present volume collects two major essays by Robert W. Jenson from that project in the hope of reintroducing them to a new generation of readers.

Part I

The Triune God

Introduction

The dogmatic *locus* about God is not and cannot be a description of God, though it often intends to state facts about God. Nor is the *locus* on God a piece of metaphysics, though it will raise and try to answer metaphysical questions. The dogmatic *locus* about God is a convenient gathering of certain questions that regularly arise in the Christian church, those that are most straightforwardly about God. These do, of course, turn out to have systematic relations to each other, and tracing these is a main task of dogmatics. But the specific set of questions that coalesce to make the *locus* "on God" is more the fruit of liturgical and catechetical history than of timeless logic.

The primary religious question is always about the identity of God: *Which* is God? Of history's putative or possible deities, which will sustain the claim? To whom may I—do I—pray?

Within biblical faith or within culture influenced by it, the question *whether* there is God can also acquire religious potency, for biblical faith poses the possibility of nihilism, of absolute distrust of reality, as not all religion does. And as long as it appears that there is only one plausible candidate for deity, that the biblical God's only competitors are such straw gods as "money" or "the belly," the awful issue between faith and nihilism is the first to claim attention. If we are sure who would be God if there were any, "Is there God?" heads our perplexity.

But history has already made clear that the "post-Christian era" will not be one of efficient and religionless secularity, but a combination of nihilist communal life, whether collectivist or chaotic, with a compensating efflorescence of non-Christian private religions. In the immediate future, Western streets will present a new divine claimant on every corner, as did those of the declining ancient world, and we will first have to make clear to ourselves which one we mean by "God" before we wager God's reality. In a religiously plural age, the question of God's identity reasserts its natural priority.

The question of *what* God is like cannot fruitfully be taken first. The big theological words—"salvific," "merciful," and so on—share a logical peculiarity: They are so determinedly analogous and open to interpretation that by themselves they mean almost nothing. "X redeems," for example, is not even an ordinary open sentence making a specific assertion about an unspecified subject, for until X is specified we do not know what "redeems" says about her/it/him. Only when "Baal," for example, replaces X does "redeems" acquire the operational value "sends rain." A theology of no-god-in-particular or of all-gods-at-once would be, if not quite vacuous, wholly unhelpful. Prior to identification of God, all that can be said about it/him/her is "God is the object of ultimate concern" or "God is whatever you hang your heart on." The most that "X redeems" could mean is "X restores whatever state X defines as good." A doctrine that went no further would be of purely analytical use and no religious use.

We begin, therefore, and spend most of our space, with the *identity* of the gospel's God, and discuss the existence and nature of God afterward. That is, we begin with "the doctrine of the Trinity," for within Christian theology it is the identification of God which this body of teaching seeks to accomplish.[1] In following this order, we follow a minority tradition of dogmatics;[2] the minority, we claim, is right.

We must next note that the doctrine of the Trinity is no one teaching or homogeneous set of teachings, as is, for example, the doctrine of justification by faith alone. It is a complex of expressions of various forms and various relations to the identification of God. We distinguish four bodies of trinitarian discourse. Their classification makes the gross outline of the part of the following devoted to trinitarian doctrine (Chapters 1–4). Allotment of space among the four reflects relative complexity, not relative importance.

The doctrine of the Trinity is moribund in large sections of the church; indeed, it often serves as a prized example of useless theological hairsplitting. The book perhaps most frequently used in Protestant seminaries for instruction in systematic theology, Gustaf Aulen's *Faith of the Christian Church*, scarcely mentions the matter, and what it does say is inaccurate.[3] Other standard works are more informative, but little more helpful in seeing the point and vivacity of trinitarian language.[4] Such positive works as Leonard Hodgson's *The Doctrine of the Trinity*, Claude Welch's *In This Name*, or even Karl Rahner's pioneering *The Trinity* have not had the impact that might have been expected.[5] And when a "Trinity" is affirmed, it is often that of John Macquarrie or Paul Tillich, an interesting fruit of speculation but only distantly related to the church's trinitarianism here to be discussed. In general, such an enterprise as that of the present essay is a minority report in the present church.

It is to be feared that modern incomprehension of trinitarian discourse often expresses a morbidity of the faith itself; against this, dogmatics as such can do little. Error and incompleteness, both in the inherited body of trinitarian teaching and in current standard theological suppositions, play the chief role. We hope to make several contributions to overcoming these, but one suspects that the sheer bulk of inherited trinitarian discourse, of various functions and from various mostly distant times and places, also makes it hard simply to grasp what all this stuff is for. It is to the aid of this last perplexity that the organization of Chapters 1 through 4 was adopted, attempting to sort the mass of trinitarian language.

From discussion of God's triune identity, we must continue to the questions traditionally discussed as the doctrine of "the one God": what God is, whether God is, what God is like. The more clearly and dialectically specific our talk of God is, the more drastically—but perhaps also hopefully—it will in our time be challenged. The acids of modernity attack every aspect of belief. Is it even meaningful to talk of God? Is there any reason to affirm God's reality? Is it not rather evil or absurdity that is God, rather than fatherly goodness? And how do we find out what to think about God anyway? Would it not be better simply to adore God in silence or by meaningless speech?

It cannot be the task of dogmatics to complete faith's response to all challenges, but dogmatics can make a necessary contribution. In the course of theological history, three bodies of teaching have developed which seek to explicate the single reality of God. By no accident, each does in fact respond to an aspect of the modern perplexity. By no accident—for the questions just recited are historically faith's own questions, merely now reflected back in secularized form.

Doubt that talk about God makes sense is pervasive through the modern period. In the modern theological tradition, analysis of the logic of theological language has become an enterprise of its own. In response to this development, this book contains a separate *locus* on the knowledge of God, where direct discussion of the meaningfulness of God-language will be found. But the logical oddity of talk about God is not as such a modern discovery. Theology traditionally discussed it in the material mode and asked: What kind of "being" is God? How am I using "is" when I say "God is such-and-such"? These investigations have often led and may yet again lead to important material assertions about God and must therefore be pursued also in this *locus*, as Chapter 5.

The more or less biblical God of Western religion was long the only serious candidate among us. Just so, there has long been a standard topic: whether it is reasonable to think that God is. This question is often part of the present *locus*, but in this work it will be discussed in the next, epistemological, *locus* and is therefore omitted here.

Finally, since theologians must make sentences of the form "God is such-and-such," they must be concerned not only with the "is" but also with the such-and-such, with the predicate. What should we say about God? And why should we say one thing instead of another? Such questions make the problem about what are traditionally called the attributes of God and are here discussed in Chapter 6.

CHAPTER ONE

The Triune Name of God

In functional continuity with biblical witness, "Father, Son, and Holy Spirit" is the proper name of the church's God. That God have a proper name is a demand of both the Hebrew Scriptures and the New Testament gospel. That God has this proper name is an immediate reflex of primary Christian experience.

The Sense of "God"

What can be said prior to God's identification must, to be sure, be said. What do people use this word "God" for, that we ask so urgently to whom or what it is truly applied?

The horizon of life and its concerns is time, the inescapable already, no-more, still, and not-yet of all we know and will. Every human act moves from what was to what is to be; it is carried and filled by tradition but intends new creation. Just so our acts hang between past and future, to be in fact temporal, to be the self-transcendence, the inherent and inevitable adventure, that is the theme of all religion and philosophy. But also, our acts threaten to fall between past and future, to become boring or fantastic or both, and all life threatens to become an unplotted sequence of merely causally joined events that happen to befall an actually impersonal entity, "me."

Human life is possible—or, in recent jargon, meaningful—only if past and future are somehow bracketed, only if their disconnection is somehow transcended, only if our lives somehow cohere to make a story. Life in time is possible only if there is such a bracket, that is, if there is eternity. Thus in all we do we seek eternity. If our seeking becomes explicit, we practice "religion."

If our religion perceives the bracket around time as in any way a particular something, as in any way the possible subject of verbs (as in, e.g., "The eternal speaks by the prophets"), we tend to say "God" instead of "eternity."

But already we are becoming intolerably indefinite, for manifestly there are many kinds of bracketing that can be posited around past and future, many possible eternities. There is, for example, the eternity of tribal ancestors who have become so old that nothing can surprise them anymore and in whose continuing presence all the future's putative novelties are therefore mastered by traditional maxims. There is the eternity of nirvana, where a difference of past and future is just not permitted. There is the eternity of existentialism, in which decision brings time momentarily to a halt. So multiform is eternity that the mere assertion that it is, that there is some union of past and future, that life has some meaning, is for practice as good as the suspicion that there is none at all. Life is enabled not by a posit *that* life means but by a posit of *what* it means. The plot and energy of life are determined by which eternity we rely on, and the truth of any mode of life is determined by the reality of the eternity it posits. If we speak of "God," our life's substance is given by which God we worship, and our life's truth is given by whether this is the God that really is.

Meditating on the foundation of biblical faith, the exodus, Israel's first theologians made Moses' decisive question be: "If I come to the people of Israel and say to them, 'The God of your fathers has sent me to you,' and they ask me, 'What is his name?' what shall I say to them?" If Israel was to risk the future of this God, to leave secure nonexistence in Egypt and venture on God's promises, Israel had first and fundamentally to know which future this was. The God answered, "Say this to the people of Israel, [Yahweh], the God of your fathers, the God of Abraham, the God of Isaac, and the God of Jacob, has sent me to you, this is my name for ever, and thus I am to be remembered throughout all generations" (Exod. 3:13–15).[1]

The answer provides a proper name, "Yahweh." It also provides what logicians now call an identifying description, a descriptive phrase or clause, or set of them, that fits just the one individual thing to be identified. Here the description is "the God whom Abraham and Isaac and Jacob worshiped." The more usual description is that found in a parallel account a few chapters later: God said to Moses, "Say . . . to the people of Israel, 'I am [Yahweh], and I will bring you out from under the burdens of the Egyptians . . . ; and you shall know that I am [Yahweh] your God, *who* has brought you out. . . . I am [Yahweh]'" (Exod. 6:2–7; emphasis added).

In general, proper names work only if such identifying descriptions are at hand. We may say, "Mary is coming to dinner," and be answered with, "Who is Mary?" Then we must be able to say, "Mary is the one who lives in apartment 2C, and is always so cheerful, and . . . ," continuing until the questioner says, "Oh, *that* one!" We may say, "Yahweh always forgives," and be answered with, "Do you mean the Inner Self?" Then we must be able to say, "No. We mean the one who rescued Israel from Egypt, and. . . ."

Linguistic means of identification—proper names, identifying descriptions, or both—are a necessity of religion. Prayers, like other requests and praises, must be addressed. Thus the typical prayer-form of Western Christianity, the collect, usually begins with some identifying description such as, "O God, who didst give thine only-begotten Son to be. . . ." The moral will of God must be proclaimed as a particular will if we are to follow it. Paul set a pattern for Christian preaching when he wrote to the Philippians: "Have this mind among yourselves, which you have in Christ Jesus, who . . ." (Phil. 2:1–11). Eschatological promise must be specified. Proclamation of a final union of humankind is gospel because the gathering is to be around Jesus, but it would be quite something else were the gathering to be around Stalin. It was precisely the wrong address of praise in which Paul saw the perversion of heathendom (Rom. 1:24–25).

Trinitarian discourse is Christianity's effort to identify the God who has claimed us. The doctrine of the Trinity comprises both a proper name, "Father, Son, and Holy Spirit," in several

grammatical variants, and an elaborate development and analysis of corresponding identifying descriptions.

We live in the present; that is a tautology. But the content
of present life is memory and expectation, in some union. We
speak of "God" to name that union. Or rather, we speak to and
from God to invoke it. Just so, we need to know who God is, to
know how our lives hang together. Trinitarian discourse is
Christianity's answer to this need.

Israel's Identification of God

What the word "Yahweh" may once have meant we do not know.
Since historical Israel did not know either, the loss is not theologically great. "Yahweh" was for Israel a pure proper name which
no doubt had once been applied on account of its sense but had
survived the knowledge thereof.[2] Indeed, in the famous passage
in which Moses asks for an explanation of the name, Yahweh is
depicted as replying with a play on an ad hoc etymology precisely to reject such curiosity: "I am who I am" (Exod. 3:14).[3]

It is remarkable that "Yahweh," with its variants, was the
only proper name in ordinary use for Israel's God. Other
substantives, predominantly "Elohim," were used as common terms and appellatives. Other ancient peoples piled up
divine names.[4] The comprehensiveness of a god's authority
was achieved by blurring the god's particularity, by identification of initially distinct numina with one another, leading
to a grandly vague deity-in-general. Israel made the opposite
move. Israel's salvation depended precisely on unambiguous identification of its God over against the generality of the
numinous. In the Yahwistic account of Yahweh's decisive self-
revelation at Mount Sinai, the central passage is "And [Yahweh]
descended . . . and proclaimed the name [Yahweh] . . . : '[Yah-
weh, Yahweh], a God merciful and gracious'" (Exod. 34:5–6),
as gods in general could not be supposed to be. Therefore it was
included in Israel's fundamental description of righteousness,
the ten commandments, that Israel must not demean the name
of Yahweh (Exod. 20:7).

A proper place for prayer, sacrifice, or consultation of the oracles was therefore one where the name Yahweh was known (Exod. 20:24). What happens at such a holy place can be compendiously described as "calling on the name [Yahweh]" (e.g., Gen. 12:8). Blessings are "applications" of the name Yahweh (e.g., Num. 6:27), and prayers are addressed by it (e.g., 1 Kings 18:24). The worshipers' use of "Yahweh" is their reason for confidence that their offering will be acceptable and their petitions heard (e.g., Pss. 20:1–3; 25:11), for those who know God's name are God's people, to whom God is committed. When God did not want to be grasped, he withheld his name (Gen. 32:30); the heathen are heathen just because they do not know it (Ps. 79:6).

To go with the name, Israel necessarily had identifying descriptions. At the very foundation of Israel's life, the introduction to the basic Torah of the ten commandments, the two are neatly side by side: "I am [Yahweh], your God, who brought you out of the land of Egypt" (Exod. 20:2). There were many descriptions that could be used to identify Yahweh, but this one, the narrative of Exodus, was that on which Israel's faith hung.[5] The exodus was the chief content of Israel's creed: "And you shall make response before [Yahweh] your God, A wandering Aramean was my father; and he went down into Egypt. . . . And the Egyptians treated us harshly and afflicted us. . . . Then we cried to [Yahweh] . . . , and [Yahweh] brought us out of Egypt with a mighty hand . . . and he brought us into this place and gave us this land'" (Deut. 26:5–9; see also Josh. 24:2ff.) The entire narrative of the Hebrew Scriptures is probably best understood as an expanded version of the creedal narrative just cited.[6] And the whole Torah was explication of the exodus' consequences: "You have seen what I did to the Egyptians, and how I. . . . brought you to myself. Now therefore . . ." (Exod. 19:4ff.) To the question "Whom do you mean, 'God'?" Israel answered, "Whoever got us out of Egypt."

The act of calling God by name was in Israel so tremendous that, as the identification of the true God over against other claimants ceased to be a daily challenge, and use of the name therefore ceased to be a daily necessity, actual pronunciation of the name ceased, at least for all but the mightiest occasions.[7] This is reflected in the pointing of "YHWH" in our Hebrew text with the vowel points for "Adonai" (Lord) as a signal to speak this word instead, and in the Septuagint translation of "Yahweh" by Kyrios.

Identifying God in the New Testament

The gospel of the New Testament is the provision of a new identifying description for this same God. The coming-to-apply of this new description is the event, witness to which is the whole point of the New Testament. God, in the gospel, is "whoever raised Jesus from the dead."[8]

Identification of God by the resurrection did not replace identification by the exodus; it is essential to the God who raised Jesus that he is the same one who freed Israel. But the new thing that is the content of the gospel is that God has now identified himself also as "him that raised from the dead Jesus our Lord" (Rom. 4:24). In the New Testament such phrases become the standard way of referring to God.[9]

To go with this new identifying description there are not so much new names as new kinds of naming. "Yahweh" does not reappear as a name in use. The habit of saying "Lord" instead has buried it too deeply under the appellative.[10] But in the church's missionary situation, actual use of a proper name in speaking of God is again necessary in a variety of contexts. It is the naming of Jesus that occurs for all such functions. Exorcism, healing, and indeed good works generally are accomplished "in Jesus' name" (e.g., Mark 9:37ff., par.). Church discipline and quasi-discipline are carried out by sentences pronounced in Jesus' name (e.g., 1 Cor. 1:10), and forgiveness is pronounced in the same way (e.g., 1 John 2:12). Baptism is described as into Jesus' name (e.g., Acts 2:38), whether or not it was ever actually performed with this formula. Undergoing such baptism is equated with that calling on the name "Yahweh" by which, according to Joel 3:5, Israel is to be saved (Acts 2:21, 38). Above all, perhaps, prayer is "in Jesus' name" (e.g., John 14:13–14), in consequence of which the name can be posited as the very object of faith (e.g., John 1:12). Believers are those "who call on the name of our Lord Jesus Christ" (e.g., Acts 9:14).

So dominant was the use of the name "Jesus" in the religious life of the apostolic church that the whole mission can be described as proclamation "in his name" (Luke 24:47), "preaching good news about the kingdom of God and the name of Jesus Christ" (Acts 8:12), indeed, as "carrying" Jesus' name to the people (e.g., Acts 9:15). The gatherings of the congregations can be described as "giving thanks . . . in the name of our Lord Jesus Christ" (Eph. 5:20), indeed, simply as meetings in his name (Matt. 18:20). Where faith must be confessed over against the hostility of society, this is "confession of the name" (e.g., Mark 13:13). The theological conclusion was drawn in such praises as the hymn preserved in Philippians in which God's own eschatological triumph is evoked as cosmic obeisance to the name "Jesus" (Phil. 1:10), or in such formulas as that in Acts which makes Jesus' name the agent of salvation (Acts 4:12). However various groups in the primal church may have conceived Jesus' relation to God, "Jesus" was the way they all invoked God.

One other new naming appears in the New Testament, the triune name: "Father, Son, and Holy Spirit." Its appearance is undoubtedly dependent on naming God by naming Jesus, as just discussed, but the causal connections are no longer recoverable. It is of course toward this name that we have been steering. That the biblical God must have a proper name, we have seen in the Hebrew Scriptures. In the life of the primal church, God is named by uses that involve the name of Jesus. "Father, Son, and Spirit" is the naming of this sort that historically triumphed.

"Father, Son, and Holy Spirit" as Proper Name

That "Father, Son, and Holy Spirit" in fact occupies in the church the place occupied in Israel by "Yahweh" or, later, "Lord" even hasty observation of the church's life must discover.[11] Why it came to be so is the matter of the next chapter; for now we register the fact. Our services begin and are punctuated with "In the

name of the Father, Son, and Holy Spirit." Our prayers conclude,
"In his name who with you and the Holy Spirit is. . . ." Above all,
the act by which people are brought both into the fellowship of
believers and into their fellowship with God is an initiation "into
the name 'Father, Son, and Holy Spirit.'"

The habit of trinitarian naming is universal through the life
of the church. How far back it goes, we cannot tell. It certainly
goes further back than even the faintest traces of trinitarian
reflection, and it appears to have been an immediate expression
of believers' experience of God. It is in liturgy, when we talk
not *about* God but to and for him, that we need and use God's
name, and that is where the trinitarian formulas appear, both
initially and to this day.[12] In the immediately postapostolic literature there is no use of a trinitarian formula as a piece of theology or in such fashion as to depend on antecedent development
in theology, yet the formula is there. Its home is in the liturgy, in
baptism and the eucharist. There its use was regularly seen as
the heart of the matter.[13]

There are two New Testament occurrences of a trinitarian
name-formula. The earliest is the closing benediction of Paul's
second letter to Corinth (2 Cor. 13:14). The epistolary benedictions of the New Testament reflect epistolary custom, liturgy,
and no doubt personal style. They occur in the opening saluta-
tions and at the closing. If we sort them out, there is a surprising result. The opening benedictions all name both "God the
Father" and "the Lord Jesus Christ." The closing benedictions—
with one exception—either name no one and are simple wishes
of "grace," or name only the Lord Jesus. Moreover, the naming of
the Lord Jesus occurs in all and only the authentic letters of Paul
and is obviously Paul's idiosyncrasy. Then suddenly, in one
Pauline letter (and that neither the earliest nor the latest) a trinitarian naming replaces the naming of the Lord Jesus only: "The
grace of the Lord Jesus Christ and the love of God and the fellowship of the Holy Spirit be with you all."

These circumstances prohibit all thought of development
from one-membered to two-membered to three-membered
formulas.[14] As far as the texts let us see, all forms are equally

immediate,[15] the choice depending on epistolary custom. The particular trinitarian formula that ends 2 Corinthians looks very much like Paul's creation of the moment, apropos of nothing special in the letter and done only because it was natural to do. The purely christological benediction that was Paul's habit ("The grace of our Lord Jesus Christ be with you") expands in both directions by its own logic. Or if Paul did not create it here, he took it from liturgical use in the same unmotivated and obvious fashion.

The most important New Testament trinitarian naming is the Matthean baptismal commission (Matt. 28:19). Baptism is the church's chief sacrament, its rite of passage from old reality to new. Within such a rite, the new reality must be identified, for the neophytes must be directed into it. In baptism, as often elsewhere, this is done by naming the God whose reality it is. The name stipulated in the canonical rubric for baptismal liturgy is "Father, Son, and Holy Spirit."[16]

It is often supposed that the tripartite baptismal formula developed from unitary or bipartite formulas: "In Jesus' name" or "In the name of God and of the Lord Jesus." There is evidence from the second century of baptism with such formulas. But as to an origin of the trinitarian formula from these, there is no evidence.[17] In any case, the tripartite formula was soon there, and it is the only one in the New Testament.

The trinitarian name did not fall from heaven. It was made by believers for the God with whom we have found ourselves involved. "Father" was Jesus' peculiar address to the particular transcendence over against whom he lived.[18] Just by this address he qualified himself as "the Son," and in the memory of the primal church his acclamation as Son was the beginning of faith.[19] "Spirit" was the term provided by the whole biblical theology for what comes of such a meeting between this God and a special human of his. It is involvement in this structure of Jesus' own event—prayer to the "Father" with "the Son" in the power of and for "the Spirit"—that is faith's knowledge of God. Thus "Father, Son, and Holy Spirit" summarizes faith's apprehension of God; this is the matter of the next chapter. But in the event so summarizable, "Father, Son, and Holy Spirit" came together also simply as a name for the one therein apprehended, and apparently did so before all analysis of its suitability.

One further matter must be discussed here: the masculinity of "Father." Emerging consciousness of the historic oppression of women rightly watches for expressions thereof also, or perhaps principally, in inherited interpretations of God. When such are found, Christianity has every reason to eliminate them. We will in fact find a decisive area where male sexism has shaped the structure of doctrine. Trinitarian Father-language cannot, however, be one such; and the widely spread supposition that it is reflects a breakdown of linguistic and doctrinal knowledge and judgment.

The church's trinitarian naming incorporates Jesus' filial address to God. That Jesus called God "Abba," which can only be translated "Father," must settle the matter for trinitarian naming, since it is Jesus' historical reality that created the name. But of course, that we may not substitute for "Father" in the triune name may only mean that the whole name is irremediably offensive. Nor can the use of "Father" within the trinitarian name be altogether separated from its more general use in Christian speech to and about God.

For filial address to God, the choice of words is limited, for us as for Jesus. "Parent" and its natural or artificial equivalents cannot be regular filial terms of address because they do not individuate. That leaves "mother" and "father." It is decisive for Israel's God that we are not of God's own substance, that God's role as our parent is not sexual, that God is not even metaphorically a fertility God.[20] The choice between "Mother" and "Father," as terms of filial address to God, was and must be made according to which term is more easily separable from the reproductive role.

Sexuality, as the union of sensuality and differentiated reproductive roles and apparatus, is the glory of our specific humanity. It is the way in which our directedness *to* each other, both among those now living and between generations—and that precisely by differences between us—is built into our bodies, into our sheer created givenness. Moreover, within the mutuality of male and female, the female is ontologically superior. She is the more ineradicably human, for while sensuality and reproduction can socially be ripped apart in the male, by alienating economic or political structures, not even abortion can do this to the female—short, of course, of the "brave new world" or of humankind's decision to die out. In societies that value members by especially inhuman standards, as in capitalist or technocratic-socialist societies that value only by contribution to the gross national product, the female's human superiority will indeed cause suffering, and many will understandably seek to be rid of it.

In religions where the direct religious analogy from human perfection to divine perfection is undisturbed, the female gender has therefore usually been religiously dominant, even in otherwise male-dominated societies. The whole of Christianity's soteriology can be summarized in the observation that in it this analogy is broken. Vice versa, it is just the ontological inferiority of the male that offers "Father" rather than "Mother" as the proper term of address to Israel's sexually transcendent God, when a filial term is needed.

That the biblical God is sexually transcendent does not, of course, mean that God is less than sexual, but rather that what we are by sexual differentiation God is without the various relations of more and less which sexual differentiation indeed involves. That Jesus, and we after him, have called God "Father" thus involves no valuing of masculinity above femininity. On the contrary, it is the only available way to satisfy the determination of Israel and the church to attribute neither to God. As for "Father and Mother," which incredibly has actually been used in services wishing to be Christian, it is most objectionable of all since by insisting on both it makes the attribution of sexual roles entirely inescapable and repristinates the deepest fertility myth, that of divine androgyny. The biblical God is not both our begetter and our bearer; he is neither.

In general, the assumption that it is a deprivation not to address God in one's very own gender is a case of humankind's

general religious assumption of direct analogy from human perfections to divine qualities. In the faith of the Bible, this direct
line is, for our salvation, broken. All speech about God is of
course, in a commonsensical way, by analogy. But the gospel is
free to take its analogies sometimes from human perfections and
sometimes from human imperfections, depending on theological need. Sometimes it takes them from death and sin. If we
must, irrelevantly, worry about whether calling God "Father" is
praise or dispraise of earthly fathers, the answer, in the structure
of Christian language-use, must be that it will be in some contexts the one and in some contexts the other.

The Triune Name as Dogma

So far we have merely noted an historically contingent fact about
the church's discourse. Now we must note that it is a fact with
authority, for in view of the function of canonical sacramental
mandates, the biblical stipulation of a triune formula for baptism must be regarded as dogma.[21] Moreover, the impact of this
dogma extends far beyond the baptismal rite itself.[22] The function of naming God in initiation, in baptism as elsewhere, is to
address the initiate to new reality, to grant new access to God. In
the community of the baptized, therefore, the divine name spoken in baptism is established as that by which the community
has its particular address to God.[23]

It has in fact worked out so in the church, both liturgically
and theologically. In the church's life of prayer and blessing,
threefold invocation is established at every decisive point. And
in the theological history we will trace in a following chapter, we
will find the role of the baptismal formula so predominant that
there would be reason to call "Go . . . baptizing in the name of
the Father and of the Son and of the Holy Spirit" the founding
dogma of the faith.

This dogma is not about something we are to think but about
something we are to do. When we pray or give thanks or otherwise invoke God, it is by this formula that we may most precisely address our utterance. There are other such orthopractic

dogmas. The very stipulation of washing in God's name as the church's initiation is one. So is the stipulation of a meal of bread and cup, with christological thanksgiving, as the church's chief gathered occasion. So, for that matter, is the stipulation that final authority in the church is to function by our reading of the Bible.

From time to time, various concerns lead to proposed replacements of the trinitarian name, for example, "In the name of God: Creator, Redeemer, and Sanctifier" or "In the name of God the Ground and God the Logos and God the Spirit." All such parodies disrupt the faith's self-identity at the level of its primal and least-reflected historicity.

Such attempts presuppose that we first know about a triune God and then look about for a form of words to address that God, when in fact it is the other way around. Moreover, "Creator, Redeemer, and Sanctifier," for example, is, like other such phrases, not a name at all. It is rather an assemblage of after-the-fact theological abstractions, useful in their place but not here. Such assemblages cannot even be made into names, for they do not identify. Every putative deity must claim, for example, somehow to "create," "redeem," and "sanctify." There are also, to be sure, numerous candidates to be Father or Spirit, but within the trinitarian name, "the Father" is not primarily *our* Father, but the Father of the immediately next-named Son, that is, of Jesus. The "Holy Spirit," within the name, is not any spirit claiming to be holy, but the communal spirit of the just-named Jesus and his Father. By these relations inside the phrase, "Father, Son, and Holy Spirit" is historically specific and can be what liturgy and devotion—and, at its base, all theology—must have, a proper name of God.[24]

These last remarks again claim that "Father, Son, and Holy Spirit" is not an arbitrary label, like "Robert" for the author of these pages. A proper name is proper just insofar as it is used independently of aptitude to the one named, but it need not therefore lack such aptitude. "Father, Son, and Holy Spirit" is appropriate for naming the gospel's God because the phrase immediately summarizes the primal Christian interpretation of God. It is this second level of trinitarianism to which we must now continue.

CHAPTER TWO

The Trinitarian Logic and Rhetoric

"Father, Son, and Holy Spirit" is a slogan for the temporal structure of the church's apprehension of God and for the proper logic of its proclamation and liturgy. Within the Hebrew Scriptures' interpretation of God, trinitarian discourse remains unproblematic and so generates new language and images but not analysis.

The Trinitarian Logic

"Father, Son, and Holy Spirit" became the church's name for its God because it packs into one phrase the content and logic of this God's identifying descriptions. These in turn embody the church's primal experience of God. In turning from the trinitarian name to the history and logic by which it became the name, we therefore also move out from the church's specific life of praise and petition, in which a name is most needed, to the wider whole of the church's life and reflection.

The gospel identifies its God thus: God is the one who raised Israel's Jesus from the dead. The whole task of theology can be described as the unpacking of this sentence in various ways. One of these produces the church's trinitarian language and thought.

If for any reason we attend to the temporality of "God is whoever raised Jesus," we note certain temporal features, which have been noticed at least liturgically, from the church's very beginning. God is here identified by a narrative that uses the tense-structure of ordinary language, whereas divine identification is more ordinarily done by time-neutral characters, as in "God is whoever is omnipotent to bolster my weakness" or "God is whatever is immune to the time which takes my life." Nor is this narrative mythic, so that the tenses would not be used in their ordinary way, for its power to identify depends on mention of an historical individual and so, in turn, on the historical narrative by which that individual—as any such individual—must be identified. Such a procedure is religiously peculiar, as has often been noticed, for while religions often mention some historical event (a "revelation") as epistemologically necessary for their knowledge about God, they do not normally identify the subject of this knowledge by that event.

To identify the gospel's God, we must identify Jesus. In this sense we may first say that God "is" Jesus. Every reality is somehow identifiable, and we cannot identify this God without simultaneously identifying Jesus. This also displays why religions do not normally pin their identifications of God to the identity of an historical event, for drastic restrictions are imposed on the ways in which we can go on to talk of a God so identified. If God, in any sense, is Jesus—or were Abraham Lincoln or the British Empire—we cannot rightly talk of this God in any way that would make the temporal sequences, the stuff of narration, unessential to his being, and that, of course, is just how religions normally want to talk of God. Indeed, the posit of one to whom tenses are insignificant and in whom, therefore, time may be evaded is the whole usual point of their enterprise.

God, we may therefore identify, is what happens with Jesus. But if we said only that, we would show no reason why it should be *God* that happens with Jesus and not merely, perhaps, an important religious epoch. Moreover, it is not as if we in any case knew about God, and then for some reason decided to "identify" God by reference to Jesus. It is what in particular happens with Jesus that compels us to use the word "God" of *this* Father in the first place.

Following much of the New Testament, let us use "love" as a slogan for what humanly happened with the historical Jesus. Then we may say that Jesus was a lover who went to death rather than qualify his self-giving to others; the love which was the plot of his life is an unconditional love. Of this person it is said that he nevertheless lives, that he is risen. Said of this particular person, such an assertion—whether true or not—is at least appropriate, for love means an unconditional self-giving, an acceptance of death; and a successful love would be an acceptance of death that resulted not in the lover's absence from the beloved but in his or her presence. Love *means* death and resurrection. For this particular man, resurrection, if it happened, was therefore but the proper outcome of his life.

Moreover, if this lover's resurrection happened, then there also now lives an unconditional lover with death—the limit of love—already behind him, so that his love must finally triumph altogether, must embrace all people and all circumstances of their lives. If he is risen, the human enterprise has a conclusion: a human communion constituted in its commonality by one man's unconditional self-dedication to his fellow creatures and thus embracing each individual and communal freedom established in the history so fulfilled.

Thus, if Jesus is risen, his personal love will be the last outcome of the human enterprise. If he died, his self-definition has been written to its end, as each of ours will be, but if he also yet lives, just this life so defined is not thereby a dead item of the past, but an item of living, surprising time, an item of the future and indeed of the last future. Only of a person whose life had been defined as this particular man defined his would these propositions be appropriate. And it is because they are appropriate, and in that they are made, that "God" is an appropriate word for the reality identifiable as what happened with Jesus. A God is always some sort of eternity, some sort of embrace around time, within which time's sequences can be coherent, and if Jesus is risen he is to be both remembered and awaited.

Conversely, we may identify God so, now a second time: God is what will come of Jesus and us, together. In our original proposition, "God is whoever raised Jesus," the event by which God is identified, Jesus' resurrection, is the event in which Jesus is future to himself and to us.

In the Bible generally, the "Spirit" is God as the power of the future to overturn what already is, and just so fulfill it. The Spirit is indeed a present reality. But *what* is present is that there is a goal, and that we therein are free from all bondage to what is. The Spirit is the power of the eschaton now to be at once goal and negation of what is. In the New Testament, this Spirit is identified as Jesus' spirit, as every human being has spirit. That Jesus' particular spirit is the very power of the last future is the "spirit"-form of the identification of God by Jesus from which trinitarian language begins. Therefore the biblical "Spirit" is the inevitable word for this second identification of God, although developed trinitarian doctrines, since they respond to postbiblical problems, need by no means be bound exclusively to this name.

Finally, this particular embrace around time must be universal, for it is the embrace of an unconditional love. It must grant a universal destiny. Therefore this God may also be identified so: God is the will in which all things have Jesus' love as their destiny. Jesus, we saw, "is" God only *as* God's identifiability. In our original identifying proposition, "God is whoever raised Jesus." "Jesus" is the object of an active verb. God is—a third time—identified as the one who does Jesus' resurrection, as a given active transcendence to all that Jesus is and does. As what happens with Jesus is its own and our end, so also it is its own and our given.

In the New Testament, "Father" is Jesus' address to the transcendence *given to* his acts and sufferings, the transcendence *over against* whom he lives and to whom he is responsible—addressed in trust. For Jesus' disciples, therefore, "the Father" is God as the transcendent givenness of Jesus' love, the one in whom we may trust for that love.

Thus we have a temporally three-point identification of the gospel's God. If we think of an identification as a pointing operation (as in "Which one?" "That one"), we must point with all three of time's arrows in order to point out this God: to the Father as Given, to the Lord Jesus as the present possibility of God's reality for us, and to the Spirit as the outcome of Jesus' work. The identification is triple—rather than, say, double or quintuple—because time docs have three arrows. The past, present, and future of all that is, is doubtless a peculiar sort of fact, but it is also the most inescapable.

That the gospel's identification of God is threefold rests, therefore, on the way the gospel modulates a generally inescapable metaphysical fact. What is peculiar about the gospel's identification of God is not the number three but rather that it follows the three arrows of time without mitigating their difference. It is the very purpose of most discourse about gods to mitigate the threatening difference of past, present, and future. Among us Greeks, this is ordinarily accomplished by a doctrine of God's being as a timeless persistence in which past, present, and future are "really" all the same. The gospel's theology cannot produce such a doctrine, for thereby it would saw off the limb of narrative identification on which all its talk of God sits. But if such a doctrine is not produced, we are left with the three peculiar identifications of God just described and with their even more peculiar mutual relation.

The God of the gospel is the hope at the beginning of all things, in which we and all things are open to our fulfillment; this God is the love which will be that fulfillment; and this God is the faithfulness of Jesus the Israelite, which within time's sequences reconciles this beginning and this end. All else being equal, no more need be said. The rhetorical and soteriological space opened here is vast and permissive. Ignatius of Antioch was once moved to say, "We are drawn up [to God the Father] by Jesus Christ's crane—the cross—suspended by the rope that is the Holy Spirit" (*To the Ephesians* ix, 1).

The temporal structure we have analyzed is the unreflected open and free temporal horizon of the church's life and proclamation. Trinitarian discourse becomes problematic, and the difficult metaphysical dialectics we first think of as "the doctrine of the Trinity" become necessary, only when mitigation of time becomes tempting, that is, only in confrontation with more normal identifications of God. The confrontation of that sort which historically occurred is the matter of the next chapter.

The Hebrew Scriptures as the Root of Trinitarianism

There is a famous saying of an anonymous first-century preacher that we must "think about Jesus Christ as we do about God."[1]

The dictum formulated a principle that was immediate and self-understood through the apostolic and immediately postapostolic time,[2] for to think of God in the way this chapter has so far analyzed is to think of Christ "as of" God.[3]

Whether such thinking remains immediate and obvious or is difficult and problematic, and so also whether we just *do* such thinking or also reflect on what we do, depends on how one does in fact antecedently think about God.

As the Hebrew Scriptures, and so the earliest church, think of God, there is no problem, and none was felt. As the religion and philosophy of the Greeks and ourselves think of God, there are many great problems, which will be the matter of the next two chapters.

To be sure, superficial reflection supposes the opposite. It is commonly thought that trinitarian language about God marks Christianity's discontinuity with the Hebrew Scriptures. Increasingly Hellenist Christians were supposedly led by their devotion to Jesus to "divinize" him and so to mitigate God's uniqueness. This common supposition is false.

It is true—as we will see in the next chapter—that from about A.D. 150 Christianity's confrontation with Hellenism led to formulations which initially smacked of divinization. But—as we will also see—the whole developed doctrine of the Trinity was the church's effort to resist this temptation. And at the level of immediate trinitarian witness and experience which we are now discussing, and during the period before massive confrontation with Hellenic theology, there was not even incipient conflict between trinitarian and Hebrew interpretations of God. On the contrary, this immediate trinitarianism was the only possible fulfillment of the Hebrew Scriptures.

Israel's interpretation of God was undoubtedly the historical result of a multitude of factors, many now untraceable. But systematically and at least in part historically, Israel's theology can all be derived from the identification of God by the exodus. If God is, more than trivially, *the one who* rescued Israel from Egypt, the main characteristics of this God are immediately evident.[4]

First, Yahweh is not on the side of established order. The usual God, whose eternity is the persistence of the beginning, has as his very honor among us that in him we are secure against the threats of the future. Ancient imperial peoples poignantly experienced the fragility of their achievement: The situation in which seedtime and harvest return each year had barely been secured, and the barbarian destroyer was each year at the door. The gods of the ancient civilizations simply *were* the certainty of return, the guarantee of continuance. Marduk, for example, was *the one who* back at the beginning divided the Mesopotamian swamps into irrigated land and channeled water, and in that he was always still there the people could transcend the ever-renewed threat of relapse into precreation disorder. The damnation against which Yahweh fought for Israel was the precise opposite.

Israel understood itself not by an established order but by rescue from oppression under the archetypically standing order, that of Egypt. Throughout its history, Israel longed to become an established state "like all the nations" (1 Sam. 8:4-5). But God always saw to it that Israel would fail, and the prophets regularly denounced the very attempt (see 1 Sam. 8:7-9). Indeed, and most uncanny of all, Yahweh remained free to undo the standing order of his own people: "For, behold, [Yahweh, Yahweh] of hosts, is taking away from Jerusalem and from Judah stay and staff, the whole stay of bread, and the whole stay of water; the mighty man and the soldier, the judge and the prophet, the diviner and the elder" (Isa. 3:1-2).

Second, Yahweh's will is not identical with natural necessity—that is, Yahweh's will is indeed what we mean by "will." In great ancient myths, the beginning of the people's worship of God is in each case identical with the absolute beginning of all things. Therein lay assurance: Nothing can overthrow the people's basis, since outside it there is nothing. Israel, on the other hand, knew very well of a history, including a history of Israel's own ancestors, that preceded the exodus. The great myths of other peoples tell of a primeval event which set the pattern of time and is therefore above time, which never really ceases to happen—as

Marduk's primeval separation of water and land recurred at each yearly inundation and draining. Israel's story told of an event which, for all repeated cultic celebration, had happened only once, in time rather than above it.

Israel, of course, could and did attribute general creation to its God. But Yahweh's creation of the world and of Israel were two acts, not one. Israel knew that created reality did not necessarily include it, that Israel might not have been. Since Israel did nevertheless exist, by an act of Yahweh, that act was just so understood as a choice:[5] "You have seen what I did to the Egyptians, and how I . . . brought you to myself. Now therefore . . . , you shall be my own possession among all peoples" (Exod. 19:4–5).

Third, since there was history before there was Israel, and yet the God of Israel ruled that history, this question must be asked: How was Yahweh the God of Israel before there was Israel? The developed form of Israel's tradition had an answer: Between creation-times and the exodus was the time of the fathers, of Abraham, Isaac, and Jacob. But how were these Israel? The solution of the ancient narrators was that patriarchal Israel was Israel by the promise of a land and a land's possibility of nationhood.[6] Abraham and the other fathers had lived in response to the promise that their descendants would be a great people. Having as yet no established order, the fathers had lived by the word that promised one.

Thus Israel knew itself as created by God's word, in the exact sense in which we until recently spoke of "a gentleman's word." Yahweh made a promise and kept it, and so Israel came to be. From the start, salvation for Israel is given by promise of what is not yet, of the future that is real only in the word that opens it. What other nations could say of a visible and tangible presence of God in holy images and places, Israel could say only of God's utterance: "The grass withers, the flower fades, but the word of our God will stand for ever" (Isa. 40:7–8). Moreover, Israel knew of a time when Israel had been Israel only by this word, without security, when Israel's whole existence had been hope. There remains only to note that with the exile of 587 B.C., when all secure national existence was (at least until A.D. 1948) taken away, historical Israel was put in exactly the position posited for the fathers.[7]

Thus the identity of Israel's God, his difference from other gods, is precisely that Israel's God is not eternal in the way the other gods are, not God in the same way. That the past guarantees the future is exactly the deity of the gods, but Yahweh always challenges the past and everything guaranteed by it, from a future that is freedom. The key steps of the trinitarian logic described in the previous section are the very specificity of the Hebrew Scriptures' interpretation of God.

As to how, positively, Yahweh is eternal, Israel's interpretation is that he is faithful. Where other ancient religions said that God is beyond time, Israel said: "Forever, [Yahweh], thy word is firmly fixed in the heavens. Thy faithfulness endures to all generations; thou hast established the earth, and it stands fast" (Ps. 119:89–90). *Emunah* (faithfulness) is the reliability of a promise; thus the Revised Standard Version often translates it "truth" (e.g., Prov. 12:17; Hos. 5:9), and a promise which is verified by events is "made *emun*" (e.g., 1 Kings 8:26). If God continues to bless Israel in spite of everything, it is because he "is keeping the oath which he swore" to the fathers, "because [Yahweh] is the *faithful* God who keeps covenant" (Deut. 7:8–9). And when the fulfillment comes, when "kings shall see and arise," it will be "because of [Yahweh], who is faithful" (Isa. 49:7).

In one famous passage, the interpretation of God's eternity as faithfulness approaches a metaphysical definition. Within the tradition of the covenant with David, the most beautiful statement of Israel's hope proclaims: "I will make with you an everlasting covenant, my steadfast, sure love for David" (Isa. 55:3).

Unlike the normal gods, Yahweh does not transcend time by immunity to it. The continuity of Yahweh's being is not that of a defined entity, some of whose defining characteristics persist from beginning to end. It is rather the sort of continuity we have come to call "personal." It is established in Yahweh's words and commitments, by the faithfulness of later acts to the promises made in Yahweh's earlier acts. The continuity of Yahweh's being is eternity, transcends time, in that Yahweh keeps all promises, in that time cannot take any commitments away. It is just this interpretation of God's eternity that we introduced as the logical necessity—given the resurrection and the resultant necessity to identify God by Jesus—of trinitarian identification of God.

Primary Trinitarianism

Therefore, so long as Christian interpretation of God was in unshaken continuity with that of the Hebrew Scriptures, Christian discourse and reflection shaped themselves naturally and unproblematically to the triune logical and rhetorical space. This can be seen in the New Testament and so long thereafter[8] as the communities were not strongly confronted with Hellenic interpretation of God.

That "God" and God's "Spirit" form a rhetorical and conceptual pair for proclamation of God's work and interpretation of our life is entirely unproblematic in the New Testament. The use was imposed by the experience of Pentecost and needed no conceptual or linguistic innovation over against the Hebrew Scriptures. Also that "Christ" and the "Spirit" form such a pair in that the Spirit is *Christ's* Spirit was direct and historically legitimate interpretation of the Hebrew Scriptures, asserting merely the fulfillment of certain expectations in fact contained therein and involving no conceptual or linguistic innovation. These matters are analyzed in detail in another *locus* of this work.

That "God the Father" and "Jesus Christ his Son" form a similar pair is more complicated. It was of course the immediate consequence of that identification of God by Jesus' resurrection which is the whole import of the New Testament. But although the identification of God by historical events is fundamental in the Hebrew Scriptures, that the conclusively identifying events turn out to be the life of an individual person requires language beyond that of the Hebrew Scriptures, though in the New Testament itself never incongruous therewith. We cannot avoid a quick survey of these developments, though in detail they too belong to another *locus.*

The emergence of a semantic pattern in which the uses of "God" and "Jesus Christ" are mutually determining is fundamental. That pattern is firmly established before the earliest Pauline writings,[9] for example, the formula quoted by Paul "If you confess with your lips that Jesus is Lord and believe in your heart that God raised him from the dead, you will be saved" (Rom. 10:9). The pattern is the logical backbone of all Paul's own discourse about God.[10] In Paul the standard Hebrew theological predicates take either God or Jesus as subject, or both at once;[11] for example, "grace" is interchangeably "of God" (Rom. 5:15) or "of Christ" (Rom. 16:20) or bestowed "from God our Father and the Lord Jesus Christ" (Rom. 1:7). Parallel constructions have "God" in one part and "Christ" in the other.[12] "So we are ambassadors for Christ, God making his appeal through us" (2 Cor. 5:20). For Paul, *God* will rule the kingdom, Jesus is *Lord*, and these two circumstances are one fact only: "For the kingdom of God [means] righteousness and peace . . . ; he who thus serves Christ is acceptable" (Rom. 14:17–18, e.g.). Christ simply is "the power of God and the wisdom of God" (1 Cor. 1:24), the manifestation of that "righteousness" in which Judaism summed up the godliness of God (Rom. 3:21–22). Yet "God" and "Christ" are not simply identified; thus prayer and thanksgiving are always directed to God, through Christ or "in his name."[13]

This semantic pattern best displays the relation between the Father and Jesus, "the Son," as the apostolic church experienced it. The titles and images by which various groups more directly attempted to grasp the relation are for our present concern of secondary importance. We need only note primal Christianity's eclecticism in the drafting of such conceptions, and their general concord with the Hebrew Scriptures. Such mythic christology as appears, for example, in Philippians 2 or the Book of Hebrews or John's Gospel, where Christ is a "pre-" or "postexistent" heavenly being of unstipulated relation to God, displays a kind of thinking fully shared by contemporary Judaism[14] and well grounded in the Old Testament.[15] The various "christological titles" by which the risen Lord was addressed and proclaimed are without exception functional in their import. They do not say what sort of "being" Christ has, but merely what role he has. Most typical in its logic is "Lord."[16] Initially merely Jesus' disciples' term of address to their master, it was naturally resumed for their risen Lord after the resurrection. But now this Lord is enthroned in God's own power and directs their mission by a Spirit that is God's own. In these circumstances, the Hebrew Scriptures' use of "Lord" for God cannot help but resonate the in-itself still purely human title. With the experience of the ancient church in our inheritance, *we* cannot but ask what sort of being ("divine," "human," or what) this title and the others used by the primal church attribute to Jesus. It is vital to understand that they raised no such question for the primal church itself, that the analysis, for example, just given of "Lord" completely describes what it did or could do for the apostolic users.

The resurrection compelled the apostolic church to find new language. Only for us does this language raise questions over against the Hebrew Scriptures. The language once available, and given the logic of the Hebrew Scriptures' talk of God, Christian invocation, exhortation, and explanation seem to have taken triune form merely by following the path of least difficulty and quite without need for explicit reflection on the pattern itself. We will best assure ourselves of this by means of samples cited at near random from different strands of the New Testament: "But you, beloved . . . , pray in the Holy Spirit; keep yourselves in the love of God; wait for the mercy of our Lord Jesus Christ" (Jude 20–21); "But it is God who establishes us with you in Christ . . . ; he has . . . given us his Spirit in our hearts as a guarantee" (2 Cor. 1:21–22);[17] "For through him [Christ] we both have access in one Spirit to the Father" (Eph. 2:18).[18] Nor is this merely a matter of stock phrases; the essential temporal logic appears in triune formulas lacking one or another of the standard titles, for example, "I charge you in the presence of *God*, and of *Christ Jesus* who is to judge the living and the dead, and by *his appearing and his kingdom*" (2 Tim. 4:1).[19] Again, "May the *God of hope* fill you with all joy and peace in *believing*, so that by the power of the *Holy Spirit* . . ." (Rom. 15:13).

The initial place in life of such language is doubtless displayed by the writer of Ephesians at 5:18–20: "But be filled with the Spirit, addressing one another in psalms and hymns and spiritual songs, singing and making melody to the Lord . . . giving thanks in the name of our Lord Jesus Christ to God the Father." The essential Christian experience was of assemblies gripped by the dynamism of a particular future—"his appearing and his kingdom"—which dynamism the Scriptures taught them to call "the Spirit" and in which grip all prayer and praise was to "God the Father" and in the name of the one under whose lordship we are indeed God's children and share his Spirit. Given this sort of liturgical experience, it was utterly natural for the work of salvation to be compendiously described simply by reversing the order and going through the same sequence starting with God, as does the same writer to the Ephesians: "In him according to the purpose of him who accomplishes all things . . . , we who first hoped in Christ have been destined . . . to live for the praise of his glory. In him you also, who . . . have believed in him, were sealed with the promised Holy Spirit, which is the guarantee of our inheritance" (Eph. 1:11–14). Just so this writer obtains a complete framework for theology and can describe the entire Christian reality in the coordinates of "God's grace," "the mystery of Christ," and revelation "by the Spirit" (e.g., Eph. 3:2–6).

The most remarkable trinitarian passage in the New Testament, amounting to an entire theological system, is Romans 8. Its conceptual and argumentative heart is verse 11: "If the Spirit of him who raised Jesus from the dead dwells in you, he who raised Christ Jesus from the dead will give life to your mortal bodies also through his Spirit which dwells in you." The subject phrase displays in the uttermost conceptual compression the precise structure we have called "the trinitarian logic": The *Spirit* is "*of* him *who* raised *Jesus*." And from the prepositional structure of this phrase, Paul then develops a rhetoric and argument which sweeps justification and the work of Christ and prayer and eschatology and ethics and predestination into one coherent understanding. With somewhat less dialectical and rhetorical complexity than Romans 8, many other passages display what can only be called a standard Pauline trinitarian conceptuality. "God" is named as the agent of salvation, which is accomplished in an act described by such phrases as "in Christ Jesus," the purpose of which act, both eschatologically and penultimately, is a "sending" of the Spirit with "gifts" (e.g., 1 Cor. 1:4–8; Gal. 4:4).

The new thing that appears in the immediate postapostolic church is the attempt to *grasp*—mostly in mythic images—the constitution of God by Christ and the Spirit, that is, not merely to speak in a trinitarian fashion but to speak about the Trinity. What we have here to examine is the trinitarianism of what Danielou somewhat misleadingly called "Jewish Christianity,"[20] that is, all Christianity up to the direct challenge of Hellenic thought around A.D. 150, and thereafter the Christianity of those areas not heavily so challenged.

The principle of all this trinitarianism is classically stated by the epexegetical continuation of the saying of Clement earlier cited: "as of God, *as of the judge* of the living and the dead."[21] The equation of Christ—and the Spirit—with God is in all this thinking an attribution of *function* inseparable from God.

There were many "Jewish" Trinity-images.[22] The most important evoked the Son and the Spirit as "angels." In the most ancient postapostolic church there was undoubtedly an angel christology immediately dependent on apocalyptic Judaism's angel speculation, but there was an angel pneumatology too, on the same basis.[23] And so the full trinitarian experience of God found expression, as in the apocalyptic vision of Isaiah: "And I saw him [Christ] ascend into the seventh heaven, and all the saints and angels praised him. And I saw him sit down on the right hand of the Glory. . . . And the Angel of the Holy Spirit I saw sitting on the left hand."[24] This vision of God and two great angels seems to have had great continuing importance for the later development of trinitarianism: Origen, creator of the first great trinitarian theology, repeatedly proof-texts with Isaiah 6:1–3, interpreting the two great seraphim of that passage as allegories of the Son and the Spirit and explicitly attributing this interpretation to a Jewish teacher.[25]

We now find this angel christology and angel trinitarianism alarming. It seems to create a large class of demigods and to locate Christ and the Spirit among them, surely a case of "divinization," and halfhearted at that. But this happens only because we anachronistically project our question about kinds of being back on this essentially Semitic discourse, and are then disappointed[26] to find Christ and the Spirit not fully divine, and Christ not fully human either. But in this thinking itself, an "angel" is simply one to whom God gives a mission and whose own reality is constituted by this mission. *Nothing* is thereby suggested about what sort of being is possessed by either God or this manifestation.[27] It can well be that the mission is in fact God's own mission. If it is, this will simply appear in descriptions of what the angel does—judges all people, forgives sin, or whatever.[28] And that Christ and the Spirit are transcendent over "other" angels appears iconographically, as in Hermas, where Christ is bigger than the other archangels and is a seventh, when all know the full number of archangels is six, or as in the *Ascension of Isaiah* where God and the two great angels are together worshiped by the other angels.[29]

The kinds of trinitarian discourse developed in the New Testament and in the immediately subsequent period have continued through the history of the church. With use of the triune name, they are the substance of living trinitarian apprehension of God. Christians bespeak God in a triune coordinate system; they speak *to* the Father, *with* the Son, *in* the Spirit, and only so bespeak *God*. Indeed, they *live in* a sort of temporal space defined by these coordinates, and just and only so live "in God." And they represent the God with whom they have thus to do in iconography and metaphor that is functional in its attribution of deity. Where, as in the medieval and modern Western church, these modes lose some of their power to shape actual proclamation and prayer, an alienation of the church must be suspected.

Pastors often believe that the Trinity is too complicated to explain to the laity. Nothing could be more misguided. Believers *know how* to pray to the Father, daring to call him "Father" because they pray with Jesus, God's Son, and so enter into the future these two have for them, that is, praying in the Spirit. Those who know how to do this, and who realize that just in the space defined by these coordinates they have to do with God, do understand the Trinity. All the intellectual complexities we must shortly embark on are a secondary phenomenon, whose proper location is the back of teachers' and preachers' minds, determining the way they guide and, when necessary, explain this relation to this God.

The Dogmatic Status of Primary Trinitarianism

The structures of language and experience analyzed in the previous two sections are not merely in fact present in the life of the church. They are daily and explicitly acknowledged and proclaimed as fundamental by the worshiping assemblies of all Christendom, being embodied in the great liturgical creeds of the apostles, and of Nicaea. The three-article creeds are the daily education and public self-definition of the Christian community in all its branches, recited at baptism and often at the Supper or other main services. And they are acknowledged such by Eastern, Roman Catholic, and Reformation bodies alike—as, for example, in the Lutheran *Book of Concord*, where they are set in first place and aptly called "the ecumenical" creeds.

Creedal formulations are as old as the gospel.[30] For our immediate purposes, two forms are important. First, the initial preachers and catechists and their successors used and passed on narrative summaries of the chief claims and facts about Jesus (see 1 Cor. 15:1-7).[31] Second, there is the rubric that baptism is to be "in the name of the Father and of the Son and of the Holy Spirit." We do not know what liturgical form this naming initially took, or even if it took the same form in all communities. But by the time ancient baptismal practice emerges into clear view,[32] in the writings of Hippolytus at the turn of the second and third centuries, the naming is an interrogation of trinitarian confession: "Let the baptizer ... say, 'Do you believe in God, the Father Almighty? Do you believe in Christ Jesus, the Son of God ... ?' [etc.]."[33] There are signs that such interrogation may have been the—or an—original way of baptismal "naming"; in any case, the primal church did demand confession of faith at baptism,[34] and this confession was shaped by the triune pattern of baptismal naming, however the latter was done.

The sort of declaratory creeds we know and use, such as the Apostles' Creed or the creeds used as bases by the councils of Nicaea and Constantinople, developed from the fusion of these two forms: the baptismal questions with their canonically stipulated triune pattern, and the summaries of christological narrative.[35] It seems likely that the location of this development was catechetical discipline, which had both to prepare for baptism and to reinforce the main items of christological missionary preaching. The shift to declaratory form from interrogatory form—which was retained at baptism itself—was probably occasioned by the demand that catechumens, before baptism, report to the congregation their participation in the faith into which the congregation had been baptized: "I believe—as do you—in. . . ." It also seems likely that the earliest stable product of this development was the forerunner of the Apostles' Creed, the old creed of the church of Rome, fixed sometime toward the end of the second century. This old Roman creed was created by addition of the christological kerygma "who was conceived by" to a trinitarian baptismal interrogation about "God the Father Almighty, and . . . Christ Jesus, his only Son, our Lord, and the Holy Spirit, the holy church, the resurrection of the flesh."[36]

What is dogmatized by the classical three-article creeds is thus not only or even primarily any one list of kerygmatically vital christological events or necessary theological items. There has never, in fact, been any one universally accepted creedal list of either. Even now, when we have reduced the creeds in practical use to two, they do not present quite the same list. What is first of all dogmatized are the kerygmatically narrated history itself, the triple-name structure, and the union of the two. Moreover, the popular impression is precisely wrong, that first there is a three-step history of God's works—the "three articles"—and that then the triune name is a sort of summary and the trinitarian logic a kind of explanation thereof. The reverse is the case.

The Apostles' Creed and those like it were created by the cat-echetical and liturgical affinity, and the logical fit, between the triune baptismal name of God and the evangelical history nar-rated in the gospel. That is, it is exactly the logic analyzed in this chapter which the creeds declare to be the true and necessary logic of the gospel.

CHAPTER THREE

The Nicene-Constantinopolitan Dogma

Over against the Hellenic identification of God, the church's discourse about God was and still is tempted to alienation from its proper trinitarian logic. The dogma of Nicaea and Constantinople was a decisive victory over this temptation.

The God of the Greeks

In much of this chapter we have a story to tell. The gospel mission did in fact meet with another and fundamentally incompatible identification of God, that of the Greeks, which could not be ignored. Christianity as we know it, and especially our inherited body of developed trinitarian dogma and analysis, is the result.

If the gospel had not met the challenge to its strange identification of God in the form of the Greek interpretation, it would have met it in some other—and indeed it did and does in those branches of the mission that lead into great culture areas other than that in which our narrative is set. Moreover, the clash will always be at the same point: religion's normal reluctance to take time seriously for God. Thus any possible great non-Western theology must contain some functional equivalent for the developed trinitarianism on which we are about to embark. But such possibilities are beyond the scope of this work.

From its beginning, Hellenic theology was an exact antagonist of biblical faith.[1] Israel's interpretation of God was determined by the rescue of wandering tribes from oppression under an established civilization, Greece's by an established civilization's overthrow by just such tribes.[2] The flourishing religious and material world of Mycenaean Greece was swept away by the flood of Dorian tribes from the north. But in certain areas the memory and traditions of lost glory survived. When Greek civilization began to revive in the ninth century, it was these surviving Ionians that led the way. Thus the historical memory of Greece began with catastrophe, with a national experience of sheer irrational contingency and power, and of death and destruction brought by it. Greek religion and reflection were tragic from their root. They were a sustained attempt to deal with the experience that we must "not reckon any mortal blessed . . . until he has reached the end of his life without suffering disaster."[3] Greek religion and reflection were thereby imprinted with five characters important for our purpose.

First, their driving question was: "Can it be that *all* things pass away?" The assurance they needed, as formulated by Aristotle, had to be: "Being as such neither comes to be nor perishes."[4] In the myth of Chronos, "Father Time" who devoured all his children, the Greeks stated their experience of time and its surprises. Their religion was the determination that "Time" not be supreme, that he be overthrown by a true "Father of gods and men." Greek religion was the quest for a rock of ages, resistant to the flow of time, a place or part or aspect of reality immune to change. The gods' one defining character was therefore immortality, immunity to destruction. Whereas Yahweh was eternal by his faithfulness *through* time, the Greek gods' eternity was their abstraction *from* time. Yahweh's eternity is thus intrinsically a relation to his creatures—supposing there are any—whereas the Greek gods' eternity is the negation of such relation.

Second, Greek religion and reflection were an act of human self-defense against mysterious power and inexplicable contingency, that is, against just what humankind has mostly called "God." The Ionian survivors willed that history have a humanly comprehensible pattern, of such a kind that its events be in principle predictable and plannable. If superhuman (i.e., immortal) actors were needed to explain some events and so vindicate their sense, these too had to be understandable and predictable in their motivations and reasons. Such were the Olympian gods, the Ionian Homer's rationalized versions of various inherited nature and clan deities, whose singular lack of holiness and mystery scholars have always noted. The Ionians rescued themselves from chaos by enlightenment, by explanation of time's seeming mysteries.

Homer's successors, as religious thinkers, were the Ionian philosophers.[5] With them the reduction of all godly characteristics to one, immortality, and the inclusion also of the gods within one comprehensible scheme of events, led (and this is the third character on our list) to the concept of "the divine," a unitary abstraction of godly explanatory power in and behind the plural gods of daily religion; for example, Aristotle reports, "The Unbounded has no beginning . . . , but seems rather to be the Beginning of all other realities, and to envelope and control them. . . . This is the Divine. So the opinion of Anaximander and most of the natural philosophers."[6] For the educated class of Greece's classic period, this abstraction, often called "Zeus," was the true religious object: timelessness simply as such. So also the word "God" is understood as an adjective, applicable to various manifestations in various degrees.

Fourth, the quest for timeless reality is never satisfied by anything directly presented in our experience. All the world we see, hear, and touch does indeed pass away. If there is the divine, it must therefore be above or behind or beneath or within the experienced world. It must be the bed of time's river, the foundation of the world's otherwise unstable structure, the track of heaven's hastening lights. Greek religion and reflection, by their inner function, were metaphysical, a quest for the timeless ground of temporal being that just so is a different sort of being than we ever immediately encounter.

And fifth, Greek religion and reflection were precisely the quest we have been calling them, for since the timeless ground is never directly presented in experience, it has to be searched for. A whole complex of motifs that will be centrally important for our story is involved here. Greek apprehension of God is accomplished by penetrating through the temporal experienced world to its atemporal ground. This theology is therefore essentially negative: The true predicates of deity are negations of predicates that pertain to experienced reality by virtue of its temporality. God is "invisible," "intangible," "impassible" (i.e., unaffected by external events), "indescribable." This theology is essentially analogical,[7] for while it consists in negations of predicates that apply to the temporal world, it cannot dispense with such predicates. The pattern is always "Deity is F, only not as other, temporal reality is F." This theology necessarily raises the question of true deity, of the characteristics marking the final and so real ground, for if deity must be searched out, we have to be able to recognize it when we find it. And finally, all this penetration is accomplished by "mind" (*nous*), that is, not by discursive analysis or argument but by instantaneous intellectual intuition, by a sort of interior mirroring, for what is to be grasped is precisely a timeless pattern.[8]

So far the essentials of Greek interpretation of God, in practiced religion and in the philosophy to which it gave birth. Before returning to the main line of our narrative, we must note one great event in the history of this religion.

The posit of timelessness was initially a sustaining posit: Deity was the reliable meaning and foundation of the human world. But only a sort of blink was needed for the value signs to reverse themselves. Timeless and temporal reality were posited as different kinds of being, defined by mutual negation. All meaning and value were located in timeless being. If we are given a metaphysical shock, we may suddenly see the line between time and eternity as a barrier, shutting us out from meaning, for we are temporal. Without attempting to assign a cause, it is enough for our purpose to note that in the transition from the local communities of classic Greece to cosmopolitan Hellenism exactly this reversal of values occurred.[9]

Thus the dominant religious apprehension of late antiquity was of deity's distance, created by the very characteristics that made it deity. We are in time and God is not, and just so our situation is desperate. Therefore the religion of late antiquity was a frenzied search for "mediators," for beings of a third ontological kind between time and timelessness, to bridge the gap.[10] Already Socrates had posited such a third kind, Eros, the child of Fullness and Want, and perceived that the language appropriate to speak of this realm is myth, that is, stories about divine beings, speech about eternities as if they were in time.[11] Discourse about deity was in any case understood to be analogical; "god" is basically adjectival and thus applicable in various grades to deity itself and to any mediators one or more steps down. In cosmopolitan Hellenism, such interpretation was put into practice. All the vast heritage of the world's savior-gods, demigods, reified abstractions, and mid-beings generally were pressed into mediatorial service. It was inevitable that when the gospel appeared on this scene, Christ would be too.

The Initial Christianizing of Hellenism

When the gospel mission confronts the Hellenic interpretation of God, it cannot and could not simply reject it. Israel proclaimed Yahweh as God for all peoples. In confrontation with Hellenism, this had to mean the claim that Israel's is the real God posited by Hellas' philosophers.[12] Moreover, Hellenism's interpretation of God both caused and expressed late antiquity's chief religious problem, the distance of God; the gospel had to address the problem. It was at the middle of the second century that Christian thinkers first posed the Hellenic analytic tasks to themselves as explicit matter for reflection. It is there we begin our narrative.

However the confrontation might have begun, it was in fact begun thus: Both bodies of discourse about God, the biblical and the Hellenic, were simply set alongside each other and more or less well carpentered together, depending on skill. On the one side this meant that Christians took over the procedure of penetrating to the "real" God by abstracting from time with negative analogies.[13] Accordingly, Christians also adopted the negative predicates by which Hellenism had qualified true deity, and made one composite list with items from biblical language.

Already Ignatius, in A.D. 125, adopted the central and least biblical concept of late Hellenic theology: God is "impassible," immune to being acted upon (*To the Ephesians*, vii, 2). This concept was to be the clearest and most troubling mark of Hellenic interpretation within Christian theology.[14] Justin Martyr, the most influential second-century theologian, defined God as the eternally self-caused and changeless cause of the being of all other beings (e.g., *Dialogue with Trypho*, 3), to the satisfaction of believers and unbelievers alike. For Justin and his fellows, God is therefore "unoriginated," "unutterable," "immovable," "impassible," "inexpressible," "invisible," "unchangeable," "unplaceable," "immaterial," "unnameable."[15]

Yet the same theologians could also speak of God in incisively and even creatively biblical fashion. So Justin again: God is concerned with us; God is the "just overseer" of our lives (*Apology*, ii, 12); God is compassionate and patient (the flat contradiction of "impassible") (*Dialogue*, 108); God's omnipotence is exercised above all in Jesus' resurrection (*Apology*, i, 19); God actively intervenes to reward and punish (*Apology*, i, 12); God's course of action is determined by regard for us (*Apology*, i, 28). The true God, indeed, is to be identified as the one who led Israel from Egypt (*Apology*, i, 11).[16] Such language is not mediated with the negative theology; the two conceptions of God are not so much synthesized as merely added together.[17] It is this additive tactic that has, from the apologists to the present, remained standard in theology. The notion of divine timelessness, once thus given room in Christian interpretation, then promptly attacks liturgical and proclamatory immediate trinitarianism.

The immediate question of every Hellenist, hearing the gospel's talk of God the beginning and God who is our fellow Jesus and God the fulfillment, must be But what is the timelessly self-identical something that is all these three? What is the time-immune continuity that must be the being of the real God? If we are not firm enough to challenge the question, there are only two possible answers: It is a fourth, of which the three are only temporal manifestations, or it is one of the three (which must then be the Father, since the other two are "from" him), of which the other two are only temporal manifestations. Historians label the first move "modalism," the second "subordinationism." Together, they comprise the whole list of ancient trinitarian heresies. They are heresies because they speak of God in just the way that saws off our narrative limb. They are precisely as common and contrary to the gospel now as in the second and third centuries. In history, they had to be worked through to be found out.

Modalism is the teaching that God is above time and the distinctions of Father, Son, and Spirit, but appears successively in these roles to create, redeem, and sanctify.[18] From its first recorded appearance in Rome, around A.D. 190, it was the standard theory of the congregations, as it still is. It was, indeed, a direct attempt to systematize congregational piety on the assumption of the timeless God. It keeps Father, Son, and Spirit in the same row and so stays close to liturgical use of the triune name and to the linear past, present, and future of baptismal and eucharistic life. But it was nevertheless as much a compromise with Hellenic deity as subordinationism. Indeed, it was and is the more complete submission, since the whole biblical talk of God is deprived of reference to God. None of the three is God. This is not noticed in immediate liturgical and proclamatory experience, but it is immediately noticed upon reflection. At the levels of learned or dogmatic theology, therefore, modalism has always been rejected promptly on its appearance.[19] We hear of only two actual modalist theologians in the ancient church, Paul of Samosata and Sabellius. Of the details of their thought we know next to nothing; only their names survived, as the ancient church's labels for modalism.

Subordinationism appears able to identify at least the biblical "Father" with God. Moreover, it had the missionary advantage that it answered directly to late Hellenism's religious need. Since it puts the Father on top, and ranks the Son below the Father—in vertical order, so to speak—it makes the Son just such a middle being between God's eternity and our time as late antiquity longed for.

Whenever Christ is grasped as a halfway entity between the supposedly timeless God and the temporal world, the subordinationist scheme is established. This can be, was, and is done strictly mythologically, with a demi-God descending and ascending.[20] But it is the sophisticated subordinationism inaugurated around A.D. 150 by the so-called apologists, the famous Logos christology, which we must describe, since it created the theological system within and against which developed trinitarianism was to be worked out. Christ, said the apologists, is—almost—God in that "the Logos" is incarnate in him.

However Justin, Theophilus, and the rest derived or invented their Logos concept, what they meant by it is plain. In the Greek philosophical tradition,[21] "logos" is at once discourse and the meaningful order which discourse discloses. If then the universe has such order, this is a divine Logos which is both deity's self-revelatory discourse and the reasonable order of the cosmos. Just so the apologists spoke of "the Logos." Moreover, as the divine reason *in* our world, the Logos could become the mediator of deity *to* our world, a "second God," and with the intensifying religious anxiety of late antiquity that is just what happened.[22] With or without dependence on this extra-Christian development, the apologists paralleled it and made "the Logos" the name of a typical personalized mediator-entity of second-century religiosity, "the next power after the Father of all, a Son. . . ."[23] Right or wrong, they thought that in all this they were but continuing John's testimony to the Logos who "was in the beginning with God," "illumined every man," and came in flesh to make God known (John 1:1–14).

In that the apologists shared the interpretation of God as the one who grounds all being by negating time, they shared also late antiquity's great problem, this God's distance. If we are to be saved, God must somehow dwell in our world, all agreed. And in the Old Testament, Christians possessed a narrative of God's activity here. But God has been defined just by his elevation above temporal action. It cannot have been God himself who walked in Adam's garden or shut the door of Noah's ark or talked to Abraham and Moses, for—as Justin asked—how should he "speak to anyone or be seen by anyone or appear in a particular part of the earth. . . . ? Neither Abraham nor Isaac nor Jacob nor any other human saw the Father, the unutterable Lord . . . , but rather they saw that other, who by his will is his Son and the messenger ('angel') to serve his purpose." An "other God," one step down the hierarchy of being, is needed to bridge the chasm between God and time.[24]

This "other God" is the Logos, the self-manifesting God, "the angel of the Lord" of the Hebrew Scriptures. Subordination is explicit. The Logos is "called" God, but over against "the creator of all things, above whom there is no other God," this predication is not literal. The Logos has "come into being," unlike the Father; he is "from" the unnameable and unoriginated Father, and just so is worshiped "after him."[25]

Since God is rational, the Logos is eternally in himself, as his own rationality. Then when God moves to create, that is, to be related to a reality other than himself, his Logos becomes external to him, as the rationality of artisans is manifest in their creations, and so also as God's relation to creation, that is, as revelation. Thus the Logos is the "first originated being" or even simply "first creature,"[26] over against the Father, who has no beginning. No distinction is yet made between different ways of deriving from God, so the difference between the Logos and the world is stated by adjectives like "first." It is this divine bridge to time that is then present in Jesus,[27] thus anchoring the bridge more securely at our end. For the second God's derivation from the Father, "Son" suggests "born" and "Logos" suggests "uttered"; both appear and combine in the neutral "gone forth."[28] He is numerically distinct from the Father, yet not set off from him.[29]

Not much has been said of the Spirit, which leads us to a vital point. The Logos theology is *not* the origin of developed trinitarianism. In itself, it is not in fact trinitarian at all.[30] The primal trinitarian naming and liturgical pattern make a temporal structure horizontal to time and inherently triple as time is. The God/Mediator/World scheme is timelessly vertical to time and of itself would posit either a deity of God and God's one mediator, or of God and infinitely *many* mediators. The space between God and the temporal world may be thought of either as one space or as indefinitely divisible, but there is no reason to think of two subspaces. In fact, the status of the Spirit was ambiguous in the whole apologetic theology. Since God "*is* Spirit" according to John (4:24), Spirit can be the name of the divine in Christ.[31] But how then is "the" Spirit a third? In the trinitarian pattern itself, on the other hand, there is no problem. On the contrary, we have seen that it is precisely in the self-posit of Spirit that triune Godhead is established. It was the Spirit's lack of place within the worldview to which subordinationism was an adaptation that prevented the assimilation of all three items of the baptismal faith into the subordinationist scheme and preserved the three-article formulas of baptism as the chief counterinstance against it.

Insofar as the apologists were nevertheless trinitarian, sometimes they tried to stack all three vertically to time, with little conceptual success, and sometimes they assigned the Spirit his biblical role outside their mediator scheme altogether.[32] What kept them trinitarian in intention was the presence of factors outside their system: the continuing trinitarian life of the church; the developing three-article creedal structure, based on baptismal confession as just noted;[33] perhaps the continuing availability and influence of a picture by which to imagine God in accord with this creed, the "Jewish-Christian" picture of the Father and the two great angelic advocates; and churchly critique of the religious and metaphysical basis of subordinationism.[34]

In the interplay of all these factors, apologetic theology reached its historical fulfillment in two great figures of the early third century. In the West, Tertullian taught a more creedal and terminological trinitarianism; in the East, Origen taught a more speculative trinitarianism. Each set the style of his region for centuries to come.

For Tertullian, Logos theology was not so much the solution of his own religious problems as part of the now available intellectual repertoire for use on quite a different problem: the Trinity itself, the proper explication of the Christian interpretation of God.[35] For him, the trinitarian rule of faith was already a given (*Against Praxeas*, ii, 1–2). Tertullian was moved to trinitarian analysis by a propagandizing explanation of the rule, the modalism urged in Rome by one Praxeas, around A.D. 190. He rightly thought this explanation explained the creed away, and set out to refute it and offer a better. As it turned out, he set the terminology of all subsequent Western analysis: There are in God "three persons" (*personae*) who are "of one substance" (*unius substantiae*).

Tertullian's chief trinitarian concern was to show how God's "monarchy" and "economy" could be simultaneously preserved (ibid., vii, 7). "Monarchy" was his opponents' slogan for the abstract oneness of God as such, which Tertullian made mean instead the uniqueness and self-consistency of God's rule, of his divine work.[36] Tertullian himself adapted "economy" to be a term of trinitarian analysis from Irenaeus, for whom it meant the historical unfolding of God's saving work; Tertullian uses it for God's own inner self-disposition to this saving history.[37] It is "the economy . . . which disposes the unity into trinity" (ibid., ii, 4). Plainly, it is theological interpretation of the three-step creed that is Tertullian's task. *Both* the one and three are those of God's reality in saving history.

For the three, Tertullian used *personae*, establishing the word for all subsequent Western theology. *Persona*[38] had been first the actor's mask, through which the actor spoke, then the role the actor thus played, and by Tertullian's time was the everyday term for the human individual, established in individuality by social role, by speaking and responding. The immediate background of the word's trinitarian use was an established exegetical use. The Logos was considered by ancient theology as the agent of all revelation; therefore when Scripture attributes speech to the Father or the Spirit, this was said to be the Son speaking "in the person" (*ex persona*) of the Father or the Spirit. Exegetically, Tertullian was thus accustomed to the three, in their distinction from one another, being called "persons." The step to use in trinitarian analysis was apparently taken before Tertullian; it was in any case a short one.

Tertullian's assertion of three *personae* in God is thus the assertion against modalism that the role distinctions, the relations of address and response found in Scripture between the

Father and Jesus and the Spirit, establish reality in God, just as such relations do among human individuals.[39] Tertullian's cases of the distinction of "persons" all come down to the distinction of Father, Jesus, and Spirit in scriptural narrative (ibid., xxiff.). They are three in that they speak to and about one another (ibid., xi, 9–10) in such scriptural incidents as Jesus' baptism. They are three because they have three mutually recognized proper names (ibid., iv, 4). Also the inner-trinitarian eternal roles are defined by the roles in saving history; when God said, "Let us make man," "he spoke, in the unity of the trinity, with the Son, who was to put on man, and with the Spirit, who was to sanctify man, as if with ministers and councillors" (ibid., xii, 3).

In his use of *substantia* for the unity of God, Tertullian followed his own philosophical tradition. This was not adhered to by later Western theology, so that "one substance" came simply to mean somehow one thing[40] and then to be interpreted within whatever philosophy was in vogue.

The resultant terminology was useful both for good and for bad. It gave the Western church language with which to get on with its daily proclamatory and disciplinary business, 175 years before this urgent necessity was filled in the East. But in its conceptual blandness, it also served to cover the very real religious and intellectual problems posed by the Christian identification of God. These were to be faced in the East.

That event was prepared by the first truly great thinker and scholar of Christian history, Origen of Alexandria, who carried subordinationist trinitarianism to its unstable perfection and created a way of thinking that dominated the Eastern church for the remainder of its theologically creative history. Though he was a far greater theologian than Tertullian, his role in our special story is so much that of the fulfiller of already-described tendencies that our treatment can be brief. One great aspect of his work may be simply noted here, for future reference: He was the creator of hermeneutically self-conscious biblical exegesis.

Origen's God the Father is Hellenic deity in purest form: sheer mind, utterly removed from the temporal material world, utterly undifferentiated, and just so unknowable (*On First Principles*, i, 1, 5–6). The unknowability of God is identical with the difference between the temporal and the timeless (*Fragments to John*, i, xiii). God is knowable only as ground of his works, by the intuition of *nous* (*On First Principles*, i, 1, 6; iv, 3, 15).

Accordingly, Origen's entire soteriological concern is for mediation of the knowledge of God. He succeeded in creating a consistently subordinationist system to mediate this deity that had place for the Spirit and so did not obviously clash with the trinitarian creeds and liturgies. He created a grandiose version of late antiquity's vision of a hierarchy of being—the Christian pair to Plotinus'—descending in successive mediations from God, like the rays from the sun, down finally to the material universe.[41] The "birth" of mediating deity from God is an eternal event: God just is self-mediating (ibid., i, 2; i, 9; lv, 5). Also, the Spirit is eternal, given from God without beginning (ibid., i, 3, 4).

The problem of the place of the Spirit is ingeniously solved. The Spirit's work is sanctification; its sphere is the church; Origen includes the church's special reality in the mediation system. He conceives the work of Father, Son, and Spirit as three concentric circles, along the line of mediation between God and us, as an inverted, stepped cone. The Father gives being to all beings; the Son gives the knowledge of God to all beings capable of knowledge; the Spirit gives the holiness in which such knowledge is fulfilled to those among rational beings who are to be saved. Both the downward mediation of being and the upward mediation of fulfillment are thus essentially triple—if dubiously triune (ibid., i, 3, 5; i, 3, 8).

The Arian Crisis

The Origenist system was unstable, since the initial mere compromise between biblical and Hellenic interpretation of God still lay at its heart. In historical particular, it could not stand the question "Well, which *is* the Logos, Creator or creature?" The secret of subordinationist trinitarianism, perfected by Origen, was the posit of an unbroken continuity of being from the great God, through the Logos, the Spirit, and other "spiritual" beings, down to temporal beings. Across this beautiful spectrum the biblical radical distinction of Creator from creature could only make an ugly slash somewhere. But the intense and open study of Scripture which was the other great achievement of Origenism itself had sooner or later to pose the Creator-creature difference.

The intellectual and religious instability of Origenism was also a confessional instability of the Eastern church. At the turn of the third and fourth centuries, the great bishoprics and professorships of the East were almost all occupied by Origenists of one shade or another, from a left wing of those most drawn by Origen's intellectual respectability, to a right wing most drawn by his christological passion.[42]

Subordinationism's inevitable breakdown was triggered by the students and other disciples of Lucian of Antioch.[43] Lucian's theology is not well known. In the last decades of the third century and the first of the fourth, he was a great teacher in the style of Origen, a martyr, and the founder of Antioch's scholarly fame. His students learned a methodical exegesis of Scripture more devoted to the literal sense than Origen's, and therefore more likely to intrude the dangerous Creator-creature distinction. They also learned a more coolly analytical—Aristotelian—Platonism, amenable to such commonsensicalities as that each thing is itself and not another. This made Origen's spectrum of being look more like a set of steps than a glissando, and so emphasized its subordinationism. If the Logos is a distinct entity only a very, very little bit different from God, then he is, said the Lucianists, in fact different.[44]

The struggle began among the Egyptian clergy. The priest of an Alexandrian parish, a second-rate Lucianist named Arius, attacked the Origenist right wing's tendency to attribute full divine eternity to the Son.[45] Since the attack touched the bishop, Alexander, a synod of Egyptian bishops deposed Arius and a few sympathizers from office.

Thereupon Arius appealed to the old-school tie. Leaving Egypt, he and his fellow rebels sought and found place with the most notable of the Lucianists, Bishop Eusebius of Nicomedia. Eusebius launched a correspondence campaign among the Eastern bishops to have Arius restored to office. Alexander responded, and a general uproar ensued which can only be explained by the theological development being ripe for it.

What Arius and his friends were concerned about is explicit and clear in the first document of the conflict, Arius's appeal to Eusebius of Nicomedia. As Arius understands it, those who attribute to the Son coeternity with the Father must either regard the Son as some sort of emergent from within the Father's being or as a parallel unoriginated being. Both are termed "blasphemies."[46]

For Arius, and for the whole Lucianist group to which he appealed, and indeed for all the more left-wing disciples of Origen, there were only two identifying characteristics of God. First, God is "unoriginated." As we have seen, the theology deriving from the apologists did not differentiate between possible different ways of having an origin; left-wing Origenism made the catchall negative definitive of deity.[47] Second, God is altogether devoid of internal differentiation. For Arius, therefore, to say that the Son is "co-unoriginated," or anything of the sort, posits two "co-gods,"[48] while to say that the Son is an emergent from within the Father introduces differentiation into even the Father, that is, denies that there is any real God at all.[49] Arius therefore teaches: "The Son is not unoriginated, nor is he in any way a part of the Unoriginated."[50]

It is plain that what moves Arius is the late-Hellenic need to escape time, become utterly dominant. If we are to be saved, there must be some reality entirely uninvolved with time, which has no origin of any sort and whose continuity is undifferentiated and uninterrupted. Just so, it is because Christ is involved with time that he will not do as really God: "How can the Logos be God, who sleeps like a man and weeps and suffers?"[51] It had long been decided, against the modalists, that the longed-for absolute timeless and impassible One cannot be a divine essence other than Father, Son, and Spirit. Then it must be the Father. Very early, the Arians put their whole case in two sentences: "As the monad, and the Source of all things, God is before all things. Therefore he is also before the Son."[52] All other considerations must be sacrificed to this logic and the religious need behind it.

It was around the converse that the controversy was to be conducted. Arius had to say, "There was once when he [the Logos] was not,"[53] that is, the Logos is a creature. In the direction of the transcendence from which we come and into which we are to return, the way, according to the Arians, leads beyond what happens in time with Christ, to a God who is not yet the Father of the Son, who is a sheer unoriginate, above all differentiation and relation. As we climb back up the ladder of being, the Logos, so long as he is above us, is God *for us* but is not God in himself.[54] The great thinker of later Arianism (350–380), Eunomius, was finally to draw the religious conclusion: The last goal is precisely to transcend the revealer and see God as does he.[55]

In the long term of the conflict, the opposition to Arius was to be carried above all by Athanasius, Alexander's adviser and then his successor as bishop. He attacked precisely the Arian vision of God as not that of the gospel. If God is not intrinsically Father of the Son, he is not intrinsically Father, for "father" is relational (*Discourse II against the Arians*). But being fatherly defines the God Christians worship. Therefore he can no more be God without the Son than light can be without shining (*Epistle on the Decree of Nicaea*, 2; 12). It is Origen's doctrine of the eternal generation of the Son—that the origin of the Son from the Father is not *in* time at all—that is here adapted. The very being of the Father would be unfinished without the Son; God's goodness is that God is Father; God's truth is the Son (*Discourse I against the Arians*, 14, 28; 20); and the Son cannot be a creature willed by the Father because the Son *is* the Father's will (*Discourse III*, 68). It is not too much to say that, for Athanasius, *what* the Son reveals about God is exactly that God is his Father.

Since relation to us, as the Father of our Lord, is internal to God's being, there is no need for bridge-beings between God and us. The great religious need of late antiquity is not filled by the gospel; it is abolished. Then Athanasius is free to label the adjectival and graded use of "God" as what it is: "polytheism, for since they [the Arians] call [the Son] God, because it is so written, but do not call him proper to the Father's being, they introduce a plurality of . . . forms of divine being" (*Discourse III*, 15).

Assimilating created beings to God is the very principle of the non-Christian religion: "This is the characteristic of the Greeks, to introduce a creature into the Trinity" (*Discourse* III, 18). The middle realm is gone altogether: "If Son, not creature; if creature, not Son" (*Nicaea*, 13).

Nicaea and Constantinople

Therefore, driven by equal and opposite ultimate concerns, the churchmen of the eastern Empire fell on one another when Arius said, "when he was not." Just at this point the first Christian emperor assumed power. Constantine came as an agent of universal peace, dreaming of the *pax Romana* restored by the new religion of love, and he found the very bishops in a brawl, the most learned in the front. After initial efforts to restore peace failed, he commanded a general council of the bishops of the eastern Empire, to meet at Nicaea in 325 in succession of an earlier Egyptian council.

Those who attended found themselves at the first great meeting of ecumenical Christianity, in a world suddenly turned from persecution to supplication. Understandably, they were in no more mood for disturbers of unity than was Constantine. They confirmed the condemnation of Arius and deposed his more intransigent supporters. And they produced a rule for talk about Christ which excluded Arius and his immediate followers but which all others, even Eusebius of Nicomedia, contrived to sign. Into a typical three-article liturgical creed, they inserted four theological explications: Christ, they said, is "out of the being of the Father," "true God of true God," "begotten not created," and "*homoousios* (of one being) with the father."[56] This is the dogma of Nicaea, the first deliberately created dogma and a main object of this whole *locus*.

"Out of the being of the Father" affirms just that origin of Christ within God's own self that Arius most feared. The phrase says that the Son is not an entity originated outside God by God's externally directed choice, that he is not in any sense a creature. And it says there *is* differentiation within God, that the relation to the Son is an internal relation in the Father, a relation necessary to his being God the Father. *To be God is to be related.* With that the fathers contradicted the main principle of Hellenic theology.

"Born, not created . . ." makes exactly that distinction between two ways of being originated from God, the lack of which enabled the subordinationist glissando from God himself, who is unoriginated, to us, who are originated, through the Son, who is a bit of each. On the contrary, we are "created," the Son is "begotten," and these are just two different things. Nobody claimed to know exactly what "begotten" meant in this connection. Yet a tremendous assertion is made: There is a way of being begun, of receiving one's being, which is proper to godhead itself. To be God is not only to give being; it is also to receive being. And there went the rest of Plato.

"True God of true God" prohibits all use of the analogy principle in calling Jesus "God." He is plain God, not qualified God. What the clause prohibits is the whole Greek use of "God" as an adjective applicable in various degrees.

Finally there is the famous and fateful "*homoousios* with the Father." The history of the word *homoousios* was checkered.[57] Its first theological use was by gnostics, for the mythic emergences of their sundry divine entities. Origen used the word, but rarely, to say that the Son had all the same essential characters as the Father, but on another ontological level.[58]

We do not know how or why this came to be Nicaea's big word. Perhaps it was introduced precisely by Arius's negative use simply to contradict him. Arius had said, "The Son . . . is not *homoousios* with [the Father]" to reject Western-type trinitarianism or any notion of Father and Son being two by division of one substance.[59]

The bishops seemingly did not have any one meaning in mind when they used *homoousios*. Constantine's Western advisers at Nicaea, thinking in Latin, no doubt took *homoousios* as a simple translation of Tertullian's "of one substance" and had no further problem. For those who thought in Greek it was not so simple. Did *homoousios* mean the same as it did in Origen? The most ardent anti-Arians, such as Athanasius, suspected it might, and might therefore be a poor guard against subordinationism; they were for a time wary in their use of it. Did it mean that Father and Son both had all the characteristics of godhead, whatever these are? Then are there not two (or three) Gods? Or did it, in more Aristotelian fashion, mean that Father and Son were numerically one actual entity? But how then could modalism be avoided? The Lucianists feared modalism could not be avoided, and when one of the chief Nicene anti-Arians, Marcellus of Ancyra, turned out in fact to be a modalist, they had a horror example ever after.[60]

Yet so much was clear: *Homoousios* meant that Arius was a heretic. Affirmatively, there is only one divine being, and both Father and Son have it. Whatever it means to be God, pure and simple, Christ is. And that suffices to make the needed and revolutionary point: Christ is not at all the sort of halfway entity that normal religion needs and provides to mediate time and eternity. He is not a divine teacher or example, a personal savior, a mediator of grace, or any of the beloved semigods of standard religion. He is constitutive of God, not merely revelatory—or if one develops a whole theology of revelation, then being revealed in Christ is itself constitutive of God.

Abrupt and almost instinctive though they were, the Nicene phrases make the decisive differentiation between Christian and other interpretations of God, then and now. Proclamation of a God or salvation that do not fit cannot be the gospel, however otherwise religious or beneficial. The Arian incident was the decisive crisis to date, and the Nicene Creed the decisive victory to date, in Christianity's self-identification. The gospel—Nicaea finally said unequivocally—provides no mediator of our ascent to a timeless and therefore distant God. It rather proclaims a God whose own deity is not separable from a figure of our temporal history and who therefore is not and never has been timeless and distant from us.

The bishops were not clearly aware of what they had said with this creed, except that Arius had gone too far. When they went home, they slowly became aware. Then the real fight began, to last for sixty years. In some ways, it still continues.

Subordinationist trinitarianism had not yet undone itself
from within; it had only been renounced in a crude version. A
variety of moves could seemingly yet be tried to combine the
glissando of being with the difference between Creator and
creature. In the next forty years each such move would produce
a new creedal proposal and a new alignment against Athanasius. Moreover, the Nicene dogma was incomplete; what about
the Spirit? So soon as the matter was noted—in Egypt again—a
whole new spectrum of disputes displayed itself.

The Lucianists begin the new struggle, refusing to take Nicaea
as the last word and working for possession of the bishoprics
and for ecumenical acceptance of a more moderate creed.[61] The
lineup shifted with each new theological attempt. At one end of
the spectrum were two groups: Athanasius with his followers,
and the Western bishops, who stuck to Tertullian's formula,
never quite understood the Easterners' problems, and supported
Athanasius when they dared. It took some daring, for after
Nicaea the anti-Nicene reaction usually contrived to look like
the peace-loving middle of the road, and so to secure imperial
support. At the other end were actual Arians, some willing to be
called that and others not, sporadically recruited from the Origenist middle. In between were the majority of Eastern churchmen, whose common purpose was to preserve the traditional
Origenist theology of the East. But, once the challenge of the
homoousios was there, their ground proved slippery, and the left
wing constantly slid into practically Arian positions.

After initial hesitation Athanasius made *homoousios* his
slogan, to mean that the Father and the Son—and the Spirit—
together make the one reality of God: It is the Trinity as such that
is God.[62] Whatever sundry bishops at Nicaea meant by *homoousios*, it is with this point that the word enters dogmatic history.
The various anti-Nicene coalitions took the Father *by himself* as
really God, and the Son, next down on the spectrum of being,
as very closely—perhaps even altogether—assimilated to God.
Confused as the terminologies were, the issue was and is clear
and vital to faith. The issue is not so much about the status of
Jesus as about who and what is God himself.

Anti-*homoousian* slogans waxed and waned.[63] None quite worked; then a new one would be tried. The final result of the anti-Nicene movement was the discrediting of subordination-ism, by the destruction of the confessional unity of the Eastern church. For example, in Antioch just before 360 there was a complete denominational system: a congregation of out-and-out Arians, a congregation of sophisticated Arians, the official church with a Eusebian bishop, a pro-Nicene group that had submitted to the bishop but held their own meetings, and a separate congregation of intransigent Nicaeans.[64]

As the weary creed-making went on, many not originally of Athanasius's party began to see that the vision of God evoked by *homoousios*—as used by Athanasius—was theirs too.[65] What was needed for the East was an explanation of how this could work, of how one might indeed say that Father and Son are one God, and that this is not a matter of levels, without thereby falling into modalism, that is, how one could hold to Origen's decisive insight that Father, Son, and Spirit are indeed three in God, otherwise than by ranking them ontologically.

Such a theory was finally provided in the 370s by a brilliant new generation of teachers and bishops, again schooled by Origen but using his dialectic to overcome his subordinationism. The most powerful thinkers among these were the Cappadocians: Basil, primate of Cappadocia, his brother, Gregory of Nyssa, and his protégé, Gregory of Nazianzus. Analysis of their thought belongs to the next chapter. Here a rough characterization will suffice. The Cappadocians took Origen's three hypostases and his real distinctions among them, in Origen a ladder reaching vertically from God to time, and tipped it on its side, to make a structure horizontal to time and reaching from point to point in God. Just such a stroke of dialectic was what was needed to enable general acceptance of Nicaea's dogma.

Emperor Theodosius I, determined like his predecessors to reunite the church, summoned yet another council at Constantinople in 381.[66] It was a council of Basil's followers, and it succeeded where all before had failed. It proclaimed the Nicene confession as the official confession of the East by adopting another regional baptismal creed that in Nicene use had been enriched with the Nicene phrases. And it added an affirmation of the full deity of the Spirit, with insertions into the third article: ". . . the Lord, the Giver of life, proceeding from the Father, worshiped and glorified with the Father and the Son . . ." In this article, the word *homoousios* was itself avoided, so as not to start the struggle about terminology again.

The article on the Spirit completed the trinitarian dogma. Since the Spirit was, on the subordinationist hierarchy, one more step from God than the Logos, affirmation of the full godhead of the Spirit marked final rejection of the whole subordinationist principle. On this affirmation the middle of the road sorted itself into those who entered the reconstituted ecumenical church and those who continued in waning opposition or sectarianism.[67]

One step remains in the story of the Nicene dogma. In 451, long after these battles were over, the Council of Chalcedon formally proclaimed both the creed of Nicaea and the creed of Constantinople as dogma for the whole church, East and West.[68] Since then, the Constantinopolitan creed—incorrectly called the Nicene Creed—has come to dominate liturgical use, since it contains the phrases for the Spirit. Both creeds together are the dogmatic documents. It has since been an ecumenical rule of all talk in the Christian church: In all three temporal directions of our relation to Jesus Christ, we have unsurpassably to do with God, and just by this circumstance our God differs from the culture-God of Western civilization, even in his Christianized versions.

CHAPTER FOUR

The One and the Three

*Developed trinitarian dialectics, such as the proposition
that God is "three persons of one substance," are metaphysical analysis of the gospel's triune identification of
God, and especially of its difference from the Hellenic
interpretation of God. The need for such analysis has not
passed; indeed, at present it is more urgent than since
antiquity.*

The Eastern Trinitarian Terminology

Two centuries of passionate reflection brought the Eastern
church back to the rule of faith with which it began. But now
there is an agreed conceptuality, provided by the Cappadocians:
"one being (*ousid*) of God in three hypostases (*hypostaseis*)." The
conceptuality was derived from expressions of Origen[1] and at
a second session of Theodosius' council, in 382, was taken into
approved ecclesiastical use.[2] In elucidating it, we will both explicate the Cappadocian analysis and continue to some analysis of
our own.

At a first level, "one being in three hypostases" was merely a
sort of linguistic settlement, stipulating terminology for a perceived need that somehow we be able to refer both to one reality
of God and to three realities of God. In most theological use,
ousia and *hypostasis* had previously been handled as rough
equivalents. The decree of Nicaea used both indiscriminately
in the singular in asserting the oneness of the triune reality, as
did Athanasius all his life.[3] The entire Origenist spectrum used
both in the plural in asserting that there really are three somehow different realities in the Trinity.[4] The new terminological

regulation, finding two words for "what is real" in trinitarian use, split the difference and took one for the one and the other for the three.

Thereby the East was provided with a trinitarian terminology extensionally equivalent to the West's "one substance (*substantia*) in three persons (*personae*)." But it is vital to understand that the two terminologies are not intentionally equivalent: If a proposition in the one is simply set into the other, its meaning is not necessarily preserved. Failure to observe this has been and is the cause of a great deal of confusion. "Substance" and "person" had never been interchangeable. Just so, their distinction evoked no new insight. Nor did they carry any history of trinitarian controversy.[5]

Ousia and *hypostasis* both came into theology from the philosophical tradition.[6] There they were used almost interchangeably, for *what is*—conformably to Hellenic apprehension, for what is by possession of some specific complex of permanent characteristics. Just so, they are also used for the "being" so possessed, that is, for both this complex of characteristics and for the stability through time their possession bestows.

Between *ousia* and *hypostasis* there were nevertheless slight nuances of difference. *Ousia* tended to be used for the reality that real things have and so to evoke, for example, the humanity Socrates has, but not so much the marks by which he as human differs from other beings, while *hypostasis* sounded more strongly the notes of distinguishability and identifiability. When trinitarian use divided the terms, the division was made along the line of these nuances. *Hypostasis* now meant simply that which can be identified, while *ousia* meant *what* such an identifiable *is*.[7] This necessarily dropped *hypostasis* to the level of individuals and located *ousia* at the level of the being any one kind of individuals are in common—except that *hypostasis* brought with it an aura of metaphysical dignity that previous terms for the individual lacked.

Just this is the starting position of the Cappadocian analysis: Father, Son, and Spirit, they say, are three individuals who share Godhead, as Peter, Paul, and Barnabas are three individuals who share humanity.[8] The one being of God is common to the three hypostases, which are distinguished by the individually identifying characteristics of "being unbegotten," "being begotten," and "proceeding."[9] Clearly this lays them open to this question: "As Peter, Paul, and Barnabas are three men, why are Father, Son, and Spirit not *three gods*?"[10] The Cappadocians' metaphysical creativity appears in their answer to this challenge.

The Three Hypostases

The Cappadocians reworked the concepts *ousia* and *hypostasis*. We will consider *hypostasis* first. The plural individuals that share humanity differ from one another by characteristics adventitious to—indeed, in the usual Hellenic view, privative of—the humanity they have in common: by brown hair, moderate intelligence, Athenian ancestry, or whatever. Just so, they are plural humans. But, said the Cappadocians, Godhead can receive no such adventitious or privative characteristics. Therefore there is no way for a plurality of divine hypostases, if their plurality is somehow established, to make a plurality of Gods.[11] Their argument, it should be noted, holds only if the graded adjectival use of "God" has become utterly inconceivable, which is just what Christian theological self-consciousness had achieved.

And there is indeed a way, without characteristics adventitious to or privative of Godhead, for the three to be individually identified. Their individually identifying characteristics are the *relations* they have to each other, precisely with respect to their joint possession of deity. God is the Father as the source of the Son's and the Spirit's Godhead; God is the Son as the recipient of the Father's Godhead; and God is the Spirit as the spirit of the Son's possession of the Father's Godhead.[12] The different way in which each is the one God, for and from the others, is the only difference between them.[13]

We have arrived at a certain completion of the dialectic. We have also arrived at a point where some more than historical interpretation and reflection is needed. There are two matters to consider.

First, we must remind ourselves what all these word games are about. The "hypostases" are Jesus, and the transcendent will he called Father, and the Spirit of their future for us. Just as vital to remember, the hypostases' "relations" are Jesus' historical obedience to and dependence on his Father and the coming of their future into the believing community. "Begetting," "being begotten," "proceeding," and their variants are biblical terms for temporal structures of evangelical history, which theology then uses to evoke relations constitutive of God's life. What happens between Jesus and his Father and our future happens in God—that is the point.

It was the achievement of the Cappadocians to find a conceptualized way to say this, by arranging Origen's hypostases and their *homoousia* horizontally to time rather than vertically to time, making the hypostases' mutual relations structures of the one God's life, rather than steps from God down to us.[14] Then the Trinity as such is the Creator, over against the creature, and the three in God and their relations become the evangelical history's reality on the Creator side of the great biblical divide. Across the Creator/creature distinction, no *mediator* is needed;[15] "Creator"/"creature" names an absolute difference, but no distance at all, for to be the Creator is merely as such to be actively related to the creature. Each of the inner-trinitarian relations is then an affirmation that as God works creatively among us, so he is in himself.

It was time, we said, to remind ourselves of these things. The Nicene dogma and the Cappadocian analysis were victories in the confrontation between the gospel's and Hellenism's interpretations of God. But the confrontation is by no means concluded. One continuous post-Nicene threat has been the temptation to interpret the Trinity as a whole by the Hellenic negative theology, so that the Trinity in its turn disappears into the old distant timelessness, carrying its internal reflection of evangelical history right with it. Already in the Cappadocians there is a danger signal: their tendency to take refuge in mystery when asked what "begetting" and "proceeding" *mean*.[16] Why should there be a problem? There is none about what these words mean as slogans

for saving historical events. No more should there be about their
trinitarian meanings—unless the understanding of the triune
life itself is infiltrated with impassibility, immobility, and so on,
with reference to which a word like "proceeding" cannot indeed
mean much.

Once the temporal reference of trinitarian language is reaf-
firmed, we can turn again to the conceptual problem of the
three hypostases. As a piece of trinitarian language, *hypostasis* is
merely an item of linguistic debris knocked from Hellenic philosophy by collision with Yahweh. Present understanding would
be advanced if we replaced it with a word now philosophically
active. Readers will not be surprised that we propose "identity,"
for as is apparent from the history of the adaptation of *hypostasis* to trinitarian use, it is exactly the ontological function
now marked by "identity" that the trinitarian *hypostasis*, in its
separation from *ousia*, invoked. We explicate this function in
two steps.

First, something's identity is the possibility of picking it out
from the maelstrom of actuality so as to talk about it. The enu-
merability of the world, whereby we can say "this, and this, and
then this" is one of the world's deepest metaphysical characters.
This character, taken of any one such "this," is an identity.

We identify in various ways. We point and say "this." But
often we cannot point. Then we have two linguistic resources:
proper names and identifying descriptions, as discussed earlier.

Accordingly, that there are three identities in God means that
there are three discrete sets of names and descriptions, each sufficient to specify uniquely, yet all identifying the same reality.
Among them that which says "God is what happens with Jesus"
has the epistemological priority of the present tense, so that in
each of the other two, terms will appear which, if interpretation
is required, can only be interpreted by reference to Jesus' story.
For example, if we say "God is the hope at the beginning of all
things" and then are asked "Hope for what?" we must answer,
"Hope for Jesus' triumph."

The three identifications can otherwise be performed independently. But the predicates we use of the one identified in any

of the three ways can be made unambiguous—should ambiguity threaten—only by running them across all three identities. For example, "God is good in the way that a giver is good; and God is good in the way that a gift is good; and God is good in the way that the outcome of a gift is good."

Second, "identity" is now regularly used to interpret personal existence, as we may say that someone is "seeking identity." This sense is connected to the first; it names the mode of identifiability proper to certain entities, those we currently call "personal" in a sense very different from the trinitarian "person." As person, in this modern sense, I am what I am only in that I remember what I have been and hope for what I will be. If Jones is a person, in this modern sense, the "is" in "Jones is lazy" is not quite a normal copula; it is more like a transitive verb, modifiable by adverbs. It is the word for a specific act of positing oneself in and through time. Existentialist thought has invented words like "existence" or *Dasein* for this act. *Hypostasis* in its pretrinitarian and prechristological uses did not have this sense, but in the often tortured ways in which the theological tradition has used *hypostasis*, just this sense for the peculiar identity of person-realities struggled for expression already in the Cappadocians.

Accordingly, that there is even one identity in God means that God is personal, that he *is* God in that he *does* Godhead, in that he chooses himself as God. That there are three identities in God means that this God's deed of being the one God is three times repeated,[17] and so that each repetition is a being of God; and so that only in this precise self-repetition is God the particular God that he in fact is. God does God, and over again, and yet over again—and only so does the event and decision that is this God occur.

The One Being

Back to the Cappadocians. They needed also a correlated analysis of the divine *ousia* to show how it could be the being of three individuals without these being three instances of God.

They had a variety of arguments; we will follow one by Gregory of Nyssa.

Since there is only one Godhead, the Trinity is somehow individual and must therefore be identifiable if real. And Gregory indeed provides an identifying description of the one *ousia* of God—but this is precisely that God's being is infinite.[18] We can identify God's one being as and only as life that knows no boundary and that therefore will always go on to surpass each— even true—identifying description.[19] This need not mean we cannot at all identify God affirmatively: God is "the one who raised Jesus," but then we are with the three rather than with the one.

Gregory is fully aware of the break he is making with philosophical tradition. He states the view "of the many," which he rejects. According to that view, "God" is, like "human" or "rock," "an unmetaphorical name by nature," "predicated to identify by the nature of the thing" (*To Ablabius*, 121). Such a word evokes some entity's entire set of essential characters all at once, insofar as these make an organic complex so that each character is itself only together with the others. Just so, such a word uniquely displays "the underlying individual subject" (ibid.), that which in any real thing *has* all the characters by which that thing is what it is, and is itself established as the possible possessor of these characters and no others. For God, says Gregory, there is no such word (ibid.).

Thus—and we are finally to the point—Gregory's answer to the question why three individuals sharing God's *ousia* do not make three gods is that "God" and all its equivalents are not predicated of the divine *ousia* at all, singly or trebly. "God" is a predicate, and how many gods are asserted depends on how many logical subjects it is attached to. A plurality of instances of the divine *ousia* is not a plurality of *gods*, for the *ousia* is not the logical subject of "God" to begin with, and neither then are the *ousia*'s instances; how many individuals are instances of God's *ousia* is irrelevant to how many gods there are.

What then *is* "God" predicated of? Gregory's revolutionary answer: of the divine *activity* toward us (ibid., 124). And since all divine action is the structuredly mutual work of Father, Son, Spirit, their divine activity is but one logical subject of "God": "All action which comes upon the creature from God . . . begins from the Father and is present through the Son and is perfected in the Holy Spirit. Therefore the name of the action ('God') is not divided among the plurality of the actors" (ibid., 127). Gregory of Nazianzus once revised an old trinitarian illustration in an astonishing way. Instead of comparing Father, Son, and Spirit to the sun and its beams, he compared them to three suns, so focused as to make but one beam: The beam is God (*Oration XXXI*, 14).

The divine *ousia* does not drop out of the picture, for the inner-trinitarian relations, by which there are three to begin with, are defined in terms of it. It is precisely deity as infinity which the Father gives, the Son receives, and the Spirit communicates; by their relations, the action of each is temporally unlimited, to be *God's* action. But it is the *work*, the creative event, done through Jesus' life, death, resurrection, and future advent, done by his Father for their Spirit, that is the one God.

Surely this tendency is biblically right, at least by that understanding of the biblical witness sketched above. Stipulating an event as the subject of "God" imposes a task of ontological revision, to which we must eventually turn, as did Gregory. But leaving that for the moment, and recalling the discussion of "identity," we obtain the following formula: There is one event, God, of three identities. Therewith this essay's proposed basic trinitarian analysis.

The Western Version

The struggle and creation we have narrated in this and the previous chapter took place in the Eastern church. Its results were assimilated into the West from the late fourth century on. The circumstances of the assimilation have been decisive for the thought and life of the Western church. Without attempting to judge relative importance, we may list three such circumstances.

First, the doctrine of the Trinity came to the West as a finished product. Thus it was more something to be explained, than itself an explanation.

Second, in conducting trinitarian analysis and speculation in Latin, the Greek results were pressed into a terminology previously established in the Latin tradition: There is one "substance" of God (or "essence" or "nature"), in three "persons." But these terms had been through none of the Eastern conceptual wars; and when it came to the creative thrusts of such Easterners as Gregory of Nyssa, Western readers invariably missed the point. Augustine himself confessed incomprehension of the key Greek distinction: "I do not know what difference they intend between *ousia* and *hypostasis*."[20]

Third, the work of synthesis between Eastern thought and Western language and need was almost entirely the work of one man, Augustine, one of history's few history-shaping geniuses. Augustine's personal spiritual and intellectual experiences impressed themselves on Western theology in a way unparalleled in Christian history. In much of theology, this has been a blessing, but it has blighted our trinitarianism, for Augustine's particular religious experience led him to understand the triune character of God as one thing, the history of salvation as quite another. Thus the trinitarian formulas completely lost their original function.[21]

All these circumstances promoted a sort of reversion to pre-Nicene thinking. Hellenic interpretation of God had never been fully overcome in the general theology of the Eastern fathers, only within the trinitarian dogma and analyses themselves, and there by subtle and easily lost distinctions. The way thus remained open for Western theology to repristinate the old apologists' additive tactic in a new form. And that is what happened over the long history of Western theology. The inheritance of Hellenic interpretation was received as what the scholastics would come to call "natural" theology, a body of truth about God shared with the heathen and so taken to be resultant, at least in principle, from the merely created circumstances of life and the merely created religious and intellectual capacities of the soul. Such of the biblical discourse about God as was not shared by the heathen was therefore thought not to be thus generally available; it was received as a higher supernatural body of truth about God, given only by revelation. But when the matter is put so, the natural knowledge of God becomes the foundation of the supernatural; Homer and Parmenides get to write the first chapter in the *locus* on God. Consequently, the supposed timelessness and impassibility of God inevitably determine all that follows, including the trinitarian discourse.[22]

Augustine laid down this axiomatic status of divine timelessness for all subsequent Western theology: "Speak of the changes of things, and you find 'was' and 'will be'; think God, and you find 'is' where 'was' and 'will be' cannot enter."[23] God not only does not change; he cannot. Just so, "he is rightly said *to be*" (*On the Trinity*, v, 2).

This uncritical repristination of Greek assumptions had two consequences directly relevant to our interest. One was the doctrine of divine "simplicity," which became a key technical device of all consequent Western trinitarian analysis. Since it is by having "accidents," that is, characteristics that can come and go, that ordinary realities give hostages to time, God, it was agreed, has none such (ibid., v, 3). As Thomas Aquinas argued it, accidents are the mark of potentiality, of capacity for becoming other than one is; this is absent from God (*Summa Theologica*, i, 3, 6). But so long as there is a real difference between the thing and its characteristics, it must be possible for the substance to remain while at least some characteristics come and go, that is, some must be accidents. Therefore in God there is no such difference; as Augustine puts it: "God is not great by a greatness other than himself . . . ; he is great by that greatness . . . he himself is" (*On the Trinity*, v, 11). "God is called 'simple' because he *is* what he *has*" (*City of God*, 1, xi, 10, 1).

The second consequence was the reintrusion into the heart of trinitarianism of the old late-antique worry about the relation of a supposedly timeless God to his temporal creation, with evil results. Augustinianism forbade any assertion about God's relation to time that could suggest change in God himself. That there is a difficulty here, Augustine himself acknowledged: "To see how God . . . creates temporal things and events without any temporal movement of his substance . . . is hard" (*On the Trinity*, i, 3). Nevertheless, he lays down the rule: When we speak of God being "our Lord," which he could not be before we existed, or of God's "becoming our Father at baptism," or of all the like, we must understand that "nothing is added to God, but only to that to which God is said to take up a relation." Thus, for example, "God begins to be our Father when we are reborn. . . . Our substance is changed for the better when we become his children; therewith he also begins to be our Father, but without any such change" (ibid., v, 17).

The single most disastrous trinitarian result of this rule is that Western teaching, rigorously sorting out usages that had in the East been beneficially vague, makes the trinitarian "processions" in God (i.e., "begetting" and "breathing") and the divine persons' "missions" in time (i.e., the Son's Incarnation and the Spirit's entry into the church; i.e., again, the whole triune reality as Tertullian or Athanasius evoked it) be two simply different and metaphysically separated things: "'mission' and 'sending' . . . are predicated only temporally, 'generation' and 'breathing' only eternally."[24] That the Son, for example, is "begotten" by the Father, and that he is "sent" to redeem humanity, are now thought of as distinct events, one in eternity and the other in time: "The Son is said to be sent, not . . . in that he is born of the Father, but either in that he appears in this world as the Word made flesh . . . , or in that he is inwardly apprehended by a temporal mind."[25] Indeed, Aquinas' argument why there must be exactly the two processions is that the Son emerges by an act of the Father's mind and the Spirit by an act of his will, and that thinking and willing are the only two personal movements that do not necessarily emerge from the agent, that is, here, from God to a temporal object (*Summa Theologica*, i, 27, 5). In this theology, there are in effect two distinct sets of trinitarian relations, one constituting an "immanent" Trinity, the triune God himself, and the other the "economic" Trinity, the triune pattern of God's work.

The final consequence of these developments is that the trinitarian language of "persons" and "relations" in God loses its original meaning and indeed threatens to lose all meaning of any sort. That God is "one and three" becomes the sheer mystification Western churchgoers accept—or reject—it as: something we assert because we are supposed to, not knowing even what we are asserting. Augustine provided Western theology with a neat formula to sum up the decades of Eastern trinitarian reflection: The Father is God, and the Son is God, and the Spirit is God; and the Father and the Son and the Spirit are not the same one; and the three are but one God.[26] But the formula no longer represents an activity of analysis to help to understand God. It is instead a paradox formula: Since God is infinite, so that addition and subtraction do not apply, "one is as much as three are together." (*On the Trinity*, vi, 12). And with his invariable clarity Augustine sees very well what then happens to the trinitarian language. He explicitly stipulates that when we say one "substance" or three "persons" we communicate nothing whatever, using the words only to say "somehow one" and "somehow three" and using these particular words only because they are traditional (ibid., v, 10; vii, 7–11). Later theology then makes pious mystery-mongering of the vacuity; for example, it is standard from Lombard on that the Son's "being begotten" differs from the Spirit's "proceeding" only by a difference that cannot be "known in this life" (*Sentences*, i, 13).

That the saving works of God, the "works *ad extra*," are works of the whole Trinity no longer can mean that each work is the joint work of Father, Son, and Spirit, in which each identity plays a distinct role,[27] but that the saving works are *indifferently* the work of each person and all; the "inseparability" of God's works is now identified with a mathematically equal abstract divinity of the triune persons. Creation is undifferentiably the work of the Trinity as one God. And the "sender" of each divine mission is the Trinity, or any of the persons, including the one sent.[28]

So also there is no longer any necessary connection of the trinitarian persons to roles and structures of saving history. According to Augustine, the theophanies of the Hebrew Scriptures could have been appearances of any trinitarian person, or of the Trinity as such; only exegesis decides for each instance, and no theological difference is made by the result (*On the Trinity*, ii; iii, 3). Finally, with Lombard it becomes standard for all scholasticism that "just as the Son was made man, so the Father or the Holy Spirit *could* have been and can be now" (*Sentences*, iii, i, 3). With this last proposition, the bankruptcy of trinitarian meaning is complete. "The Son" or "the Logos" were originally titles for Jesus in respect of his role in God's saving reality; now they name a pure metaphysical entity, not necessarily related to Jesus at all and—equally with the other divine persons—available for whatever divine duty comes along.

The original meaning of "Father," "Son," "begets," "gift," and so on, as words for the reality of saving history in God, having evaporated, Western theology was compelled to find other ways of sustaining the trinitarian terminology's meaningfulness— unless, of course, the whole doctrine was to be abandoned, which was not thinkable before the sixteenth century. Since the relation between the creature and God is now back to the old Hellenic standoff between temporality and its abstract negation, also the Hellenic way of giving meaning to talk of timeless deity was inevitably adopted: "Persons" and "relations" are taken to be reality in God describable by *analogy* from temporal reality.[29] The whole pattern of Western theology is already set in the sequence of Augustine's *On the Trinity*. The first seven books analyze inherited trinitarian formulas by the axiom of divine simplicity and end with their reduction to vacuity. This result demands the search for created analogues of triunity that occupies the remaining books.[30] And the chosen created reality is the human soul, where from Socrates on the "image" of timeless deity had been chiefly sought.[31] In that God is triune, and in that temporal being is ontologically dependent on inner analogy to timeless being, and in that for the intrinsically self-conscious soul the grasp of this analogy is its own active reality, we can meaningfully say "Father, Son, and Spirit" about God[32]— according to Augustine and his followers. Therewith the whole relation of God to his work in time reverted to the pre-Nicene conception of the temporal imaging of timeless reality. Arius was the winner after all.

All temporal being, according to Augustine and his Platonist teachers, is dependent on God in respect of its being, of its intelligibility, and of its activity. The triune image of God in the soul is the realization of these dependences in the mode appropriate to consciousness:[33] "We *are*, we *know* that we are, and we *love* this being and this knowing" (*City of God*, xi, 26, 7–9). And since this self-consciousness is necessarily also God-consciousness (e.g., *On the Trinity*, viii, 3–6), the triple structure of consciousness is an image of divine triplicity: "This . . . trinity of the mind is not the image of God only because the mind remembers itself and knows itself and loves itself, but because it can also remember and know and love the one by whom it is created" (ibid., xiv, 12).

All Augustine's trinitarian analogies, the stock-in-trade of subsequent Western reflection, are but variant descriptions of this structure of simultaneous self- and God-consciousness. The triple dependence is most directly reflected in this formula: being/knowledge/love.[34] Since in the soul's dependence its being is love, this formula can turn into: the soul as lover/the soul as object of its own love, that is, as known to itself/the soul as love (ibid., viii, ix, 1–3). The love trinity in its turn, translated into a description of the soul as a substance, becomes: mind/knowledge/love (ibid., ix, 3–4). And translating yet again, to a more functional analysis, we get memory/knowledge/will (ibid., x), for the mind as consciousness is identical with itself as being in that it is memory, and love is the action of will.

Our discussion of Western trinitarianism must alternate between lamentation and admiration of the virtues of its defects. We must now note the first such virtue. In turning to the soul for a meaning-giving analogue of divine triunity, Augustine necessarily exposed his introspection to some pressure from inherited trinitarian language. Thus he discovered the dialectical complexity of the soul's own reality. That the soul is complex, all antiquity knew. But that the complexity is living and dialectical, that in it each factor is what it is only by and for the other factors,

Augustine was first to note. "The soul would not seek to know itself..., if it did not in some fashion love itself, with a love which again depends on the knowledge given in memory."[35] In effect, Augustine, looking for analogues of triune deity, discovered the ontological difference of conscious from unconscious being, the great theme of all subsequent Western philosophy.[36] And then Augustine does, however grudgingly, reflect all this back again on God: "Or are we indeed to suppose that the consciousness that God is, knows other things and does not know itself...? Behold therefore the Trinity: consciousness, and knowledge of self, and love of self" (ibid., xv, 10). Several steps removed from authentic trinitarian insight though this interpretation of God is, it is a great intellectual achievement in itself, and one made under the pressure of Scripture. That God is personal is a deeply Christian notion and an abiding contribution of Western theology.

The second virtue of Western trinitarianism is that precisely the ultimately hopeless task of thinking the plurality of persons within the notion of a temporally undifferentiable God, and within so abstract a notion of God's unity as represented by the simplicity axiom, compelled Western theology to work out the abstract dialectics of tri-identicality to perfection.[37] Lombard, following Augustine, laid down the dialectical boundary conditions: "The Father is not greater than the Son nor the Father or the Son than the Holy Spirit; nor are two persons together any greater something than one, nor three than two; nor is the divine essence greater in three persons than in two, nor in two than in one." In consequence, "the Father is in the Son and the Son in the Father and the Spirit in both, and each is in each and all" (*Sentences*, i, vix, 4–5). The rule acquired conciliar status: "The three persons are one . . . substance, one essence, one nature, one divinity, one immensity, one eternity; all divine reality is one where an opposition of relation does not prevent it."[38]

Distinctions in God are posited by inner divine "processions," of which there are two: the "begetting" of the Son and the "breathing" of the Spirit.[39] A "procession" is a "movement to an other"; the other of generation and spiration in God is God himself; therefore the divine simplicity is supposed not to be violated.[40]

Therefore also, since every procession establishes relations, there are relations in God. Moreover, these are "real" relations, that is, not merely external as between two coins possessed by one owner, each of which is the same as if not so related. For since *both* terms of each such relation are God, the relation cannot be external to its terms.[41]

This immediately gives a list of four relations: The Father "begets," the Son "is begotten," the Father and the Son "breathe," and the Spirit "is breathed."[42] And then we have five "notions" applicable to the inner-divine distinctions, the four relations plus "unbegotten" or "unoriginated" of the Father, marking his position as the starting point of all the processions, who himself does not proceed.[43] If now we seek identifying properties for each of the persons, "unoriginated" drops out, since it applies also to the Trinity as such, and so does "breathes," since it applies both to the Father and the Son. Thus, by the sheer geometry of the relational structure, we arrive at exactly three "properties" or "personal notions": "begets," "is begotten," "is breathed."[44] It surely must be said that the mere aesthetic rightness of this analysis somehow commends it. Figure 1 shows a flow chart of deity.

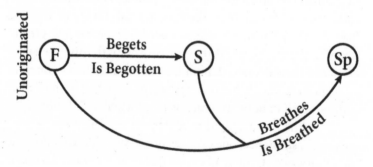

FIGURE 1

Then come the great metaphysical assertions. First, the relations, and so the personal properties, are each identical with the one divine substance, "with respect to the entity," that is, as we would say, "objectively," for "paternity" and "breathing forth" are in themselves divine attributes, and by the simplicity axiom each divine attribute is "with respect to the entity" the divine substance. The relations-properties differ from the divine substance only "with respect to the way we know them," except that "only" is misleading, since this necessity of our knowing is itself founded somehow in the divine reality. The relations and the essence are really the same, but the distinction we cannot help making is necessitated by that one reality.[45]

But if the relations are not merely real in God, but real insofar as and only insofar as they are identical with the divine substance, then they are real in God in the same way the divine substance is real. Thus they "subsist," that is, they are possessors of attributes (here the divine attributes) and doers of deeds (here the divine deeds). That is, again, they are proper "persons" in the regular Latin sense of the word.[46] And now, conversely, we can say what the "persons" truly are: "'Divine person' . . . means a relation as a subsistent."[47]

Within the metaphysical tradition, the notion of a subsistent relation is of course sheer nonsense. The scholastics labored mightily to mitigate the offense of their definition to what they accepted as natural truth. But so radical a doctrine of the reality of relations cannot be contained by Plato or Aristotle. That some relations, such as paternity, are founded in the related terms, inherited wisdom can accept. But this doctrine identifies the substantiality of the related terms with the internality of the relations between them. Even the classification of the personal properties to which the scholastics are driven—that they are *both* "relative" and yet "eternal and immutable"[48]—is a defiance of all Hellenic common sense.

This assertion of the substantiality of relations, that is, of their ontological independence and possible priority over against the related terms, is the main place at which the metaphysically revolutionary power of the gospel breaks out in Western theology. In the lead of the Greeks, our inherited ways of thinking suppose that there must first be *things* that in the second place may be variously related. But there is nothing intrinsically obvious about it; in fact, by biblical insight, it is the other way around.

The general consequences of this reversal of interpretation have long appeared in Western philosophy, most explicitly in some aspects of German idealism, as Hegel's definition of spirit as the relation between self and not-self, which just so is the being of the self.[49] The task of drawing out the more specifically theological consequences has lagged, as it must until the Augustinian doctrine of divine simplicity is discarded. That, indeed, is one purpose of this study, to which we have made various approaches and to which we will return.

The Athanasian Creed

The extent to which Augustinian trinitarian teaching can be taken as official doctrine of the Western church depends on the extent to which the so-called Athanasian Creed[50] establishes such doctrine. The long first section of this composition is a rhetorically splendid and theologically astute brief statement of Western trinitarian language-rules. The basic principle is that we "are neither to confuse the persons nor divide the substance."

The unity of substance will be preserved if we are careful to attribute all divine attributes equally to each person, but never so as to posit three logical subjects: "Uncreated is the Father, uncreated the Son, uncreated the Holy Spirit . . . ; and yet there are . . . not three Uncreateds . . . but one Uncreated . . ." and so on. This is hammered home in rolling repetitive periods, choosing just those attributes of God that were decisive over against the Arians: "uncreated," "immense," "eternal," "omnipotent," "infinite." In the straight line from Athanasius, the posit of three kinds of deity is rejected as polytheistic: "For just as we are compelled by Christian truth to confess that each person singly is God and Lord, so we are forbidden by the catholic religion to say that there are three gods or lords."

The distinction of persons is to be achieved by the language of relations, though this technical term does not appear. "The Father is from no one, not made nor created nor begotten. The Son is from the Father only, not made nor created but begotten. The Holy Spirit is from the Father and the Son, not made nor created nor begotten but proceeding." It should be registered that the most unfortunate features of Western analysis do not explicitly appear.

The Athanasian Creed seems to have originated around the turn of the fifth and sixth centuries in Spain or southern France. It became the text for trinitarian instruction in the Carolingian theological institutions, and enjoyed great prestige through the Middle Ages. From the eighth century on, it was sung as a canticle, usually at the first Sunday office. Most Reformation compendiums of official doctrine included it. It does indeed state the unproblematic part of the Western church's trinitarian inheritance.

Yet the text of the Athanasian Creed was never adopted by an ecumenical gathering in the style of Chalcedon. In the modern period, many committed to its doctrine have nevertheless had great difficulty in affirming it, especially in using it liturgically. The problem has been, generally, the creed's identification of "the catholic faith" with a particular theological analysis, and specifically the opening anathema, "which if anyone does not preserve integral and inviolate, he will without doubt perish eternally." That one should be damned for bad, or even merely out-of-date, theology has seemed a bit hard.

Perhaps the difficulty will at least appear in a different light if indeed, as now seems proven,[51] the text was written and initially used neither as a liturgical or personal confession but as a memory piece for seminary instruction. It is one thing for future preachers to understand that salvation hangs on their preaching and that they are to preach thus and so. It is quite another thing for a congregation publicly to proclaim curses on the theologically maladroit or anachronistic. At any rate, the retreat of the Athanasian Creed back into the classroom may be regarded as a return to the proper locus of its authority. There, however, it surely deserves the highest respect.

Vicissitudes of Western Trinitarianism

The danger of the West's abstract trinitarian analysis is not only that it is false, but also that it is likely to reflect negatively on the fundamental liturgical and proclamatory levels of trinitarian discourse. It seems plain that this has in fact happened, though tracing the history is beyond the scope of this work. One need only think of such phenomena as popular Catholicism's replacement of the triune structure for prayer with one or another piety of the "Jesus-Mary-Joseph" type, or of denominational Lutheranism's centuries-long affection for forms of prayer and praise with only second-article remembrance-content and no invocation of the Spirit, or of Calvinism's concentration of fear and hope on a pretemporal deity resembling nothing so much as Eunomius' "Unoriginate."

From Augustine on, the doctrine of the Trinity tended to become increasingly a "revealed mystery," taught in the proper place of theological systematics because it was supposed to have been supernaturally revealed that God was in fact triune, but having less and less interpretive force for the actual concerns of believers. As such, it was a setup for destructive critique. The critique has come from both the church and the world.

The doctrine has not easily been seen as functional within religious life. Thus one sort of critique, from within the heart of the church, has been benign neglect. The first Reformation system of theology, Melanchthon's *Loci communes* of 1521, omitted the developed doctrine altogether, on the grounds that "to know God is to know his benefits," thus clearly supposing that trinitarian discourse is not about God's benefits. Pietists in all branches of the church have regularly taken the same attitude,[52] as did John Locke[53] and other forerunners of the Enlightenment. Another sort of churchly critique has been more explicit. Western Christians have in effect found themselves, so far as experience is concerned, in a pre-Nicene situation. Many, liberated by historical or philosophical critique from affirming inherited doctrine just because it is inherited, have recapitulated pre-Nicene theological history, reinventing apologetic subordinationism and Arianism. It is this phenomenon which appears in such "unitarian" movements as have been explicitly Christian: Servetus, the Socinians,[54] or the English and American Unitarians.[55] It appears again in the "neologians," who in Germany mediated the first impact of the Enlightenment.[56] Since we have been over all that ground once, we need not here investigate any of these theologies, only note their existence and influence.

Such critique has not abated in our century. Currently influential are the arguments of Cyril C. Richardson, that inherited trinitarianism is the result of the use of inappropriate biblical and Hellenic language to state necessary theological insight into God's transcendence and immanence,[57] of G. W. H. Lampe, that we need more "personal" language and that the metaphysical problems generated by traditional language are insoluble,[58] and of C. F. D. Moule, that a "binity" would make sense but that there is no need to make a "person" of the Spirit.[59] In general, current objections are not very different from those of the eighteenth and nineteenth centuries and like them are based on the assumption that standard Western teaching is "the doctrine" of the Trinity.

The full Enlightenment, of course, rejected trinitarianism from quite another side.[60] The tradition itself posited two bodies of knowledge of God, "natural" and "supernatural," and stipulated the first as that accessible to "reason" and the second as obtained only by bowing to the authority of some agency of revelation. The Enlightenment was a declaration of reason's freedom over against authority; just so it countenanced only the "natural" part of theology. Thus the Enlightenment affirmed Aristotle's God in its purity, untouched even by such biblical contaminants as maintained by Augustine. Insofar as the Enlightenment was simply unchurchly, as in France, its unitarianism is outside our story. But insofar as it remained inside the church, as often in England or Germany or the United States, it mingled with such currents as described just before, to promote sundry modalisms and subordinationisms, as well as gentlemanly silent compacts to let sleeping "dogmatic" dogs lie. Under all these sorts of critique, the inherited doctrine of the Trinity was by the opening of the nineteenth century nearly defunct in all those parts of the church open to modernity.

The history of nineteenth-century spirituality and theology, at least in such parts of the church, was a series of attempts to overcome the Enlightenment with respect to its evacuation of religious substance, without returning to reliance on supernatural authority. Two great figures dominate the effort: Friedrich Schleiermacher and G. W. F. Hegel. Both are in fact important for current trinitarian thought. Schleiermacher typifies and largely inaugurated the dominant pattern of the nineteenth and twentieth centuries, which continues to get along without much trinitarianism. Hegel deliberately "renewed" the doctrine as a speculative insight, providing the pattern of other such attempts thereafter and much of the impetus and conceptual style for the more churchly twentieth-century renewal by Karl Barth.

Schleiermacher put his exceedingly brief section on the Trinity at the end of his systematics, as a sort of summary. There it cannot function to identify or interpret the God spoken of in the body of the work. Rather, having expounded what is effectively the contents of a three-article creed, Schleiermacher then takes such a creed's "Father . . . , Son . . . , Spirit" as a concluding memory device suggested by tradition. At the level of the immediate expression and critique of piety—which according to Schleiermacher is the only legitimate level for dogmatics—the doctrine's necessary function, he says, is to insist "that nothing less than the divine being was in Christ and inhabits the Christian church as its communal spirit, and that we do not take these expressions in any weakened sense . . . and intend to know nothing of . . . subordinate divinities" (*The Christian Faith*, 170, 1).[61] To that we must say, so far so good.

As a doctrine about the "divine being" itself, however, the doctrine of the Trinity is, according to Schleiermacher, a bungle. Such doctrine first results from "eternalizing the distinction between the being of God for itself and the being of God for the unification [with Jesus and the church]" (ibid., 170, 3). But just that move is disastrous. Schleiermacher's difficulty, it is vital to note, is precisely Augustine's: uncritical acceptance of the Greek dogma that divinity equals timelessness (ibid., 171, 52) and can therefore be spoken of only in analogies. "The divine causality [Schleiermacher's interpretation of God's reality] . . . must be conceived as utterly timeless. This is achieved through expressions which name temporal reality, and is therefore achieved by pictures; . . . one equates the temporal opposites before-and-after, earlier-and-later, and so suspends them" (ibid., 171, 1).

But where Augustine struggled to maintain some sense for the inherited trinitarian propositions, Schleiermacher just drops them. He is free to do this because of the new historical situation, but also because, according to him, specifically Christian apprehension does not reach to the basic understanding of God at all; this is borrowed (his word) from universally valid philosophical analysis (*Brief Description of Theological Study*, 43–53). In fact, despite what is usually said of him, Schleiermacher maintains a particularly simpleminded form of the disastrous old distinction of natural from revealed theology.

If, for reasons of purely intellectual harmonization, we still want a doctrine of triunity, Schleiermacher has two recommendations. First, the doctrine should be "Sabellian," a description of successive temporal manifestations of a divine reality itself unaffected thereby. Second, we should take "the Father" as a name for this divine reality, and "the Son" and "the Spirit" as names for the manifestations (*The Christian Faith*, 172, 3). Thus Schleiermacher's recommendation is exactly and compendiously Arian after all.

We need not decide whether Schleiermacher's version of the Trinity has greatly influenced nineteenth- and twentieth-century ordinary Christianity, or only marvelously exemplifies it. It is enough to note that most Protestant readers will recognize in the last paragraphs a description of what they gleaned from the catechetics and preaching of the mainline denominations.

Hegel deliberately set out to reinvigorate the inherited doctrine of the Trinity, by releasing its metaphysically revolutionary implications.[62] He made the Augustinian-Western version of the doctrine the center of his philosophy, the West's last universal and perhaps last great system of thought. Augustine, we have insisted, failed to describe a genuinely tri-identical God. But in the attempt he did perceive new truth; he perceived an in the modern sense *personal* God, whose being is constituted in the inner dialectics of consciousness, in the play of—now we will use the language of Hegel's time—immediate self-consciousness ("memory"), objective knowledge of self, and will that unites them. Hegel abandoned Augustine's hesitations, made this interpretation a universal concept of personal being, and then made all reality personal.

It was Hegel's goal to make a true synthesis of the two clashing streams of Western thought: the Greek will rationally to grasp reality's sense, and the Bible's grasp of reality as history, with all its contingencies and contradictions. This can be done, said Hegel, if we see that history makes its own kind of sense, which is the sense not of the merely beholding and sense-describing mind, but of the living and sense-creating spirit. The spirited rationality of poets and great statesmen—and of authentic philosophers like Plato—does not abstract from contingency and contradictions, only so to achieve itself; it posits them, to overcome and encompass them and so achieve an expanding, *living* meaning. Napoleon does not abhor enemies; he seeks them, to create a larger European order in the struggle. Goethe does not banish irrationality and conflict from his plots; he invents them, to achieve the meaning of drama rather than of mere chronicle. Abstractly stated: The rational subject posits the object, that which is not itself, not sheer transparent meaning. Then the rational subject achieves itself as the *process*, the *act*, of rediscovering itself in the object, that is, of finding meaning in what is not merely as such meaningful. This reconciliation of reason-as-subject with object-made-reasonable is living reason, spirit.

Since reality is historical, it is the sort of sense just described that reality has: the eternal creating and overcoming of contradiction in higher harmony. Since reality has this sort of sense, true reason is the mind that fulfills itself as just described, that works out its own reason precisely in contingent and contradiction-laden objective reality. The great metaphysical claim follows of itself: Reality-as-history makes sense only as the object of a Subject that finds itself therein, and so is itself Spirit. God is the Mind that has the world for object; he is the world insofar as Mind indeed finds sense, and so Itself, in the world; and he is the free Spirit that occurs as this event. God is the absolute Poet-Statesman-Philosopher. God is just what Augustine said: Mind and Knowledge and Love that joins them.

Hegel believed Western thought fulfilled itself with him; at least so far as its trinitarianism is concerned, he was right. Augustine's insight can be taken no further. Neither can Augustine's failure: this trinitarianism's distance from the saving history that necessitated it in the first place. In Hegel, Augustine's trinitarianism fulfills its constant tendency by finally explicitly taking the world as God's object, rather than Jesus the Son. From Hegel on, there has been a continuous tradition in which the trinitarian dialectics are exploited for their speculative possibilities, without much direction of the speculation by the dialectics' original object. The most notable recent exponents of this tradition are John Macquarrie and Paul Tillich.[63] From the point of view of this work, such efforts merely perfect ancient error.

In our century, the decisive step in repairing the great flaw of Augustinian-Hegelian trinitarianism has been taken. Karl Barth has reachieved an authentic doctrine of triunity, by what amounts to a christological inversion of Hegel's.[64] Only make *Jesus* God's object in which he finds himself, instead of Hegel's "world" or Augustine's merely metaphysical "Logos," and you have the doctrine of Barth's *Church Dogmatics*, Volume 1 I/1— which observation takes nothing from the extraordinary ingenuity of Barth's move.[65]

Barth perceives the difference between the Hellenic quest for God (he says "natural theology") and the gospel's proclamation that Jesus is God's quest for us (he says "revelation") more rigorously than any but Luther before him and uses this insight as the sole motor of trinitarian discourse. The entire doctrine of the Trinity, he says, is but the specification of which God it is that can so reveal himself as God is in fact revealed in Christ.[66]

The biblical claim of revelation, Barth says, poses three questions: Who is revealed? What does he do to reveal himself? What does revelation accomplish? The answer to each must be God, without qualification.[67] "*God* reveals himself. He reveals himself *through himself.* He reveals *himself.*"[68] And apart from each of these three sentences, the other two remain ambiguous.[69]

The key point is why the answer to all three questions must be simply God. Summarizing drastically, we may state Barth's answer: All three questions must be answered just "God," in order to negate our religious quest conceptually as revelation in Jesus' death and resurrection in fact negates it.[70] If the revelation, Jesus, or the achievement of revelation, the divine presence among us, were not simply God himself, we would by them merely be launched on a religious quest for God himself. But what the cross and resurrection reveal is exactly that such a quest, denying the sufficiency of the word of the gospel, is unbelief. Yet the God who so reveals himself does not thereby become merely identical with historical revelation and accomplished presence; that God is never thus grasped by us is, again, what the cross reveals. Also the one revealed is God utterly. Finally, having thus prevented subordinationism, Barth excludes modalism by the very same considerations. The necessity of giving the same answer to all three of revelation's questions does not amalgamate the questions themselves into one, for then again the real God would remain behind revelation and we would be back on our quest.

Since it is Barth who taught twentieth-century theology—or the living parts of it—the importance and point of trinitarian discourse, his influence has been pervasive through this entire study. That must here be explicitly acknowledged. But his contribution to required new trinitarian analysis is not so great as might be expected. Nor does he carry us to full liberation from a past-determined interpretation of God.

Trinitarian analysis is by no means complete, nor will it be until the struggle between the gospel's and Hellenism's identifications of God is over. It is time to state such of our own proposals as are not yet explicit.

The first step is to free trinitarian doctrine from captivity to antecedent interpretation of deity as timelessness.[71] In part that is already done in this work—as in Barth and some other post-Hegelian treatments—by the mere sequence of topics and by the christological concentration we, again like Barth, have insisted on at every step. In part it must be accomplished in the next chapter, where we will attempt an evangelical concept of deity, the basis of which is already laid throughout the previous chapters.

Within the trinitarian dialectics themselves it is the relation of the "immanent" and "economic" Trinities that must in this connection be reconsidered. The most important contemporary Catholic trinitarian theorist and the most important Protestant, Karl Rahner and Eberhard Jüngel, agree on a rule for the contemporary task: "The 'economic' Trinity *is* the 'immanent' Trinity, and vice versa."[72]

The legitimate theological reason for the "immanent"/ "economic" distinction is the freedom of God. It must be that God "in himself" could have been the same God he is, and so triune, had there been no creature, or no saving of fallen creation, and so also not the trinitarian history there has in fact been. Here is a second rule (which is perhaps too little observed by both Rahner and Jüngel). Reconciling it with the other just stated has always been the problem. The two rules are compatible, we propose, only if the identity of the "economic" and "immanent" Trinity is eschatological.

Within theology's captivity to the timelessness axiom, the eternity of Jesus could be conceived only as a reality that always was in God. Thus was posited the "Logos *asarkos*" the "not [yet] incarnate Word," Jesus' metaphysical double, who always was in God and then *became* the one sent in flesh to us. The Logos' relation to the Father was described as a Father-Son relation, and rightly, since it is Jesus' relation to his Father that is to be interpreted. But the begetting and being-begotten of *this* Father and Son had to be timeless; thus this "procession" could not in fact be the same as the temporal relation of Jesus to his Father, that is, as the "mission." The Greek fathers mostly ignored the difficulty, thus permitting authentic trinitarian discourse in which the processions and missions occur together. But when more rigid thinkers came along, the difficulty proved fatal. This whole pattern must be exactly reversed.

Instead of interpreting Christ's deity as a separate entity that always *was*—and proceeding analogously with the Spirit—we should interpret it as a final outcome, and just so as eternal, just so as the bracket around all beginnings and endings. Jesus' historical life was a sending by the Father, the filial relation between this man and the transcendence to whom he turned temporally occurred; and this man is risen from the dead, so that his mission must triumph, so that his filial relation to his Father is unimpeachable. Thus Jesus' obedience to the Father, and their love for us which therein occurs, will prove an unsurpassable event, that is, are a God-event, a "procession" in God. Jesus' Aramaic or Hebrew prayer, and his prophetic apprehension of God's Word, will be the Father's final self-expression, by which he establishes his identity for us and for himself. And the Spirit that is the breath of this future will blow all things before himself into new life. The saving events, whose plot is stated by the doctrine of trinitarian relations, are, in their eschatological finality, God's transcendence of time, God's eternity. Thus we need posit no timelessly antecedent extra entities—Logos *asarkos* or not-yet-given Spirit—to assert the unmitigated eternity of Son and Spirit.

Within trinitarian thought's captivity to an alien definition of deity, we have been unable to say simply that Jesus *is* "the eternal Son," that what happens between the human Jesus and his father and the believing community *is* eternity. Instead, we have had to say that Jesus is the dwelling and manifestation of his own preexistent double—and with that, all the impossibilities we have trudged through are there. It is the need for the "pre-" that causes them; that is, it is the interpretation of eternity as persistence of the first past that causes them. If instead we follow Scripture in understanding eternity as faithfulness to the last future, *these* problems merely disappear.

Truly, the Trinity is simply the Father and the man Jesus and their Spirit as the Spirit of the believing community. This "economic" Trinity is *eschatologically* God "himself," an "immanent" Trinity. And that assertion is no problem, for God *is* himself only eschatologically, since he is Spirit.

As for God's freedom, only our proposal fully asserts it. The immanent Trinity of previous Western interpretation had but the spurious freedom of unaffectedness. Genuine freedom is the reality of possibility, is openness to the future. Genuine freedom is Spirit. And it is only in that we interpret God's eternity as the

THE ONE AND THE THREE

certainty of his triumph that we are able without qualification to say that God is Spirit. If we so understand God's freedom, we are indeed unable to describe *how* God could have been the selfsame triune God other than as the Trinity now in fact given. But neither have we any call to, so long as God's utter freedom, as Spirit, is acknowledged. In that acknowledgment we are equally commanded to say *that* God could be otherwise God and forbidden to say *how*.

Therewith we are at the next required amendment of inherited teaching. On a traditional diagram of trinitarian relations, the procession of divine being is all one way, from the Father. Son and Spirit derive their deity from the Father, but Father and Son do not derive deity from the Spirit; in Augustine's formula, "The Father is the principle and source of the whole of deity" (*On the Trinity*, iv, 29). The places for relations whose arrows would point *to* the Father are vacant.

Pre-Nicene subordinationism had two closely related roots. One was the need for mediation of time and eternity. The other was the apprehension of God as fundamentally located at the beginning rather than the end, so that the trinitarian relations, even when rightly set parallel to time, had as active relations to point only *with* time's arrow. It corresponded to this apprehension that to command, beget, give, and so on, were felt as more appropriate to deity than to be given, obey, and so on.[73] Of these roots of subordinationism, only the first was pulled up by the Cappadocians. Thus it became a fixed axiom that the Father's begetting marked a sole primacy in deity,[74] that the transcendence to whom Jesus looked back was actively deity, while the Spirit he gave to the future was only passively so.

The asymmetry of the trinitarian relations is the more remarkable in that the Bible clearly presses candidates for the missing parts of the diagram. We propose to fill them in. Which biblical language we choose for the future-to-past active relations is at present of secondary importance. Using "witnesses" for the Spirit and "frees" for the Spirit with the Son, we may say the following. The Spirit's witness to the Son is equally God-constituting with the traditional relations. And so is the Son's and the Spirit's

joint reality as the openness into which the Father is freed from
mere persistence in his pretemporal transcendence. Moreover,
since the only biblical approach to a definition of deity is "God
is Spirit," the Spirit must at least be recognized as differently but
equally "principle and source" with the Father; let us mark this
with a "notion," and let that be "unsurpassed." Thus we obtain a
new diagram, shown in Figure 2.

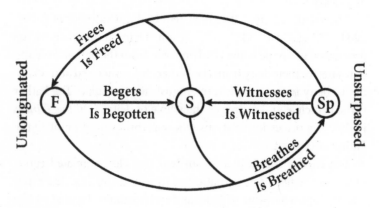

FIGURE 2

The tradition could say how sending and obedience, giving
and being given, are realities not merely between God and us,
but in God—and so final goods. But it could not say how freeing
and being freed, witnessing and being witnessed to, are equally
realities in God. Thus the tradition could show that—to use Reformation language—God's *law* is his own true self-expression.
But it could not show that the *gospel* is similarly anchored in his
being. We do not suggest that the church so persistently slides
into legalism because of gaps in a diagram; we do suggest that it
does so because of a conception of God accurately represented
by the traditional diagram, by which God is indeed God of the
law but not of the gospel, defined in his deity as the Father but
not as the Spirit. We wish to amend the conception.

This is perhaps also the place where the traditional doctrine of
God does indeed reflect male dominance. Whether or not dominance is biologically a male characteristic, it has been culturally.

The traditional trinitarian relations, unsupplemented by those we propose, display command as constitutive of deity but not obedience, assertion but not reception. Indeed, the very definition of deity as assertion against time and its chances, which lies behind the asymmetry of relations and against which we have been arguing, bears the same value preference. It has been convincingly argued that these characteristics of traditional trinitarianism are the last outpost of the ancient world's dominance of male solar and sky gods over female earth and lunar gods.[75] Teaching a symmetry of trinitarian relations is not, of course, intended to balance female characteristics with male characteristics, and certainly not to posit obedience or receptivity as inherently female. The point is rather to eliminate altogether the influence of antiquity's sex-role doctrines.

CHAPTER FIVE

The Being of God

Specification of the kind of being God is must follow the trinitarian identification. When it does, we will specify God's being as event, person, spirit, and discourse.

The Metaphysical Questions

All the creeds begin "I believe in God, the. . . ." It is dogma that God *is*. There can be no such thing as a Christian atheist, except in very special senses of "atheist."[1] But in what sense "is" God? Is God as an idea is? Or as a tree is? Or how? The question needs only to be asked to become desperately puzzling. The question of the being of God is thus dogmatically imposed on the theological enterprise and has in fact been at all times vigorously investigated. With it, we land decisively on the far side of a border we have been crossing through the previous two chapters. We land in the middle of metaphysics.

Metaphysics asks two great questions. First, What sort of being has . . . ? Second, Whatever sorts of being there are, how are they all sorts of "being"? That is, What is being? These are not esoteric questions. We will instantly see that the first is not, if we insert "I" in the blank: What sort of being have I? The sort that vanishes with time? The sort that transcends time? Or some other? That there are several kinds of being is at a common-sense level obvious; there are things, events, ideas, numbers, consciousnesses, and who knows what else. It is against the threat of time that the plurality of beings' kinds becomes portentous, as our expansion of the question in the first person assumed. Thus the Greeks' reflection about kinds of being was driven by the fear that all "things" may pass away. Ordinary things clearly are subject to time, they saw; ideas clearly are not; how about consciousnesses?[2] And if the first metaphysical question is lively, so—at one further remove—the second must be.

Theology has asked the first metaphysical question also about God: What kind of being has God? This is clearly a grammatically possible instance of the question, but it is a logically odd one, for the word "God," as we have seen, means "eternal reality." Therefore any actual religion which identifies its God and so specifies how God is eternal thereby answers the metaphysical question in advance. Adherents of an actual religion have no direct need to ask what sort of being God has. For them, the questioning runs the other way around. And it is of course only the adherents of some religion who use the word "God," in such questions or otherwise. Thus, "What kind of being has God?" can be a lively question only *between* religions, as the effort of one religion to understand itself over against another.

In fact, it is in the long confrontation of biblical and Hellenic religion, to which we have already devoted so much attention, that Christianity has necessarily and rightly asked about the being of God. The special character of these two religions has made the confrontation uniquely creative metaphysically, but it has also given the confrontation a treacherous twist. Since Greece needed criteria by which to recognize "rear" deity when its quest should reach it, its religious reflection involved an embryonic form of the metaphysical question about God: What are the marks of true timelessness? Because Christian Hellenists had to deal with the demand that Jesus' Father be displayable as *really* God, and so had to deal with the demand for criteria of true deity, it was all too easy for them to be led to pose the question of God's being in a way that begged the question to their own betrayal: What are the other metaphysical characteristics of God, besides timelessness?[3] It is in this very form that we have already encountered the question in Augustine. Insofar as the fathers thus entangled themselves, Christianity was set in the pattern we have been trying to overcome: that Christianity's interpretation of God, properly become metaphysical in discussion with Greece, assumes an initial definition of deity that aborts the discussion and merely recites Hellenic principles.

Method, therefore, is decisive. A doctrine of any putative God's being is a certain abstraction from the reflectively developed form of that God's identification: If, for example, "God is the one who raised Jesus," we have already referred to him as a person, by speaking of him as "the one who" followed by a transitive verb. Thus theology's habit of treating God's being first and his triunity thereafter is a disaster, for if the trinitarian identification of God is not made the basis of the doctrine of God's being, some other identification will too easily be unwittingly presupposed. The right question, which we will try to answer in the following, is: What sort of being must God have, since he is triune?

The second metaphysical question "What is being?" has no special theological form, since it is itself a theological question. Thus Aristotle himself sometimes defined his "first philosophy" as the investigation of deity[4] and sometimes as the investigation of *ousia*,[5] for if there is God—and the denial that there is, is also a theological position—then to be is either to be God or to be dependent on her/him/it to be whatever else. In a religious reflection, therefore, it is the "either . . . or" of the previous sentence that is the key to the question of being. The question will be answered by finding a determinant that can be switched to display the difference between God and other reality and then stating it indifferently to this switch. For example, the standard such move in scholastic Christian thought is: God is the explanation; creatures are that-which-needs-explanation; and therefore to be is to be intelligible—*ens est veritas*.

Our tradition has a standard answer to the first metaphysical-theological question: God has persistent being. And to the second: God is persistent, all else is temporary, and therefore to be is to have a past. We need not here again attack these answers. The entire story of the last two chapters told of Christianity's struggle with them; our rejection is already stated. It is the task of this chapter to display the faith's alternative. We will make four specifications of God's being: that God is event, person, spirit, and discourse.

Since the great confrontation began with the capture of bibli-cal faith by its rival and interlocutor, faith's alternative has always appeared as breakthrough, as Christian thinkers' wrenching disaccord with what they too suppose is obviously true. The full story of the long breakthrough would be a complete history of theology; we will here proceed more systematically, referring at random to a few great figures of the tradition. In what ways our own contribution is also a wrench with deep assumptions of our thinking, we cannot say; others will have to do that.

We will not explicitly investigate the second metaphysical question. That would carry us too far beyond the limits of dog-matics. But an answer to that question will at once guide and emerge from our consideration of God's being. It will be well to state that answer here, that readers may know it as they read: God anticipates; creatures recoil; therefore to be is to have a future.

God as an Event

The entire exposition of God's triunity demands our first prop-osition: God is an event. The kind of reality God has is like that of a kiss or an automobile accident. The argument for this proposition is the previous three chapters.

In the dominating tradition, God's being has been specified by the notion of "substance," whether understood more according to Plato or more according to Aristotle: for example, John Ger-hard, "God is a spiritual substance: utterly simple, infinite. . . ."[6] A substance[7] is *what is* something, maintaining itself in being by possessing some definite complex of attributes answering to "something"; or substance is the reality possessed by and as those attributes; and the word in use shimmers between the two and derives much of its metaphysical power from the ambiguity. A substance is, for example, what is "legged," "with a seat," and so on, so as to *be* a chair, and persists in being as long as it retains possession of "leggedness" and "seatingness."

Thus the metaphysics of substance realize a cluster of existentially-laden notions: of persistence, independence, and possession. To be substantial is to endure, by having reality as

THE BEING OF GOD

"attributes," that is, independently of other substances. It is plain that no immediately experienced reality quite fulfills this vision. All are subject to action by other realities, and thus from time to time gain and lose attributes: The two-legged animal, Jones, may in fact lose a leg. Thus all give hostages to time, and may endure long but not forever: The bipedal, vertebrate Jones may survive the loss of bipedality but not of vertebration. "God" is then posited as the one *true* substance,[8] all of whose attributes are securely possessed, so that times' chances are nothing to him. God has no "accidental" attributes which come and go, and so gives no hostage to time or other realities. God is the *perfect* substance. All the attributes we attribute to God—"simplicity," "infinity," "omnipotence," or whatever—merely explicate God's perfection.

That Christians cannot approve this metaphysics should have been apparent: "For whoever would save his life will lose it" (Matt. 16:25). We have seen how the greatest trinitarians were driven by the dialectics of the trinitarian identification of God to deny that there is any complex of attributes by possessing which God is, and so had to make the subject of "is God" be not a substance at all but an act, an event. We have also seen how thoroughly most theology subsequently relapsed from that insight.

Rejection of the dominant tradition just at this point is endemic in contemporary theology. We may illustrate almost at random. So the Roman Catholic radical Leslie Dewart: We must "de-Hellenize" the faith by overcoming the ideals of immortality, stability, and impassibility.[9] But so also the conservative Lutheran Peter Brunner: "In view of God's . . . self-determination to us, we must . . . abandon all pictures of God that with the help of antiquity's mode of thought read into God a fixed, unmovable, and abstract perfection, so that . . . talk of new judgments, new reactions, new deeds, and new words in God . . . appears to be naive anthropomorphism."[10]

But while the demand is general, the fulfilling thereof is less frequent. One great project of twentieth-century theology was devoted to it, Karl Barth's *Church Dogmatics:*[11] "God's deity consists, into its farthest depths, therein—or at least *also* therein—that it is event." Moreover, God's being is not eventhood, or something of the sort, but a particular event, "that event of God's activity in which we are involved in his revelation,"[12] the active relation of the triune persons.[13] Barth's doctrine of God's being as love and freedom is then the explication of this being-as-event.[14] To the extent that theology currently tends to ignore the main parts of Barth's work (and in English-speaking territories has never grasped them), it has cut itself off from the only fully realized attempt thus far to fulfill modern theology's own constant demand.

One other ponderable and very influential contemporary theological project is often thought to specify God's being as event, but in fact does not. Just so, we must devote some attention to "process theology." We will here not denote by this phrase every theology that has learned from Alfred North Whitehead or Charles Hartshorne (that would be almost all English-language theology) but only those theologies that find in their thought "the right philosophy" and so maintain the key doctrines of their interpretation of God.[15] Thus our own analysis will be of Hartshorne himself.[16]

It is true that "process" metaphysics understands all reality as concretely consisting in events, and so also God as so consisting. What there most concretely is, is in no case a substance (e.g., "this man") but the momentary events of the man's life. The enduring human is a series of the events, established as a series by certain kinds of likeness and relation between the events. "This man" is the fact that a unity can be abstracted from some particular sequential events that is more than their mere aggregate.[17]

Thus no enduring entity is, in this metaphysics, an event, but rather an abstraction from some set of events. But whereas each human, or each galaxy or indeed each other enduring entity than God, is an abstraction from its own specifiable set of events—so that it makes sense to say that this human *is* such-and-such events—the events that God concretely is are simply all the events that are the history of the world.[18] Therefore, if our discourse remains at the concrete level, the word "God" has no import of its own; we cannot with it denote any identifiable reality. Concretely (i.e., as *event*) there is only the world. There is God as *God*, as more than the world, only in God's "*abstract character*," in that sort of his reality that is grasped by our abstractions from concrete reality, that is, there is God, not as event but only as an in itself timelessly given structure of relations between all events. Process metaphysics contribute greatly to our understanding of the general character of reality. But they do not expound the assertion "God is an event," since they do not in fact make the assertion. Process metaphysics ontologically demote the notion of substance. But once we do come to speak of the enduring entities to which the notion was traditionally applied—whether "Jones" or "God"—they also apply it, and then do not really modify it at all.

We wish to say that God is an event. We see two necessary explanations.

First, traditional metaphysics are insofar commonsensically right, that an event must happen *to* some enduring entity. What does not follow and what we have denied is that the enduring entity is therefore ontologically prior to the event. What God happens to is Jesus and the world. God is the event of the world's final transformation by Jesus' love. That "all manner of things will be well" and that it is now true that all manner of things will be well is the reality of God. Thus God is not an event in time, nor even an event extended through all time. God is rather the event by which the world has a future, to *be* a world of time. Were there no eschaton, were the world as a whole not thus open to a future, the world would not occur within that unstoppable oncoming of uncertainty which we call time. God is the temporalizing of the world.

But what if no such thing happened to the world, if it were not temporalized? Then *this* world would be no-thing at all. Instead of the world that actually is, there might be another world, of which the great mythic vision of circling time were true, in which all things always returned to their beginning. And for this world there might be its appropriate God, Brahman-Atman. But that is another matter altogether. As to whether the real God could have been God without any world, we can only answer as before:

The analysis of God as free event, as spirit, equally compels us to say that he would have been and forbids us to say how.

Second, God, if real, must be a logical subject. It must be possible to make sentences with a verb and "God" as the subject. And if the God is the one we have been speaking of, it must be possible for the verb to be active, indeed transitive. With events in time, it is precisely the awkwardness of making an event a logical subject, especially of active verbs, that has led to the doctrine of the priority of substances to what happens to them. How can an *occurrence* be said, for example, to "speak by the prophets" or to "sustain the universe?"

A logical subject must be not only identifiable but also reidentifiable, as when one calls the service station and says, "This is the man who brought (note the tense) in the Horizon for tuning." For if I say, "John is angry," and you say, "Who is John?" I cannot merely respond with "the one who is angry." A logical subject must indeed be an enduring entity in some sense or other.[19] It is just this point that has traditionally disqualified events as logical subjects: An event happens, and then where is it?

It is, we suggest, in that God is the *triune* event, that God is not over after God happens. It is the tri-identicality of the divine action that makes it a logical subject. What happens to the world with Christ has plural identifiabilities bracketing time and just so reaching through time. Nor are these disconnected, leaving, as it were, gaps of time between them, for their plurality is the same as their relations with each other. Thus we may say that what happens with Christ has a self-repeating identifiability, which we may plausibly treat as the continuing identifiability of a logical subject, without this being the sort of reidentifiability the tradition has taken for the only sort: the persistence of some one set of identifying characteristics, the temporal extension of a "substance."

We will pick up one last suggestion from Gregory of Nyssa. The divine *ousia*, "deity," is, according to him, sheer temporal infinity. For Gregory, the word no longer stands for something that is God; it denotes sheerly the infinity of the act that is God. It is this *ousia* that the three hypostases derive from and with each other, that is, the acts of the Father or the Son or the Spirit, within their joint act that is God, are indeed *within* that act, are *divine* acts, in that they are subject to no temporal limits. The distinction and relation of three identities are a structure of pure triumphant possibility-as-such. They are the structure of the temporally plural ways in which the action that is God overcomes all conditions. The Cappadocians' "one *ousia*" means that whether the conditions that might be imposed on what happens with Christ are the burdens of the past (imposed on the Father, were only he God) or the risks of the future (imposed on the Spirit, were only he God) or the statistics of the present (imposed on the Son, were only he God), they are no hindrance to the action that in fact is God, which just in this utter unhinderedness can be only *one* action.

God as Person

The concept of personhood as a particular kind of being seems to be modern and, moreover, a result of Christian theology's influence on Western life and reflection.[20] But once the concept is there, it is obvious that all the Bible's talk about God in fact speaks of him as what we now call personal.[21] Indeed, most practiced religion treats deity as personal, since it addresses deity in hope of response. Yet the personhood of God is also regularly attacked religiously. Thus all actual Vedic religion assumes the personhood of deity, and nearly all sophisticated Vedic reflection denies it.[22] In the history of Christian theology, discomfort with the notion of God's personhood or, prior to the emergence of the notion, with those biblical descriptions of God which we now comprise therein, has greatly depended on the Hellenic interpretation of deity. In that this deity is the timeless ground of temporal reality and can therefore be simultaneously and successively manifested by many different persons, it is natural for Hellenic interpretation to conceive deity itself as impersonal.

There is a problem here that cannot be obviated merely by decrying Hellenic religion. As soon as the confrontation with Hellenism awakens metaphysical reflection in the church, whether in antiquity or now, it becomes clear that it will not do to call God "a person," without qualification. For "a" person is individualized by difference from other persons, and in the case of God who would they be? But if God is not "a person," can it be meaningful to call him "personal"? The problem is not esoteric. Every believer faces it, and it is safe to say that most merely take their choice and either think vaguely of God as rather like electricity or picture God entirely mythically as a mighty but invisible woman or man.

The tendency of our analysis is given in advance. In view of the clear language of the Bible we will maintain God's personhood until driven from it. We have already entered Christianity's deep stream of insight into God's personhood, as represented by Augustine and Hegel, and will not leave it willingly.

Johann Gottlieb Fichte may pose the problem. He imprinted the turn of the eighteenth and nineteenth centuries in Germany with the "atheism controversy" occasioned by his views.[23] A conscious being, said Fichte, with all the thought of his time, and rightly, establishes its individual being by *self*-consciousness. But it is not possible for there to be an object of consciousness that has no boundary distinguishing it from the rest of reality. Therefore the self of self-consciousness must be a bounded, finite self; and therefore, said Fichte, God cannot be a conscious being, since God is infinite and so cannot know himself as finite. And therefore again, God cannot be personal, since "unconscious personhood" is a contradiction.

There are two possible replies to Fichte's sort of worry. One is argument that God can be personal without being *a* person. The other is argument that there can be an infinite person, meeting Fichte head-on. We will pursue the latter.

The object as which God knows himself is Jesus. Thus God's self-consciousness is indeed consciousness of a bounded, particular individual, so that this requirement of personhood is fulfilled. But the decisive question is just *how* the reality of this individual is bounded. The reality of each created person is defined by the event sequence, the plot, of his life, as this sequence is made into a determinate whole, into indeed a plot, by his death. So with Jesus. He is defined by his particular life and particular death as "love," as a life for all other lives. He is the crucified one, whose life was lived in the promise he brought his fellows and who finally gave up his self wholly to that promise. That he is risen does not mean that this death is canceled so that this life is again undefined. It means that *this one*, this defined one, is future and present reality and not merely past, so that he can be the objective self of the living God. But if God's self-consciousness is consciousness of *this* present, bounded individual, God is conscious of his self as the person for all persons, as a particular defined love, and so is not shut in by this bounded self-consciousness, but freed.[24]

It all depends on what sort of infinity, what sort of freedom from limitation, we have in mind when we attribute infinity to God. If we think of simple absence of definition, an infinite being cannot indeed be self-conscious. But if we think of God's infinity as trinitarianism (e.g., Gregory of Nyssa) should teach us to think of it, as freedom to transcend each new definition while never lacking one, or as the Hebrew Scriptures should teach us to think of it, as unconquerable faithfulness, then that the bounded individual Jesus is God's object-self does not hinder God's infinity, it constitutes it.

The "a person" that God is, is the human person Jesus, the Son. The triune event that God is, is by its triunity a person, this one. We need not, therefore, think of the other identities, of the Father or the Spirit, as, with respect to their distinction from one another, individual personal beings in the modern sense. If the Father and the Son were singular persons, they would be metaphysical somethings in the very style of the "Logos *asarkos*" we have just eliminated, about whom we might well have Fichte's qualms. Instead, we will press the scholastic interpretation of the triune identities as "subsisting relations." We will say, All there is to being God the Father is being addressed as "Father" by the Son, Jesus; all there is to being God the Spirit is being the spirit of this exchange.

In that Jesus cries "Father if it be possible . . ." and in that he will give up his rule at the last, and in that he is not disappointed in these relations, there is the Father. In that Jesus gives his spirit, and in that he will gather all to himself in that spirit, and in that this movement is final, there is the Spirit. This does not mean that the Father and the Spirit are created by Jesus. The relations necessarily posit some individual terms, but this does not mean they are secondary to them. And finally, in that all this is true, Jesus *is* the Son (not: *there is* the Son!). About the Father and the Spirit, Fichte and those who have argued as he did were right. The sort of being possessed by them, and so by the triune God each of them is, *relatively to* each of them, is not that of a something, personal or otherwise. But that is not the entire account. God is not an individual person. But there *is* an individual person who is God. And therefore the Augustinian-Hegelian dialectics of consciousness, which define the very notion of personhood in the modern sense, can indeed in their trinitarian application to God establish the personhood of God.

We now can deal with a difficulty that may bother readers: Can it make any sense to speak of an event as a person, even in the sense just described? We respond: *Only* an event can be a person.

The life of any of us is an event, but it is also made up of many events. To grasp my life as an event, I must therefore grasp the dramatic connection, the faithfulness, of each of its constituent events to all the others. But I, as a creature, do not have this faithfulness in myself. The days of my life do not cohere in anything visible in them but only in the promises of God. And I, as a fallen creature, do not hearken to Gods' promises. My days therefore threaten to fall apart, to become an incoherent sequence that could just as well have members other than those it does, to become "absurd." Yet so long as God does not punish my unbelief by indeed loosing my identity into the flux of events, I cannot avoid recognizing some events as *my* deeds and sufferings and others as not. Thus I am driven either to faith in God or to suppose a mysterious something other than my life and its intrinsic coherence, "whose" life my life is, "whose" deeds and sufferings the events of my life are. And so arises the myth of the "person" I am as something other than the event that I am.

In our fallenness, we may in fact be unable to deal with ourselves without the myth just described. But there is no reason to
apply it to God. God is neither creature nor fallen. God is speaker
and hearer of the Word by which he lives. And he believes his
Word. With God, "person" and "event" are therefore only alternative insights into one reality.

Now we can also deal with the difficulty raised by the Bible's
drastically personal language about God: that God changes his
mind, reacts to earthly events, and the like.[25] Or rather, we can
see that there is no difficulty.

Over against and in the time established and embraced by the
occurrence of God, God is an enduring entity by virtue of his
triunity. And this enduring entity's objective self, the criterion
of its self-identity, is Jesus of Nazareth, in his openness to his
fellows. Therefore, that over against time God listens and con-
siders and truly responds is but faithfulness to himself. God's
action and reaction over against us through time, in that it is
faithful to his self that is Jesus and so is an indefatigable wooing
and rescuing, does not compromise God's eternal self-identity,
it constitutes it.

That God answers prayer, that God makes threats and
"repents" of them when the evil is past, that God makes promises and fulfills them by new and unexpected promises—all
this is not "anthropomorphic" or "symbolic" statement. It is the
strictest descriptive propositional truth. It is when *we* are said
to initiate something new, to be surprising and faithful at once,
that language must be stretched a bit. God has no problem here
at all. "From eternity the Father sees us in the Son . . . , as determined for fellowship with him. . . . In that God in the totality of
his being and from eternity thus enters the covenant of relation
he has willed, saving history as real history is possible also for
God."[26]

It is in the determinations of God's being as event and person that the main problems arise. "God is spirit" and "God
is discourse," to which we now turn, can therefore be more
briefly discussed. Nevertheless, they are the religiously decisive
determinants.

God as Spirit

Western understanding of personhood as a kind of being has classically found two great essential movements of and within personal being: mind and will. Thus Thomas Aquinas, following Aristotle, lists five powers of "the soul," but gives only two theological significance: the "intellectual" and the "appetitive."[27] Schleiermacher based the necessity of religion on the necessity for unity in our life of "thinking" and "acting."[28] Or again, all Kant's thought can be read as an analysis of personhood; his great work was in three volumes, one on knowing, one on willing, and a third on how they work together.[29]

As the examples of Schleiermacher and Kant suggest, the great analytical problem about personhood has been how mind and will are joined. Is the person a mind steering appetites, as Socrates and all his followers have taught (e.g., Plato, *Phaedrus*)? Or is the person a will, using reasoning to think through how to get his way, as Arthur Schopenhauer taught most bluntly?[30] Or are they joined in some other way? We are here not concerned with this problem as a problem about human persons.[31] But in that we see God as person, we see also God as mind and will. Augustinian-Hegelian trinitarianism defines God as consciousness established in knowledge of self—the Son, and love of self—the Spirit. And so the problem is posed also about God.

The great scholastics argued the problem in a particularly sophisticated form. Since God is Creator, what God knows and what God wills are the same. And since God is good, what God wills is the good. So the question: Does God know what is good, and therefore will it; or is the good good because God wills it? Thomas Aquinas was the great proponent of the first option, Duns Scotus and the later nominalists of the second.[32]

The matter at issue is vital for faith, despite its esoteric appearance. We may think of an absolute event and person, and yet not think of *God*—or anyway of the God of the Bible. The God whose primary reality is unmovedly to know us and all things, as what we are, in order then perhaps to make plans for us accordingly, is simply not the one of whom the Bible speaks.

The God of the Bible is a storm, blowing us like leaves from what we are to what we will be and only knowing us in this motion. The great Mind's Eye is doubtless a noble conception and may even subsist, but he is much too harmless to be God by an Ezekiel's lights. Yet neither is the Bible's God a sheerly arbitrary force. We must somehow learn to think God as *faithful* will.

One work, from all the history of theology, can be the reality test. Martin Luther's *On the Bondage of the Will*[33] is intemperate, prolix, and sometimes misguided; it is also the book after the Bible that is most inescapably about God. God is the one who "works life, death, and all in all" (*Bondage*, p. 685), who indeed cannot not work all in all (ibid., pp. 709, 712). We know this about God not because of philosophical speculation but because of the gospel. Only in confessing that God is responsible for all that happens are we so humbled before him as to need the gospel. And only in that God rules absolutely can he make unconditional promises, that is, can the gospel be true (ibid., pp. 614, 619, 632). But just so God is hidden, and exactly in his reality as God of the gospel, for the "all" that he works is at best morally ambiguous by the gospel's own lights: "This is . . . faith, to believe that he is merciful who saves so few and condemns so many . . . , so that he seems . . . to delight in the tortures of the wretched and to be more worthy of hate than of love" (ibid., p. 633). Our only hope is to flee from God in this undefined power and naked majesty, to God as he has defined himself in Christ, as redeeming love (ibid., pp. 684–85). Yet this self-definition is not a *mitigation* of God's unchecked will and majesty, nor therefore our flight to it a flight to a mitigated God, as nearly all other theology understands it. For God's self-definition as love occurs as the crucifixion, as yet another hiding, yet deeper than the first in the world's ambiguity (ibid., pp. 689–90), and so as the final event of that powerful hiddenness which, we have just seen, *is* God's majesty.

With this touchstone, we may not define God either as mere mind or mere will. We must make will the more central to our reflection, but we must posit a will that just *is* also mind. That is, we will think of God as spirit.

Were God the Father God by himself (which is contrary not merely to fact but to logic), there would indeed obtain about him precisely the scholastics' problem: Does he choose what he chooses because he knows what is good, or is what is good good because it is what he chooses? And the problem would be insoluble, given in the very conception of such a "naked majesty."

As it is, God is God the Father and God the Son, and just so God the Spirit. Therefore if we first think of the Father as *mind*, so that he has his self-identity in self-knowing, then the self as which he knows himself is Jesus, and so is a particular love and particular hope, a particular good thing *willed* by the Creator, that is, by God himself. Or if we first think of the Father as *will*, so that he has his self-identity in self-choice, then the self he chooses for himself is Jesus, who as a created person is always determined in his choices by others, that is, by his *knowledge* of them, including of the Father. Thus as God in fact is, the abstract and finally impotent dialectics of mind versus will cannot describe him. His reality is complex and alive; mind and will are given in him only in original structured unity.

That is, God is freedom. God is neither mind using will nor will using mind; God is creativity that is both. God is transforming and faithful liveliness. God is *spirit*.

We must hasten to prevent misunderstanding. The word "spirit" is often now used in a way that has little to do with its use in Scripture or here. That God is spirit does *not* mean that God is disembodied, a "pure spirit" in the vulgar sense. On the contrary, he has a body,[34] and did he not, would in fact not be spirit. That God has a body means, first, that[35] there is an *object* of our intention that is he, and that this same reality is the object of God's own intention of himself. And second, that there is an enduring entity by which God can be identified and by which he identifies himself. This enduring object that is God's body is the Jesus that walked in Palestine and was raised into present eternal life. Had God no body, he could not be spirit, for we have just seen how the freedom and complex temporal urgency of God is given in his having Jesus as his objective self.

THE BEING OF GOD

The common religious conception of "pure spirit," meaning disembodied personhood, has no application to the triune God, even though nearly the whole theological tradition has tried to apply it, led by confusion between the biblical opposition of "spirit"/"flesh" and the Hellenic opposition of "mind"/"body," and by too hasty identification of "body" with "mass in space." The suppositious mere "God the Father" of three paragraphs back would be such an entity, and just so neither free nor temporally potent. A "pure" spirit would be either an impotent mind or an aimless will. To our salvation, the real God is neither. He is the living union of the Father and the Son. He has a body and therefore can be free creative spirit, the power of the last future.

God as Discourse

"In the beginning was the Word, and the Word was with God, and the Word was God" (John 1:1). It was the first deliberate dogma of Christianity, by which the faith forever defined its difference from other religions, that with Christianity's God there is *no* "silence of eternity," that we do *not* lose our voice and ears as we approach him, that he not only has a word for us—which is eccentric enough in the world of religion—but *is* his word for us: The Word is "of one being with the Father."

God is event, person, and spirit. The three propositions achieve their synthesis, and therewith their final clarity, in the proposition that God is word. Or perhaps we should say that Christianity first knew that God is word and has been engaged in working out the other three determinants.

It is religiously offensive to say that God is word. To be sure, all religions acknowledge that God must initially reveal itself/himself/herself to us if we are to know her/him/it, for if God were simply there for our inspection, she/he/it would not be God. A communication of some sort, a "word" in some kind of sign system, must begin the relation. But then, by normal religious apprehension, we must move on to a deeper or higher grasp of God. And as we move toward God we move beyond the initial communication, for God as such is silence. The God of normal religion is not personally present in address to us; God addresses us only to call us into the distance where God truly dwells.[36]

The word is the medium of life in time. It is because the world is not merely present to us, but present as *interpreted* in signs and symbols of indefinitely many sorts, that time can be the horizon of our life. For the world experienced in and by interpretation is just so the world that could be experienced as interpreted otherwise than it is; and thus *potentiality* is present in our world. Since the word is the medium of life in time, normal gods eschew the word except as a temporary measure.

The word is the medium of our life's commonality. It is in speech about the world, in whatever kinds of signs, that we inhabit a world that is not my world only or yours only but precisely *ours*, so that we can come together in it. Since the word is the medium of mutual determination, normal gods are in themselves silent.

That the Bible's God is different in this respect became so soon apparent that there is on this point no continuing history of theological alienation such as we have traced on other points. The temptation has worked mostly in the mystical tradition, and in the tradition of piety, in hymnody and prayer. Thus an anonymous English mystic counseled: "Forsake as well good thoughts as evil thoughts, and pray not with thy mouth."[37] And we have a considerable number of vehemently anti-Christian poems that by virtue of their pious sound and associated sentimental tunes are favorites of the congregations. We cite only the most brazen: The communion between Jesus and the Father is "the silence of eternity, interpreted by love," to share in which we are exhorted to "let sense be dumb, let flesh retire."[38]

Not only does the *triune* God speak to initiate relation to us, but the initiated relation eternally remains speech, remains communication. This God's eternity is his unconquerable futurity, and it is in the word that the future is present. This God *is* fellowship with us, and it is in the word that we are there for one another. The Christian vision of the end is not of a great silence but of a great liturgy, of preaching and our eternal response of praise and acclamation (Rev. 4–5).

Nor is the triune God speech only over against *us*. The second identity is "the Word," is God's address to us. The third identity is the Spirit of this address, the Word's power to open us to the last future. It is precisely the relation between these three in which God lives. God *is* each of the identities, so he *is* the Word. And by the triune reality of whatever God is, the word that God is is an exchange, not a lecture. Thus the final characterization of God's reality must be: God is a conversation. Or choosing a more dignified word: God is discourse.

The conversation that is God is not a conversation in heaven—at least, if heaven is some other *place* than earth. The conversation that is God is the proclamation of the law and the gospel. Where human discourse occurs which opens human life to the last future, there is the occurrence of God. It is precisely as the exalted Lord, as what trinitarian theology has come to call the second hypostasis of God, that Matthew quotes Jesus: "Where two or three are gathered in my name, there am I in the midst of them" (Matt. 18:20). And it is as God *present* that the second identity *is* God. God is indeed present to every quark or every galaxy, but he is present to all things at and from the verbal event of the law and the gospel.

Thus the body of God, the object that is God and by virtue of which he indeed has a location, is "the body of Christ," the body-side of the law-and-gospel event. Every communication event has a body-side, an object-reality, as which those who address each other are there for each other.[39] If the preaching of the gospel is indeed the occurrence of God's word, then the body-side of the preaching of the gospel—the sights and sounds, the bread, the cup, the bath, the gestures of fellow believers—is the body-side of God's presence. Christ, we said earlier, is the body of God. It is into the embodiment of the gospel, that is, into the objective life of the church, that Christ is bodily risen. It is the embodiment of the gospel that is the "body of Christ" and so the body of God.

This matter has some dogmatic significance. We confess in the Lord's Prayer that God the Father is in "heaven," and in the three-article creeds that Christ is risen as a body and is at the Father's "right hand" there. But where is that?

The location of heaven, or rather the nature of heaven as a location for God, became confessionally divisive between Calvinists and Lutherans. Calvinists have maintained that heaven is a metaphysical *part* of creation, created by God as his own place within creation, so that it makes sense to speak of going and coming between heaven and the rest of creation, and of Christ's risen body being located there and therefore not located elsewhere in creation, for example, in the assemblies for the Supper. This tradition is still maintained by Karl Barth. Lutherans have, with some waverings, followed Luther's own view: that God has no *particular* space within creation, and that just so his place in creation, that is, his object-presence for us, is wherever the gospel sounds, to let us apprehend him there. Heaven is the "space" of the Word and the sacraments, the space of the Supper and baptism and however many other such events there are.[40] Readers will perceive this work's adherence to the Lutheran position, indeed, the determining force of that decision for the whole understanding of God. At the same time, we will hardly now wish to judge any continuing division on the matter itself as legitimately church-divisive.

CHAPTER SIX

The Attributes of God

Since God is, we can make factual statements about God.
The method of obtaining such statements is decisive for their
truth. True attributions to God are then forms of the gospel.

The Necessity of the Doctrine

If there is God, it must be possible to form subject-attribute sentences (such as "God is loving" or "God is a nuisance") that are and can be judged to be true or false. The traditional doctrine of God's attributes is the attempt to make a list of the important true attributes and to work out the method of their derivation. Given the initial meaning of the word "God," and given a previous specification of God's sort of being (so that we are not concerned, e.g., with whether God is liquid), the words in question as predicates will be those that name some value.

The attempt now easily assumes a comic air. There was no problem so long as certain assumptions of classical philosophy could be made: that there just are a definite number of desirable attributes, each in any given natural language with its appropriate word. But we now tend to think of language as a creative activity, and so of the good as a pie that can be divided by words indefinitely many ways. Thus the possible number of value words is infinite. On these assumptions, it is absurd to ask What are God's (six? seven? or one hundred?) perfections? Shall we put "gentle" on the list? Or hold the slot for "humorous"?

What can be retained from the traditional doctrine is the attempt to state the method of deriving predicates for use with "God" and the discussion of a sampling of cases. But so much must be retained, for if we cannot say, for example, "God is loving" and know that we speak truth, God is not real. It is dogma in the three-article creeds that God is in fact Father, Almighty, Creator, Lord, Judge, and Giver of life, and so also that such statements can be factual. It will probably also be desirable to take our cases mostly from the traditional lists since these have shaped the language of the church.

The Method of Derivation

Our first concern is method. Unfortunately we have a quarrel also with the traditional method of derivation. It is an immediate consequence of everything in the previous chapters, that Martin Luther was correct when in 1518 he presented the thesis "The true theologian is not the one who comes to see the invisible things of God by thinking about what is created; the true theologian is the one who thinks about the visible and hinder parts of God, having seen them in sufferings and the cross."[1] The key to the thesis is the chiasmus on "see" and "think about," which readers should note before proceeding.

Luther's first clause exactly captures the standard method,[2] at least since Augustine. God, in his timeless glory, is "invisible." Our initial object is therefore the created, "visible," world. About this world, thought reveals that it contains within itself no sufficient reason for its own existence or character. Unless the world is reasonless—an unthinkable possibility until recently, and perhaps in fact not capable of consistent assertion—there must be a reason of the world that is not part of the world.

This reason can be reached only by the method of negative analogy. To the world's reason can be attributed those characters which it must have to *be* the world's reason. But all our words for causation and purpose are modeled on causes and outcomes that belong to the created world. We can fit them to the world's reason only by striking their reference to the world: so, for example, "God is a loving Father—only not as created fathers love, unreliably . . . [etc.]." And we will perform this operation only on such of our words as, in their worldly use, name what is good in creation, for it is the reason, the value, of the world for which we are reaching.

The end of this path cannot be thought in the normal sense; the logic of our words has been disrupted on the way by the striking of temporal reference. The end is rather a vision, a seeing with the mind's eye[3] "of the invisible things of God." It should also be noted that there is no fundamental difference of method here between "natural" and "revealed" knowledge. The revelation in Christ simply adds special items to the total of the effects in the world from which God's character as its reason in intuited.

Luther's second clause proposes a very different method. The starting point is not our reflection on the world but particular events *in* the world, summed up as "the cross." These are directly presented to our experience, our "seeing." Nor do these exemplify the perfections of the world; they are rather "sufferings." The vision of God is then not the end of our cognitive path; it is the same act as this—cognitively normal—experience of the cross, and so the beginning. The events summarized "cross" simply *are* God insofar as God becomes our object, what we can see. This does not mean that there is no mystery in our experience of God, but the mystery is not the mystic shimmer of distance; it is that God presents himself in sufferings. What we see as God is correspondingly God's "visible" and inglorious reality, God's participation in sin and death and ignominy. And the work of the theologian is now to think hard about all this, in itself a normal rational exercise rather than a seeing at great distance. Just so, the world by no means drops out as an object of theological reflection. On the contrary, it is in at the beginning *and* at the end.

One step must be added to Luther's description, a step he either assumed or perhaps inadequately noted. That on the cross we see God is not our arbitrary choice. It is the crucified one's resurrection, which presents him and his sufferings as God-for-us, in which alone, indeed, he *is* God-for-us.[4] Whether we thereby quite follow Luther or not, we must say that the worldly object as which we have God for our object is the historic Jesus *as* the body of the risen Lord.

With the foregoing demands in mind, we propose a method of attribution to God, which can be summarized: Every true proposition of the form, "God is . . ." is a *slogan* either for the gospel's pivotal claim or for some true version of actual gospel proclamation. In this summary, "the gospel's pivotal claim" denotes one pole of all actual gospel proclamation: the assertion that "Jesus is risen," where "Jesus" can at need be backed up by such descriptions as "the one who preached the kingdom's imminence and was crucified for it." The other pole is the hopes and fears by which those of a time and place have a future, for example, hope for freedom or heaven or food. "Actual gospel proclamation" occurs as the mutual interpretation of these poles.

We should give an example of this interpretation. Large areas of the world are now swept by the hope of "liberation," of escape from conditions of institutionalized economic and political exploitation. The claim of Jesus' resurrection can interpret this hope and interpret itself by it. In the one direction, the interpretation gives an eschatological vision: Jesus, whose life and death defined him as life for others, lives in spite of the death such selflessness had to bring, so that there is now one human who need not exploit others, and so that his relation to others must finally shape all their lives. Therefore, we *will* be liberated. In the other direction, the interpretation gives ethics: Our hope for liberation is a realistic hope in that it is finally hope for Jesus' triumph; and therefore also we need not become ourselves exploiters in order to pursue it. "God liberates" is a slogan for this entire gospel interpretation.[5]

There are, we have proposed, two classes of divine attributes: slogans for the gospel's claim merely as such, and slogans for actual versions of gospel proclamation. In this dualism, we follow the tradition, in which the habit of bipartite classification is universal and deeply rooted. Thus John Gerhard lists nine possible classification systems, all bipartite (*Loci communes theologici*, ii, 105). This dualistic propensity is doubtless finally rooted in the dualism of God and creature and the correlated dualism (following Luther's scheme) of God in his naked majesty and God in his defined majesty.

But while we may approve the deep reason for bipartite classification, we cannot approve the particular bipartite classification that in fact dominates the tradition. Continuing with Gerhard: "Some [attributes] are predicated of God *absolutely,* i.e., without any relation to creatures, as when God is called 'eternal' or 'immense'; and some are predicated *relatively,* as when God is called 'creator,' 'being,' or 'judge'" (ibid.). This division betrays all too clearly the definition of God himself by abstraction from his relations, against which we have been struggling. We therefore have proposed a different classification, to serve the legitimate part of the same purpose.

Some true subject-attribute sentences about God are slogans simply for "Someone (Jesus) is *risen.*" They stipulate, over against some religious concern, what is involved in saying that he is "risen." Thus, for example, over against the question whether Jesus, this figure of historic antiquity, can mean anything to us in our so very different world, we may reply that since he is risen, his life is not in fact distant in time but brackets our time, defining all our possibilities. As a slogan: "God [always the *triune* God, of whom Jesus is the second identity] is eternal."

Other true subject-attribute sentences about God are slogans for actual proclamations of the gospel, for what is said when "Jesus is risen" and some community's or individual's penultimate hopes and fears so interpret one another as to give eschatological vision and founded ethics. We have already given an example, and will give others later. Such slogans are intrinsically historic in their validity. For the hopes and fears of humankind are not constant; their change and succession are indeed the very substance of history. Thus that because Jesus lives we will yet be free of exploitation would not have been a gospel-proclamation to, say, Paul's Corinth, and "God liberates" therefore would not have been a meaningful predication to God. Herein these attributes differ from those of the first class, which always have point.

The true God occurs as Jesus' resurrection. With some oversimplification, we may say that the two classes of God's attributes are those posited in saying that anyone is risen, and those posited in saying that it is Jesus who is risen. Had Nero risen instead of Christ, there would still be an eternal something, but it would be an eternal malignity. That there is instead an eternal benignity is what is said by attributions of the second class. And it is the actual content of Jesus' human life that interprets penultimate hopes and fears to give such content to eschatological vision. That Jesus' humanity and ours interpret each other at all depends on his resurrection, but the matter of the interpretation depends on the specificity of his humanity.

"Jesus Is Risen": Attributes for the Predicate

The first class of attributes, then, are those that explicate the notion of resurrection, bearing always in mind that this notion is itself derived not from general considerations but from the apostles' attempts to describe a particular event that happened to them and Jesus the Nazarene after his death. That stipulated, we may say that the first class of attributes are those which explicate the notion of deity as such, that deity which Father, Son, and Spirit have together in that they derive it from each other. We already have our primary explication of this deity, and so our first attribute: *temporal infinity*.

God is *infinite*. That is, God can be limited by no temporal conditions. Rules of the form "If X happens/has happened, Y must/cannot therefore happen" do not apply to God. God can accept and approve not only the godly but also the ungodly. He can use in his final fulfillment not only the virtues and successes of history, but also its sins and disasters. God can give life not merely to the not-yet born but also to the already dead. He is not predictable by the probabilities. God transcends what has happened and now is, creating what cannot but must yet be. Allowing for the skew introduced by the majority tradition's presumption of divine timelessness, we thus state the legitimate content of a traditionally listed attribute of the "absolute" class, *eternity*.[6]

Since this infinity occurs as the resurrection of Jesus, God's creative transcending is not arbitrary. It has a character: faithfulness to the historical Jesus. A second attribute: God is *faithful*. With this, we replace a second traditional "absolute" attribute, changelessness,[7] and we replace it with a fundamental apprehension of the Hebrew Scriptures. God's continuity as an enduring entity is that of a successful personal life, the very truth of which is to unite unpredictability and reliability. Aristotle defined a successful drama as one in which each event is a surprise when it happens, but makes us afterward say it was just what had to happen.[8] It is this sort of continuity that we attribute to God's temporal infinity by calling him *faithful*.

Following the lead of the traditional listing of "absolute" attributes, we next come to *omnipresence*, or as the Protestant scholastics were accustomed to say, "immensity." Here we have less quarrel with the tradition. According to Aquinas,[9] God "is everywhere by essence, presence and power" (*Summa Theologica*, i, 8, 3). He is everywhere "by essence," that is, in his own selfhood, in that he is the creator, the giver of being. Both any place and what is located in it exist only by the direct action of God, who just so is at that place (ibid., i, 8, 2). God is everywhere "by presence" as anyone is present to those things that are in the scope of his intention, that he "sees" (ibid., i, 4, 3, resp.). God is everywhere "by power," as a ruler is present to all those subject to him (ibid.). It will be seen how, partly in spite of the language, this concept of omnipresence is that of a *personal presence* to all creation: God is present to the world as I am to one I meet and effectively and creatively address.

In the Christian tradition, there has been a long rethinking of the notion of space—beginning decisively with the Greek fathers,[10] and achieving a fulfillment in the work of the seventeenth-century Lutheran metaphysicians—that has moved from the notion of a universal container to the notion of a coordinate system for mutual presence. Thus later scholastics distinguished three modes of spatial presence: an entity may be somewhere "locally," in that the entity has spatial boundaries; an entity may be somewhere "definitively," in that a bounded space can be indicated as the entity's location, even though the entity has itself no spatial boundaries, as a thought is in the brain; or an entity may be somewhere "repletively," by "containing" the space. Only in the third mode is God anywhere, and in it he is everywhere: "God, contained in no space, contains all spaces by the immensity of his being."[11]

We have only one amendment to this general tradition but that is sizable. The traditional doctrine, subtly and distinctively Christian though it is, assumes the essential disembodiment of God. Against this (but continuing in the scholastic terminology) we will want to assert the "definitive" presence of God at certain places in created space. Just so, Martin Luther made "definitive" presence the mode of Christ's presence in the eucharist.[12] God, he argues, is "repletively" present everywhere, and so therefore is Christ, "at his right hand." But if God in Christ is to be present *for us* as conscious beings, we must be able to direct ourselves toward him, to *intend* him. Though this is not Luther's language, God's subjective "repletive" omnipresence must have an objective side, constituted by his "definitive" presence at certain places to which his word calls us. If we direct ourselves to the space occupied by, for example, the eucharistic loaf, we thereby are spatially related to God, even though God has no spatial boundaries.

God's infinity, in our view, is basically his temporal infinity, the unhinderedness of his transcendence through time. God's *spatial* infinity is merely an expression thereof. He "contains" all spaces not by being a larger space but by temporally bracketing the spatial world. The subtly interrelated meanings of the word "present" are no accident and may guide our thinking. Space, the horizon of presence, is simply the experienced reality of the temporal present. God's spatial infinity is his ability to be *now there* for, to be present to, every creature. God's spatial infinity is the present tense of his faithfulness: God is wherever Jesus' self-giving reaches.

We could continue indefinitely with such absolute attributes, but perhaps infinity, faithfulness, and omnipresence are enough and sufficiently basic cases. Taking Gerhard's list as typical of the tradition, he had also spiritual, incorporeal, invisible, simple, immortal;[13] all these have in fact been considered at some place in this *locus*. We turn to the second class of attributes.

"Jesus Is Risen": Attributes for the Subject

The second class of attributes are those that state what it means that it is *Jesus* who is risen. They explicate what it means that it is the particular event that happens between *him* and *his* Father and *their* Spirit, and not some other, to which "deity"—temporal infinity—pertains. Despite the skew of which we constantly complain in this part of traditional doctrine, this logic can easily be seen also in the traditional lists. Thus Gerhard had as his second class: omnipotence, goodness, mercy, justice, omniscience, freedom of will, and truth, all of which explicate the gospel. The assertion of God's attributes of this sort, for example, "God is good," is therefore itself a mode of gospel proclamation.

It must be admitted that some traditional relative attributes seem but distantly related to the gospel, for example, omnipotence and omniscience. Yet why must God be, for example, omnipotent? Many putative Gods are not, and it would even seem possible to speak of someone as risen and yet not attribute omnipotence to that being. It is the specific character of the promises to be made because *Jesus* is the risen one that requires believers in those promises to think of God as omnipotent. These are promises of the triumph of the *unconditionally* loving one and therefore of a good so encompassing as to be realizable only by a will that encompasses all events, and so contrary to probability as to be expectable only from a will that recognizes no other mode of impossibility than self-contradiction. It must be admitted that in many scholarly deductions of God's omnipotence this evangelical derivation is not very apparent; yet even in the most abstract it can be detected in the warrants and biases of the argument. Luther goes straight to principle: "It is the one and highest *consolation* of Christians in all their adversities, to know that God . . . does all things immutably, that his will cannot be resisted nor yet changed or impeded."[14]

We will therefore not be surprised that also the creedal "almighty" had its matrix of a particular era's hopes and anxieties.[15] The great fear of late antiquity was meaninglessness: that the gap between this temporal world and eternity might be unbridgeable, or, expressed in terms of the divine, that the God who is fully divine, who is unqualifiedly eternal, may not function as God of this world. That would mean that no divine being was all-ruling. To those so tormented, the gospel speakers said:

Jesus' Father and ours is in spite of everything *all*-ruler, Lord both of this world and the next.

Once current in the church's language (and in this case even taken into the creed) a word like "almighty" tends to acquire a life of its own. "God is almighty" becomes a theological axiom, from which can be deduced soteriology for situations very different from that in which it had its own soteriological meaning. And the word itself lies in the language, ready for life when the gospel again meets fear of debility at the heart of being, as decidedly in our present time. Both these continuing histories can go well or badly for the gospel.

We continue to a second attribute of this sort, this one untraditional. If we adhere to Luther's methodological rule and then examine traditional lists of attributes, we find them radically incomplete. All the traditional "relative" attributes are characteristics that are good also in this world. That we see God in sufferings and the cross would never be guessed from them. Of possible attributes that are *not* good in this world, we will discuss the most offensive and decisive: God is mortal. God has in fact suffered death and therefore is somehow or other qualified and qualifiable by dying.

Jesus died, indeed, was executed. According to trinitarian apprehension of God, he is an identity of God. What he does and suffers, God does and suffers. Nor can his significance for us be abstracted from his death. The crucifixion cannot be made an incident irrelevant to Jesus' being as God for us, however our otherwise derived suppositions about God may make us wish it could: "but we preach Christ crucified, a stumbling block to Jews and folly to Gentiles" (1 Cor. 1:23). It is therefore an unavoidable item of Christian proclamation and reflection: "God the Son died." And such language was from the first deeply anchored in the liturgy and piety; so, for example, Melito of Sardis: "The Invisible is seen . . . , the Impassible suffers . . . , the Deathless dies. . . . God was killed."[16]

Despite the proposition's obvious gospel-necessity, it has been resisted through the whole history of the church. Arianism was at heart one long attempt to evade it: The Logos could not be God straight out precisely because he is one person with Jesus and so a sufferer of death. Indeed, the whole agony of trinitarian development was, as we have seen, occasioned by second-century acceptance of the impassibility axiom, of which "God died" is the extreme contradiction.

In the christological controversies leading to and following the Council of Chalcedon, the continuing attempt by those most committed to the impassibility axiom to evade attributing death and suffering to the Logos, and the insistence by those most committed to the biblical image of Christ that this must *somehow* be done, was perhaps the chief problem.[17] These controversies generally belong in another *locus*, but we must here note the "theopaschite" controversy at the turn of the fifth and sixth centuries, where the matter was put explicitly to the test.[18] In the first phase of the controversy, liturgical enthusiasm and theological scruples clashed directly. A new and instantly beloved version of the *Trisagion* "Holy God, Holy Almighty, Holy Immortal," enriched with "who were crucified for us," was suppressed by church authorities committed to standard theology, lest the Trinity be taken for the subject of suffering. In the second, a compromise explanation of such liturgy was proposed, phrased to make clear that the Trinity as such was not crucified: "*One of* the Trinity suffered in the flesh." But even this was resisted, by the pope among others, despite its manifest biblical authenticity and perfect agreement with orthodox tradition. It took the emperor Justinian, whose motives were mixed, to compel official churchly acceptance, sealed at a general council in 553.[19] And even though theopaschite language has thereafter had dogmatic status, it has continued to be rare in systematic theology and has remained unreckoned with in standard lists of divine attributes.

The understanding of God's mortality must indeed be trinitarian. "*One* of the Trinity" died; and when patripassionists have extended the suffering of Jesus' death to the Father, this has rightly promptly been rejected.[20] Let us set up the dialectics by posing a naive but inescapable question: What about the time between Jesus' death and his resurrection? If the second identity died on Friday and rose on Sunday, was God meanwhile a binity?

If we have grasped the point of trinitarianism, the question answers itself. Jesus' death was not an interruption of his deity; as the conclusion of his obedience to the Father, as part of what the Father intends in intending Jesus as his self, Jesus' death is *constitutive* for his relation to the Father and so for both his deity and the Father's. Jesus is not God despite his death; he is God in that he died.

This answer will still seem puzzling if we continue to understand being as persistence, if we think that something really *is* whatever it was and persists in being. Then the three days of death must be an interruption of Jesus' being and so of his godhood. But just that understanding of being is what Christian interpretation of God contradicts. Something really *is* what it will be and now is open to being.

Jesus' death is part of his eventful relation to the Father and the Spirit. In that he is risen, this relation is future and present reality. And just this event is God's eternity, in which Jesus is always God. Jesus' death and resurrection are the way the particular Christian God goes about to be eternal, to be temporally infinite. For it is what happens between the identities, of which event Jesus' death is a main constituent, that *is* the eternal God.

Participation in our finitude, alienation, and consequent disaster thus belongs to the event that in fact God is. Exegeting "belongs"; it essentially characterizes the true God that, *if* there are creatures and fallen creatures, he is able and apt so to participate in their life. It is appropriate to what it means to be this God that in his second identity he died with and for us. God is not subject *to* death, but he conquers death only by undergoing it. In this way God is indeed mortal.

Finally, one other of the traditional attributes must be discussed: *goodness*.[21] Given the creeds and the liturgy, it is dogma that God is good. It is the simplest and most encompassing interpretation of the resurrection: History will have a good outcome; goodness is the heart of events.

Yet there are two traps in the notion of divine goodness. The first is that "God is good" is construable as gospel-proclamation in any and all situations, and just so tends to become general and then empty. Second, since the traditional derivation of divine attributes by analogy from features of creation necessarily used the "*good*" features of creation, it has been easy to confuse the divine goodness proclaimed by the gospel with an abstractly necessary character of the prime reason, and so again to empty it of its gospel import. Either way, the outcome is the familiar conception of "the good God," whose goodness is unquestionable and mostly irrelevant.

"God is good" is a Christian sentence only insofar as it is used precisely equivalently for "Jesus of Nazareth will triumph." The difference between the two sentences is only that between rhetorical or metaphysical contexts in which one or the other is more convenient: One sentence is in the present tense, the other in the future.

There is no way to round off our discussion of the attributes of the second class, since in principle we can invent new ones forever. We will instead round off our entire *locus* on God by harking far back. God is the universally transforming event between Jesus the Israelite, and the transcendence he called to as "Father," and their Spirit among us. Given who Jesus is, this event is good. So we conclude the doctrine of God.

Part II

The Holy Spirit

Introduction

The phenomenon we call "spirit" is both universal in human experience and universally remarked.[1] Thus, in uncommon agreement, Hebrew *ruach* and Greek *pneuma*, with their synonyms and related words, have identical backgrounds and usage.[2] Both initially meant "wind" and "breath," and neither ever fully lost this sense or reduced it to pure metaphor. In the uses that concern us, both evoke the liveliness of life, as the elusive and ever-moving breath, the wind that blows where it will to set still things in motion. In the world, the wind is both the dynamism in and of the world and, in its untraceable origin and destination, beyond the world. In us, the breath is both the motion of our own life and drawn in from and breathed out uncontrollably into the alien world beyond. Thus spirit is self-transcendence; the liveliness of each life is precisely its origin and end beyond itself. Moreover, spirit is both life in its openness to dynamism beyond itself, and the dynamism that comes on it; any Greek could have said with the Yahwist, "God . . . breathed into his nostrils the breath of life; and man became a living being" (Gen. 2:7). The Delphic oracle and the Hebrew prophets were equally "inspired," that is, blown through. Spirit, we may say, is personal being, not as "mind," knowing and leaving the other as what he or she is, but as creative, participatory, present to and in the other.

Nor does our use of such philosophically laden words as "transcendence," "personal," or "mind" create any great distance from biblical speech or, indeed, from similar speech in many cultures and religions. The Western philosophical tradition is here very straightforwardly taught by the Bible; such teachings as Hegel's doctrine of "spirit" as personal self-recognition in the other make a current in Western philosophy that is indebted to the Christian tradition in a remarkably uncomplicated way, whatever may happen in other currents or in the eddies between them and this one. In this *locus*, we can go back and forth between biblical and some philosophical language with a freedom that elsewhere might be disastrous.

Humanity is spirit; there is no mode of human life so tradition-bound or torpid that we are not a wind breathed to and by ourselves, to elude our own grasp, and that we do not experience this in ourselves. Just so, God, if God of the living and not of the dead, must so surely be spirit that where this is fully grasped all other spirits are, over against this God, not-spirit, "flesh" (e.g., Isa. 31:3). Not only in Christian theology, the notion of spirit is a crossing place of anthropology, theology, and even cosmology.

The ways in which we, and perhaps other creatures, are spirit, and the relation between our spiritness and God's, are a concern of this *locus* in two connections; others are discussed in other *loci*. Of those to be discussed in this *locus*, one is the matter of Chapter 3; the other will be discussed in one section of Chapter 2, but perhaps should be touched on already at this point.

That we too are spirits is the possibility of God's presence to us as a spirit. Or rather, the triune God, being the mutual creative and participatory presence of Father and Son, is antecedently Spirit; and in that the triune God becomes present also to us, we too are spirit. Our reality as spirits, and our relation to God as the Spirit, is a chief concern of the Fourth *Locus*; here we introduce the matter only to warn against a prevalent perversion thereof, which misidentifies the subject of this *locus*.

That God and we are both spirits can, given a certain religious motivation, be taken to mean that "spirit" names a kind of being— perhaps an invisible kind over against the material kind—which God and we share. Religion unreformed by the gospel, outside or inside the church, regularly seeks to blur the difference between God and the human self, in order to alleviate the burden of our created distinctness and its responsibilities. In the notion of "spirit" as a common essence of God and human selves, such religion finds opportunity. Both in high mysticism and in Sunday-supplement self-help, being "spiritual" can mean melting into a just so equally indistinct and undemanding God. This temptation is an undercurrent of many of the problems we will discuss in this *locus*. And in the modern period, it has emerged in a way that has made the whole doctrine of the Spirit problematic.

In much idealist thought and in theology influenced by it, the self-transcendence, the spirit, of the creature *is* God, and conversely, the self-transcendence of God is itself the act of our creation.[3] There is historical irony here, for Western philosophy learned such profound understanding of spirit from the Scriptures and from the tradition of theology. Yet where this understanding's dialectics work in this idealist way, the biblical speech about God's Spirit is no longer comprehensible. It is fundamental in Scripture that God would be God were there no other spirits at all, and that this God's reality as Spirit precisely constitutes this independence.

The idealist dialectic has not remained the property of philosophers. Popular American religion has followed it in both theory and practice. The ideas and diction of those who now read Carlos Casteneda or Alan Watts differ little from those who once read Ralph Waldo Emerson or Mary Baker Eddy, except that the percentage of sheer blather has risen. Speaking to a congregational group about God, one will sooner or later be asked why one does not make more of "the Spirit," and on probing will discover that what is in fact wanted is an analysis of religious experience, in itself a perfectly legitimate and necessary enterprise.

At the very beginning of our discussion, we must therefore lay it down bluntly: The *concept* of "spirit," of life's self-transcendence, indeed applies to God, the gods, and us, and whatever is spirit is just thereby involved with all else that is spirit. But the particular *reality* the New Testament calls "the Spirit" is the distinct and independent "Spirit of Yahweh," the particular Spirit of Jesus and his Father, distinct from us as we are from each other. And the mode of this Spirit's presence to other spirits is always that of Creator to creatures.

There is no kind of being called "spirit." What there is, is Jones, Smith, and God, each of whom is in his own way self-transcendingly lively. The paradigmatic uses of "spirit" are and must remain those in phrases with the pattern "the spirit of. . . ." There is "the spirit of Lincoln" or "the spirit of St. Luke's Congregation" or "the Spirit of God." Spirit is precisely the person or group as not immediately identical with itself; the genitive phrase marks the nonidentity. The self with whom the person as spirit is not identical is the "body"; just so, we also speak of "the body of. . . ." If we then use "spirit" as an ontological classification, as in "Humanity is spirit," it is simply to say that human beings are marked by this self-transcendence. And if we speak of "a spirit," this is a way of referring either to an individual of such sort or to the self-transcendence, the spirit of, such an individual. There is—we here assert in advance—no spirit-reality as a kind of thing; spirit is always *of* some individual or individual group.

The division of this *locus* appears to us not narrowly determined by the matter. We isolate four contexts in which the Christian tradition speaks of the Spirit of God and discuss them in something like an order of decreasing immediacy, beginning with the context which seems both most immediate and historically originating. But if someone thinks another division would have been more helpful, or disputes the historical judgment just made, we do not think that many material assertions of our discussion would be affected.

According to this division, Christian experience of and teaching about the Spirit are partly claimed fulfillment of Israel's experience of the Spirit, and so a mode of the gospel-proclamation itself (Chapter 1); partly a mode of soteriology corresponding to such proclamation (Chapter 2); partly the appropriate self-interpretation of the church, in which all the main recurrent problems of the church's life have to be fought out (Chapter 3); and partly speculative interpretation of the created world (Chapter 4). All four bodies of experience and discourse are continuous with one another, both systematically and historically.

CHAPTER ONE

The Spirit That Spoke by the Prophets

*Israel's experience of and testimony to "the Spirit" are
fulfilled in the prophetic message and experience of the
church, by the strictly christological content of the message. The motifs of this biblical pneumatology are dogmatized in the third articles of the creeds.*

The Hebrew Scriptures

To understand the Christian experience of and teaching about the
Spirit, the compendious starting point is the New Testament
account of Pentecost—not the story of wind and flames and a
linguistic miracle, but the biblical interpretation that follows and
for the sake of which Luke tells the story:

> This is what was spoken by the prophet Joel: "And in the
> last days it shall be, God declares, that I will pour out my
> Spirit upon all flesh, and your sons and your daughters shall
> prophesy . . . , your young men . . . , and your old men;
> . . . yea . . . , my menservants and my maidservants . . .
> shall prophesy. And I will show wonders in the heaven
> above and signs on the earth beneath . . . , before the day of
> the Lord comes. . . . And it shall be that whoever calls on the
> name of the Lord shall be saved." Men of Israel, hear these
> words: Jesus of Nazareth, a man attested to you by God with
> mighty works and wonders and signs . . . , you crucified
> and killed. . . . This Jesus God raised up. . . . Being therefore
> exalted at the right hand of God, and having received from
> the Father the promise of the Holy Spirit, he has poured out
> this which you see and hear. (Acts 2:16–33)

In the primal church, the religious phenomena that the gatherings of the newly risen Lord's disciples displayed were interpreted as the fulfillment of a fundamental motif of Israel's life:
the coming of the Spirit of Yahweh to make prophets.

During and after the exile, Israel's faith became ever more
exclusively expectation;[1] in that context, prophecy could be seen
not merely as one phenomenon within Israel's religious life, but
also as itself the normative form of faithful life. Just so, the *content* of Israel's expectation could become liberation of prophetic
existence from its exceptionality. Of the signs and wonders that
are to accompany the fulfillment of God's word, the most material then can become that *all* God's people shall be speakers
and not only hearers of that word. Such a complex of expectations appears, among a very few other places, in the book of Joel
cited by Luke (Joel 2:28–32). The primal church said: In the fact
of our existence, that is, in the bursting forth of the message that
a crucified one is risen and in the manifestations accompanying
this proclamation, Joel's prediction is fulfilled. Moreover, it was
the reappearance in the Christian community, as one such manifestation, of the specific phenomenon of prophecy itself which
gave occasion for this interpretation, that is, initiated Christian
language about "the Spirit."[2] It is, therefore, the Hebrew Scriptures' talk of "the Spirit of Yahweh," and especially its connection
with prophecy, which we must first and fundamentally examine.

Through the whole Hebrew Scriptures, "*ruach* Yahweh"
maintains its primal impact. The Spirit is experienced as moving
transcendent force, to create or throw down, whether in nature
or society; this is especially true in the direct documents of religious life (e.g., Pss. 18:5; 104:29–30). At the very heart of Israel's
faith, its confession of the exodus, Israel can say that the breath
of Yahweh freed them from Egypt, in that Yahweh's *ruach*
blasted the Egyptians and drove back the waters (Exod. 15:8–
10). Above all, therefore, God's Spirit creates life: "The spirit of
God has made me, and the breath of the Almighty gives me life"
(Job 33:4). In one branch of Wisdom teaching and literature,[3]
there developed an explicit doctrine of the *Creator Spirit*: "By his
power he stilled the sea; by his understanding he smote Rahab.

By his wind [Spirit] the heavens were made fair . . ." (Job 26:12–
13). But the Spirit is also the *ruach* of judgment, especially in
the prophets: "a spirit of judgment and . . . a spirit of burning"
(Isa. 4:4; see also 27:8; 30:27–28). For "All flesh is grass. . . . The
grass withers . . . when the *ruach* Yahweh blows upon it . . ." (Isa.
40:6–7). Both the spirit that is human life (Gen. 6:3; see also Job
27:3; 32:8; 34:14ff.) and the evil spirit in which humans carry
out judgment on themselves (1 Sam. 16:14) can simply be called
God's Spirit.

In Israel's narrative tradition, the Spirit is above all God's
power on and through the charismatic leadership of Israel:
Moses, the judges, the early kings, and the prophets who appear
around these. Their activity belongs to God's creating, here of
Israel: to God's throwing down what is and bringing forth what
is to be. Thus in the stories of the judges, both the call to leadership and the release of particular actions are described with
"And the Spirit of Yahweh fell upon . . ." (Judg. 3:10; 6:34; 11:29;
13:25). Each time this happens, history gives a lurch.

Decisive for us is the regular juxtaposition of the coming of
the Spirit to evoke political action with the coming of the Spirit to
evoke prophecy. The correlation is especially striking in the stories
of Moses, who is made the archetype of both political leadership
and prophecy, and of Saul, the last judge and first king. It was the
Spirit that was "on" Moses, that enabled him to fulfill his public
role. But when he was forced to share his responsibilities, so that
"some of" his Spirit had to be given to others, the immediate result
was that they "prophesied" (Num. 11:17–30). Of Saul, we repeatedly read that the Spirit "rushed upon" him, sometimes with the
result that he undertook political action, sometimes with the result
that he "prophesied" (1 Sam. 10:10–11; 11:6–7; etc.). But also the
dynastic monarchy of the southern kingdom initially legitimated
itself by the claimed initiative of the Spirit (2 Sam. 23:1–7): When
David was anointed, the Spirit left Saul and "came upon" David
(1 Sam. 16:13). The monarch thus took over the whole activity of
the judges. This obviously meant military and political leadership,
but at least the dynastic founder, David, had to be also a prophet
(2 Sam. 23:2).

We know little concretely about this archaic prophesying by assault of the Spirit. Clearly it involved a complex of visible, indeed obtrusive and unmistakable, special behavior (e.g., Num. 11:17–30); thus of Saul we read: "And he too stripped off his clothes, and he too prophesied before Samuel, and lay naked all that day and all that night" (1 Sam. 19:24). It was often a communal phenomenon (e.g., 1 Sam. 10:10–11; 19:20ff.). It could happen either to permanent prophets or unexpectedly to anyone at all (e.g., 1 Sam. 19:20ff.; 1 Chron. 12:18). It was uncontrollable, and sometimes even unavoidably catching (1 Sam. 19:20–24). It could involve rapture, either physical or in vision (1 Kings 18:12; 2 Kings 2:11–16) and apparently other shamanistic capacities also (2 Kings 2:13–14).

But however different such Spirit-filled shamanistic prophesying may have been from the activity of the later classical prophets, one factor points to them and is decisive for archaic prophecy: the identity of the Spirit with freedom to speak on God's behalf, indeed, specifically to speak *promises* on God's behalf. What ancient evidence there is, is unanimous.[4] In an oracle legitimating the Davidic dynasty, perhaps reaching back to David himself,[5] David presents himself as one with promises to speak for God: "His word is upon my tongue. The God of Israel has spoken, the Rock of Israel has said to me: When one rules justly. . . ." And this claim is equated with the claim: "The *ruach* Yahweh speaks by me . . ." (2 Sam. 23:1–7). Only two stories actually describe a Spirit-filled prophesying with all archaic features. One, the Micaiah story, is about the making of true and false predictions about the outcome of battle; in this story, the question which prophet speaks truly is the same as the question which has the Spirit (1 Kings 22:5–28). The other, the Balaam story, depicts a shaman who despite himself speaks true promises instead of false curses; this is explained "And the Spirit of God came upon him" (Num. 22:41–24:25).

The attribution of prophetic speech to the Spirit is uncommon in the classical preexilic prophets, though it perhaps never died out (Hos. 9:7; Mic. 3:8); reasons can only be conjectured.[6] It is the more remarkable that the conception returns in full force in the exilic and postexilic prophets, that is, as Israel's hope becomes increasingly eschatological. Second Isaiah presents only the locution "And now the Lord God has sent me and his Spirit" (Isa. 48:16). But Ezekiel's entire self-conception repristinates that of archaic prophesying: The Spirit "falls upon" (Ezek. 11:5) and enters (Ezek. 2:2; 3:24) Ezekiel, enraptures him (e.g., Ezek. 3:12, 14; 8:3), and tells him what to say (Ezek. 2:2–3; 3:24–27; 11:5). Finally, in postexilic prophecy not only does this conception continue (Isa. 61:1), but there is a full-fledged doctrine of prophetic inspiration, as the agent of all revelation in Israel: All the law and the writings were "sent by his Spirit through the former prophets" (Zech. 7:12). Indeed, the whole work of God can now be identified with the presence of God's Spirit (Isa. 63:10–11). It is undoubtedly this late-prophetic impulse which accounts for the appearance in the last great history-work, that of the Chronicler, of Spirit-worked prophetic intervention as a standard event in the political history of monarchical Israel (2 Chron. 15:1–2; 20:14–15; 24:20). In any case, the Chronicler too has a total Spirit-theology of revelation: "Thou gavest thy good Spirit to instruct them . . . and didst warn them by thy Spirit through the prophets" (Neh. 9:20, 30).

It expresses the same connection of the Spirit with the word that also *wisdom* is understood as Spirit-worked, in both early and late texts. Joseph's wisdom is that the Spirit of God is in him (Gen. 41:38). Even the artisans of the desert sanctuary have their skill by the Spirit (Exod. 28:3; 31:3). And Daniel, the survivor by wisdom, is one in whom is "the spirit of the holy god(s)" (e.g., Dan. 4:8, 9, 18). The book of Job draws the point: "But it is the *ruach* in a man, the breath of the Almighty, that makes him understand" (Job 32:8).

We will understand the import of the correlation of Spirit and word only if we remind ourselves of a decisive characteristic of the prophetic word itself: It is not merely a word about the future, but a word that *creates* the future.[7] "By the word of the Lord the heavens were made" (Ps. 33:6), and here "the word of the Lord" is *terminus technicus* for the prophetic word.[8] Thus the kings feared the archaic prophets because their oracles not only predicted victory or defeat but also caused it to happen (e.g., 1 Kings 22:5–28). And centuries later, at the high point of self-conscious but still primally vigorous prophecy, we have the famous passage of Second Isaiah: "For as the rain and the snow come down from heaven, and return not thither but water the earth, making it bring forth and sprout . . . , so shall my word be that goes forth from my mouth; it shall not return to me empty, but it shall accomplish that which I purpose" (Isa. 55:10–11). That God creates by word and that God creates by the Spirit are alternative descriptions of the same event. In either description, the work of the prophets—and other word- and spirit-bearers—is Gods continuing creative work, to throw down what is old and call forth the true Israel that is to be. Putting the two descriptions together: The Spirit is freedom for, and the power of, the word that opens the future.

In later Israel, the coming and presence of the Spirit, from characterizing the *speakers* of promise, became also a *content* of promise. This requires no further initial explanation than the basic notion of spirit. Since the Spirit is God's power as the life of Israel, a promise of new life for Israel must be a promise of a new coming of the Spirit. But such promise will not be spoken until it is new life that must be promised, until Israel's hope has become not merely hope for this or that historical good fortune but hope for rescue from death. That is, it will not happen until Israel has confronted its own death, until Israel's hope has had to become eschatological. Thus the promise of the Spirit first appears in Isaiah, but there gloriously: "Until *ruach* is poured upon us from on high, and the wilderness becomes a fruitful field. . . . Then justice will dwell . . ." (Isa. 32:15–16). When there is universal peace among all creatures, it will be because "the mouth of the Lord has commanded, and his Spirit has gathered them" (Isa. 34:16).[9]

The Spirit, as the dynamism of God's life and the life God gives us, is at the heart of Ezekiel's hope, right to the spirit in the chariot wheels (Ezek. 1:4, 17, 20–21). Above all, there is the vision of the valley of dry bones. Here the Spirit is at once life, breath, and wind, all as God's Spirit (Ezek. 37:1–14). And all this archaic imagery is eschatological promise of resurrection, of God's final triumph over Israel's separation from its life in God (Ezek. 37:13–14; 39:29).

Finally, in postexilic prophecy the connections in principle are stated. There must be eschatological hope just *because* God is the giver of Spirit and therefore the God of life and not of death: "nor will I always be angry; for from me proceeds *ruach*, and I have made the breath of life" (Isa. 57:16). And the presence of the Spirit is the union of the promises made by God's past acts with their final triumph: "Yet now take courage . . . ; for I am with you . . . , according to the promise that I made you when you came out of Egypt. My Spirit abides among you; fear not. . . . Once again, in a little while, I will shake the heavens and the earth" (Hag. 2:4–8). The Spirit is the—in both senses—present reality of God's eschatological power. The Spirit is at once the guarantee and the object of final hope.

Given how definitely, through the whole tradition of Israel, the Spirit is the Spirit of prophecy and wisdom, Israel's experience and interpretation of the Spirit could fulfill itself only in some union of that experienced prophetic Spirit with the hoped-for eschatologically outpoured Spirit just described. In Ezekiel, there is a natural resonance between Ezekiel's pneumatic self-understanding and his promise of new Spirit, but there is no conceptual synthesis. Two syntheses were possible; both were made.

One synthesis is messianic: at the last, there will be triumphant life because God's people will be gathered by and around a last prophet (and king and wiseman), a final Spirit-bearer. So the great Messianic promise of Isaiah: "And the Spirit of the Lord shall rest upon him, the spirit of wisdom and understanding" that brings universal peace (Isa. 11:2–9). This line is continued by Second Isaiah, who describes "the servant of Yahweh": "I have put my Spirit upon him, he will bring forth justice to the nations" (Isa. 42:1). Since the servant is a prophetic figure, if not only that,[10] there is here a perfect union of eschatological hope with prophetic self-understanding.

The other synthesis is communal: At the last, death will be overcome because *all* God's people will be prophets, bearers of life. Hope for the coming of a nation of prophets emerges late and seldom in Israel's history, but then in full force. The main instance is the Joel passage already cited: "And it shall come to pass afterward, that I will pour out my Spirit on all flesh; your sons and your daughters shall prophesy, your old men shall dream dreams, and your young men shall see visions. Even upon the menservants and maidservants in those days, I will pour out my spirit" (Joel 2:28ff.). But there is also the remarkable if somewhat obscure oracle in Second Isaiah: "This is my covenant with them . . . : my spirit which is upon you, and my words which I have put in your mouth, shall not depart out of your mouth, or out of the mouth . . . of your children's children . . . from this time forth and for evermore" (Isa. 59:21).[11]

It is plain that the dialectics of Israel's knowledge of the Spirit will be completed only by yet one more step: hope for a people that is a community of prophets, and therefore is possessed of unquenchable life, because it is gathered by the final Prophet, hope for a people all of whom have the Spirit because among them is a Spirit-*bearer* whose prophetic mission is precisely to be the Spirit-*giver*. This step is not taken in the Hebrew Scriptures, unless in entirely transcendent-predictive fashion by Second Isaiah's "servant songs."[12]

The New Testament

The traditions deposited in the synoptic Gospels continue the Hebrew Scriptures' use of "the [Holy] Spirit." Also in the synoptic Gospels, "the Holy Spirit" usually just means the Spirit of prophecy: "said in the Holy Spirit" can stand for "prophesied" (Mark 12:36 par.), and "will be filled with the Holy Spirit" can stand for "will be a prophet" (Luke 1:15–17). The Spirit inspires utterance (Matt. 10:20 par.; Mark 13:11 par.) and works rapture (Mark 1:12 par.; Luke 2:27). But also the life-creating reality of the Spirit appears in the Gospels' use, though notably only in contexts closely tied to the prophetic work of the Spirit.

This traditional language is used with almost complete concentration of reference to the person of Jesus. There are three great centers of Spirit-language in the evangelical narrative. First and perhaps most ancient, Jesus' *baptism* is unanimously in all four Gospels a descent of the Spirit (Mark 1:9–11 par.). This descent is described as the descent of the Spirit to make a prophet: It inaugurates Jesus' preaching mission (Mark 1:12–15), issues immediately in rapture to another place (Mark 1:12 par.), and was at least initially described as a call-vision.[13]

It is of the first importance that the account of Jesus' baptism is introduced, unanimously in the tradition, with John the Baptizer's testimony: "I have baptized you with water; but he will baptize you with the Holy Spirit (and with fire)" (Mark 1:7–8 par.).[14] The prophet Jesus does not bear the Spirit only for his own empowerment; he bears him in order to give him,[15] and this gift is eschatological, a baptism with the fire of judgment. Thus is taken the final step in Israel's knowledge of the Spirit which was not taken in the Hebrew Scriptures, and it is taken apparently without laborious reflection. The entire New Testament doctrine of the Spirit is therewith achieved in principle.

Second, there is a general connection of the Spirit with Jesus' birth. God directly creates this child as a completely new thing. The connection is ancient, as shown by its appearance in both Matthew and Luke despite the disparity of their birth legends (Matt. 1:18–20; Luke 1:35). In Matthew, Mary's pregnancy is "in the Holy Spirit." In Luke, the Spirit will "come upon" Mary, exactly in the fashion of archaic prophetic seizure, to create the child: Mary will bring forth the child the way the prophets brought forth their words. Just so this child is God's eschatological new creation, called forth by "the Power of the Highest." The identity of the Spirit who creates Jesus with the prophetic Spirit is made inescapable in Luke, who depicts a positive epidemic of Spirit-filled prophecy in the vicinity of the birth (Luke 1:41, 67; 2:25ff.).

Third, Jesus' works, but especially his life-giving healings, are "in the Spirit of God" (Matt. 12:28; Mark 3:29–30). This power is explicitly equated with the approach of "the kingdom of God" (Matt. 12:28 par.); in Luke's version it is "the finger of God" (Luke 11:20). In Jesus' mission, the personal endowment of the prophet and the eschatologically life-giving power of God are indistinguishable.

It remains only to note that in Luke these apprehensions of the primal community are elaborated into a theology. Luke takes advantage of a Markan reference to a sermon of Jesus to give its supposed content (Luke 4:16–30): an interpretation of the Spirit-filled prophet of Isa. 6:1–4 as the promised last prophet of other Isaianic passages, and a claim that Jesus is he. Also, the final prophet's gift of the Spirit to his people, posited contextually in the baptism narratives, is made explicit: Luke specifies that the "good things" Q said Jesus' disciples will be given are "the Holy Spirit" (Luke 11:13 par.). It is consistent with this Lukan reflection that Luke introduces prophetic rapture where Matthew and Mark have only travel (Luke 9:14), and has the only synoptic reference to inspired speech by Jesus (Luke 10:21–24).

The Spirit-interpretation of major parts of the evangelical narrative did not occur in a vacuum.[16] An experience and a self-conception in perceived continuity with those of archaic and late Israelite prophecy were a vital part of the life of the primal church and may indeed have dominated in some areas. The integral phenomenon of prophecy reappeared and played an important role in establishing the gospel and its tradition,[17] while people at least *called* "prophets," whose actual activities are hard to describe certainly, were evangelists and liturgical leaders in many communities.[18] There perhaps were even places where bands of ecstatics made the real congregation, surrounded by an outer group of postulants and hangers-on[19]— this may be part of the background for the expectation that appears in Luke, that manifest prophetic seizure is the normal sufficient condition or consequence of baptism (Acts 8:14–18; 11:15–17; 19:2–6). Most important, evangelists and leaders of all institutional types (apostles, teachers, or whatever) understood their own work and were understood by others in the terms of Spirit-filled prophecy and in direct continuity with Hebrew prophecy.[20] "Then Peter, filled with the Holy Spirit, said . . ." (Acts 4:8) states an archetype. Paul himself is one from whom we have direct testimony,[21] while from quite other parts of the church the traditions preserved in Acts stereotypically depict the work of the church's heroes as Spirit-given[22] and attribute to them both shamanistic acts and direct instruction by the Spirit's voice.[23]

Two constant further characters of this prophetic Spirit are decisive. First, this Spirit continues to be the breath of life, the *Spiritus Creator* who raises the dead, and can even animate a statue (Rev. 11:11; 13:15). The Spirit is the ontological opposite of death;[24] both Christ and we die by "the flesh" but rise "by the Spirit" (1 Pet. 3:18; 4:6). In a traditional formula given by Paul, the Holy Spirit is the reality-sphere of resurrection (Rom. 1:4).

Second, inspiration by this Spirit is invariably understood christologically. The risen Jesus has a spirit as any living person does; and this "Spirit of Jesus" simply *is* the Spirit of prophecy (Acts 17:1). When prophecy appears in the Christian gatherings, it is the risen Christ who sends the Spirit to create it (Acts 2:33). Indeed, even the Hebrew prophets were held to have been inspired by "the Spirit of Christ" (1 Pet. 1:11). The most drastic expression of this christological doctrine of inspiration is in a prophetic word, the truly remarkable saying: "For the testimony of Jesus is the spirit of prophecy" (Rev. 19:10). In this saying the Spirit is not an enabling or energizing power adventitious to mere speaking about Jesus. Gospel-telling does not need to become something more to be Spirit-filled; where the witness to Jesus occurs, there is the Spirit, and vice versa. With that, we are back with the Pentecost text from which we began: "This Jesus God raised up. . . . Being therefore exalted at the right hand of God . . . , he has poured out this which you see and hear."

Prophetic inspiration is the one great anchor of New Testament Spirit-theology. Baptism is the other. Baptism is the church's initiation rite.[25] In the missionary situation, it was therefore necessarily seen as the gate to a promised future: "Be baptized, and you *shall* receive . . ." (Acts 2:38). And therefore, further, within understanding shaped by the Hebrew Scriptures, baptism was merely thereby inevitably proclaimed and experienced as a rite of the Spirit, of the power of God's promises: ". . . shall receive the Holy Spirit." It is possible that in some places baptism's connection with the Spirit only meant incorporation into a community in which there were Spirit-filled people. But for the traditions that actually appear in the New Testament, initiation into the believing community is identical with the gift of the Spirit for all neophytes.[26] And therefore, generally in the New Testament, all believers are Spirit-bearers.[27]

The conviction that all the baptized have the Spirit must mean either that all members of the congregation are explicitly prophets or that the experience and understanding of Spirit-bearing include phenomena other than manifest prophecy. The former may have been the case in some regions, but predominantly in the New Testament and most explicitly in Paul, the latter is assumed or asserted to be the case.

Paul makes two steps. First, he in effect if not deliberately separates the constituents of prophetic activity into distinct "gifts," so that there is at least one gift for every believer, even the least ecstatic (1 Cor. 12:1–13, 27–31; Rom. 12:6–8). Second, he identifies the common feature that qualifies all these as gifts of the Spirit, as contribution to "the common good" (1 Cor. 12:7), as "the building up" of the community and its unity (1 Cor. 14:3ff.). The charism in the charisms is therefore love (Rom. 12:9ff.; 1 Cor. 12:31ff.), the final manifestations of the Spirit's presence not religious phenomena but "love, joy, peace, patience, kindness, goodness, faithfulness, gentleness, self-control" (Gal. 5:22–23). This does not mean the Spirit loses his character as Spirit of prophecy. As given for the building of community, the gifts are all communication-acts, most of them straightforwardly verbal; and on the lists of gifts, prophecy is again chief.[28]

If the church were a standing religious society of the present world, Paul's theology of the Spirit, in which contributing funds can be a Spirit-given act, would bowdlerize the Spirit's eschatological reality. But the church does not so understand itself anywhere in the New Testament; the church is the anticipating community. Paul therefore does not merely accommodate the other great side of New Testament testimony to the Spirit, that the Spirit gives eschatological life; he is the chief witness.[29]

In one great passage (Rom. 8:1–27), Paul brings together all these sides of the New Testament's apprehension of the Spirit and nearly exhausts their dialectics in one magnificent sweep

of argument and rhetoric. This argument's exposition can conclude our biblical discussion.[30] The passage is initiated when
over against analysis of the old pre-Christ human situation Paul
asserts a decisive eschatological change: There is "now no condemnation" for those in Christ Jesus. Contrary to how it has
always been, there is now no fear that our life will have been, at
the end, without value. The reason is that the standard of judgment[31] has changed. Once we were judged in a way that con-
victed of sin and sentenced to death and by which, therefore, sin
and death maintained their control;[32] now we are judged in a
way that frees for life and by which, therefore, the *Spirit* rules,[33]
the opposite of death and bondage. This change in standards of
judgment has been worked by the incarnation (vv. 3–4).

The penultimate outcome[34] of God's act in Christ is thus
the existence of two kinds of people, those still in the situation
before the great change and those in the new situation, those
who live "according to flesh" and those who live "according to
Spirit." "The flesh" is neutrally the creature as other than God,
pejoratively the creature curved in on its otherness from God;[35]
life "according to flesh" is life of the second sort, life that holds
its breath, that tries to be purpose and energy for itself. Life
"according to Spirit" is life that rejoices in being moved and
inspired by God, to be just so itself spirit. In that we lived without Spirit lay the necessity of God's new act;[36] that we now live
by the Spirit is the new fact worked by God's act.

We cannot here trace Paul's analysis of *how* the incarnation works the shift from the old situation to the new, except to
note one point vital for our purpose: The argument functions
by positing a double opposite to "Spirit": "flesh" and "the law."[37]
The "law of sin and death" turns out to be "the Law" absolutely,
in respect of the latter's failure. But "the Law" is a mode of
God's *word*. Thus "Spirit" in this argument includes what Paul
elsewhere calls "promise" or "the gospel";[38] Spirit here is the
Power of the promises brought by the message about Christ.
Thus also in Paul's opposition of "flesh" and "Spirit," the Spirit
is the Spirit of prophecy, the Power of an utterance that creates
the future.

Accordingly, Paul must now shift from third-person argument to second-person gospel-speaking, to the actual making of such a powerful utterance: "And you *are* 'in Spirit,' not 'in flesh'" (v. 9a). The Romans may be sure of their inclusion precisely because the Spirit of God is the same as the Spirit of Christ, that is, as the Spirit of the gospel which they know they have in fact heard and into which they know they have been baptized (v. 9b–d). And so Paul is free for unfettered proclamation of the Spirit-aspect of the absence of condemnation: the resurrection of the dead (vv. 10–11). "He who raised Christ Jesus from the dead will make alive also your mortal bodies, through his Spirit that dwells among you" (v. 11).[39] The word about Christ, the word which contains no condemnation, is just so Spirit; those who have heard it may therefore know that they are already in the power of eschatological life.

Just so, since believers are *now* in the grip of life, Paul turns briefly to exhortation: Believers must not anachronistically live according to flesh (vv. 12–13). But on this occasion he is himself too inspirited to remain with exhortation. If we cling to the old ways, it is only out of fear. But—and now Paul is back with proclamation—fear is unnecessary. The Spirit from God might indeed have been an enslaving power; but in fact, as Christ's Spirit, he establishes us in Christ's own relation to God; he is a "Spirit of adoption" (vv. 14–15a). We have no more to fear than does the resurrected Christ himself! And the reality of this confidence is specifically Christian *prayer*, in which we address God as "Father"—as Christ did and does (v. 15b). Such prayer is itself legitimate only as prophetic utterance (v. 16); it is inspired by the Spirit (v. 15b).[40] "You have received the spirit of adoption, in whom we say, 'Abba,' that is, 'Father.' The Spirit himself bears witness, together with our spirit, that we are indeed *children* of God" (vv. 15b–16).

Wherewith the eschatological power of the Spirit breaks through all argument: "And if children, then heirs . . . fellow heirs with Christ" (v. 17). All creation is a mere present from God for the Child and children (vv. 17–18). Therefore it waits—or rather, cannot wait—precisely for us. Though we cannot understand it, this waiting too is verbal (vv. 19–22). The prayers of creation, perhaps the only true and necessary "speaking in tongues" are—it will appear further on (vv. 22, 26b)—the Spirit's, that is, they too are prophecy.

What it can mean to be inheritors of the universe we cannot say; we can only join the dumb creation in cries only God understands (v. 23).[41] Such a promise transforms all life into hope (vv. 23–25) and puts the true object of our prayer beyond our praying for it (v. 26). But life that is pure hope is itself prophetic ecstasy;[42] and the prayers we cannot conceive we may let the Spirit pray for us (v. 26). And just so, emptied of all that is not future to it, our life becomes even now true life: We have "the beginning of the Spirit" (v. 23).[43]

The Creedal Tradition

The ancient church was perhaps more straightforwardly, and unimaginatively, biblical in its witness to the Spirit than in any other part of its theology. This was doubtless because Hellenic conceptions in this area, being both undeveloped and in their basis very similar to the biblical, were both less challenging and less alienating than in other fields. We may, in pedestrian fashion, summarize what we have found in the New Testament so: (1) The Holy Spirit is the Spirit of the creating word, both of the Hebrew prophets and of the church; (2) the Holy Spirit is poured out in baptism, to make a prophetic community; (3) the Holy Spirit is the bond of this community; (4) the Holy Spirit is the power of the resurrection both now and eternally; and (5) the Holy Spirit is all these things because he is the Spirit of Christ. Precisely these points are the stock of patristic discourse about the Spirit. Moreover, the locations of patristic pneumatology are also the same as in the New Testament: prophecy and baptism.[44]

So long as the fathers' pneumatology remained within the sphere just defined, it was, if not overly creative, clear and unanimous.[45] The kind of alienation which in other matters both made confusion and elicited new insight appeared here only by attraction from another *locus*: In the pre-Nicene theology, the

Spirit became implicated in the Logos-theology's interpretation of Christ as a mediating mid-being between God and creatures. Since the very notion of the Spirit is of God's active presence to us, this theology threatened to make the Spirit otiose and to create a binitarian, and paganized, interpretation of deity. Conversely, baptismal confession of the Spirit was the chief hindrance to the complete triumph of this theology, and the achieving of a theology with room for confession of the Spirit was identical with the achieving of true trinitarianism. But all this belongs to the Second *Locus*.

Since in the area covered here all the fathers said much the same things, a few early examples will suffice. Ignatius of Antioch described himself as a prophet, a "God-bearer."[46] He is so as a witness to Christ, and therein is in direct succession of the Hebrew prophets, who were "disciples" of Christ "in the Spirit" (*To the Magnesians*, ix, 2), teachers in advance of the Christian congregations (*To the Philadelphians*, v, 1–2). For the Spirit is *Christ's* Spirit (ibid., introd.); what the Spirit communicates is what Christ is and does (*To the Ephesians*, xvii, 11), and Christ's will is done in the church through the Spirit (*To the Philadelphians*, introd.). At the same time, all in the congregation are God-bearers (*To the Magnesians*, introd., 7), indeed, "full of God" (ibid., xiv). Just so, the Spirit is the bond of divine unity among the congregation, identical with the presence of Christ (ibid., xv). The Spirit *is* love (*To the Trallians*, vi, 1).

A key figure in the period of patristic pneumatology's crystallization was Irenaeus, bishop of Lyons.[47] He decisively identifies the Spirit that is experienced in the church as the *prophetic* Spirit, in confrontation both with wild prophecy and with some who reacted by denying the reality of churchly prophecy (e.g., *Against Heresies*, iii, 11, 9; 12, 1; 19, 1–2). This Spirit was given to Christ by the Father, that he may give him again: "The Lord, receiving the gift from the Father, himself gave the gift again to those who participate in him, sending the Spirit into all the earth" (ibid., iii, 17, 2). The effect of the Spirit's presence, thus given, is the "mingling and mixing" of God's Spirit with the creature, to restore the creature to God's image (*Demonstration of the Apostolic Preaching*, 97), the end of the old life and the beginning of a new (*Against Heresies*, iii, 17, 2).

The chief site of patristic pneumatology is the developing creedal tradition, both as repository and as lively authority.[48] The structure of our three-article creeds seems to have resulted from the threefold baptismal name of God drawing to itself material from summaries of doctrine and evangelical narrative used in catechetical preparation for baptism. To the naming of the Spirit, creeds through the creed-making period, from the middle of the second century to the end of the fourth and from all parts of the church, constantly attached one or more of the following items:[49] inspiration of the prophets, baptism,[50] the church,[51] resurrection, and eternal life. These may simply have been items of urgent confession in the time of early Catholicism's self-definition against gnosticism and the sects, attached to "Spirit" because they logically fit there. Or they may have belonged to catechetical lists of vital theology divided among the three parts of the name, landing with "Spirit" because they were the concluding items. There was a logical fit, because the last items of a theological confession ordered on a history-of-salvation principle must occupy exactly the temporal slot, on the boundary of present and future, that is the Spirit's.

Whatever the precise formative history of the third article, the composite result is an adequate summary of New Testament witness. The Spirit inspires the word, creates the church, is given at baptism, overcomes death, and is an anticipation of final life. Only explicit stipulation of the Spirit as *Jesus'* spirit is missing; but there was no need for this, since the three-article creeds are but an expansion of the triune baptismal name of God, by which that relation is antecedently established. Dogma is often characterized as summary of Scripture; in most cases, it is not. But of the dogma established about the Spirit in the creedal third articles, the characterization is precise.

CHAPTER TWO

Pneumatological Soteriology

*Western Christianity's attention to the practical power of
the gospel must be translated from causal language about
grace to hermeneutical language about proclamation if it
is fully to achieve its own truth. This translation is done
by the Reformation doctrine of justification and issues in
a new doctrine of predestination.*

The Doctrine of Grace

If we rehearse again the items of christological faith appropriated to the Spirit in the creedal third articles, we note that this
is where *we* come into the creeds: Here appear faith, baptism,
church, and eternal life. What is sketched in a third article is our
life as it is, because reality is as the creeds otherwise describe
it. The Spirit is, as we have seen in the New Testament, the creative and transforming power of that gospel address of which the
three-article creeds are content summaries; the Spirit is precisely
the fact that the gospel makes changes in us.

In the Western church, analysis of this impact of God in
Christ on our actual lives, through proclamation and the sacraments, has been the continuing chief theological interest. It is
salvation, justification, sacramental grace, faith, predestination,
and so on, that have fascinated Western thinkers, not so much
divine triunity or hypostatic union. That is, Western theological
work has been directed mainly to the third article.

From its inception, the Latin church was practical in its concerns. Initially, this practicality of Latin Christianity amounted
to a decidedly subevangelical works-righteousness. Tertullian
was only unusually blunt: quoting at random, "Every man must

satisfy God in the same matter in which he has offended."[1] It was when Augustine joined the practical concerns of the Latin church with the doctrine developed in the East, of God and his transforming works, that Western Christianity as we know it was created, in which the central concern is precisely the practical effect of God's living reality in our lives.

Prior to the Reformation, however, this theological enterprise was handled not as a doctrine of the Spirit but as a doctrine of "grace" (*gratia*). In part, this is merely a terminological crotchet, which will cause no trouble so long as we remember it. If we want to find the medieval or Tridentine Roman Catholic equivalents for biblical, Eastern-patristic, or Reformation discussions of the work and nature of the Spirit, we must look under the heading "grace." It is Augustine's usage that shaped pre-Reformation Western theological terminology so,[2] and his usage had a basis in that of the New Testament, especially of Paul.[3] Behind the usage choice, however, there is a material theology that is deeply problematic.

The doctrine of the Trinity worked out by the Greek fathers conceptualized the creative relation of God to his faithful people in a specifically biblical way. As we have seen, the creedal statements about the Spirit merely summarized the Bible's witness; then the specific trinitarian dogma insisted that this preaching, community-gathering, and vivifying were no less than God's own reality among us. But Augustine's particular adaptation of trinitarian doctrine obscured this function of the doctrine. For Augustine, the three "persons," over against us, are functionally indistinguishable. Thus Augustine could no longer conceptualize the saving relation between God and creatures by saying that the Father and the Son are transformingly present in the Spirit, as the Greek originators of trinitarianism had done.

With the specifically Christian understanding of the relation between God and the faithful thus blocked, Augustine was left with the standard position of Western culture-religion: On the one hand there is God, conceived as a supernatural entity who acts causally on us; and on the other hand there are the results among us of this causality. In the subsequent Latin tradition, God and the objects of God's causality are then both interpreted accordingly: They are "substances," fundamentally self-sustaining and self-contained entities, who "act" over against each other, the result of which action is in us a *habitus*, an acquired disposition to behave and react in ways obedient to the will of God.[4]

That Augustine then pored over Paul for his material descriptions of God's action and our consequent "habits,"[5] is the great blessing of the Latin church; until recently, even the most alienated Western Christian showed more understanding of the great issues raised by Paul than do leading theologians of the Eastern churches. But that Paul's assertions were pressed into this utterly unsuited framework has been the Western church's great theological disaster.

The Augustinian framework of the doctrine of grace has been a difficulty, moreover, precisely over against the very dogma which is the fruit of Augustine's and the Augustinians' study of Paul: the declaration of the Council of Orange that all spiritual life is the work of grace in us and that "free choice [is] so weakened that . . . no one is able rightly to love or believe in God . . . , except by the prior initiative of the grace of God's mercy."[6] Perhaps the simplest way to see the difficulty is to note that whereas Paul can call fornication, enmity, and so on, "works," so that the *negative* phenomena of human life can indeed be fitted into a causal understanding of our relation to exterior influence, such things as love are precisely not effects but "fruits" (Gal. 5:19–23), which supposes a very different relation between God, whose fruits they are, and us, in whom they appear. More particularly, the difficulty appears historically in two ways.

First, Paul used the word "grace" (*charis*) and its derivatives both for the quality of God's behavior in Christ and for the gifts of the Spirit that are the fruits among us thereof.[7] Following his lead, Augustine used "grace" for both God's saving causality and the effects on our side, for both God's love to us and the love to God which God creates in us.[8] The terminology could have been a mere variant on Paul's, except for the conceptual framework in which it functioned. In that framework, the "grace" that is our love to God necessarily becomes an "habitual" quality[9] of the substance faithful-human, over against the "grace" that is a quality of the substance God. So Thomas Aquinas: "Grace may be understood in two ways: in one way as the divine aid that moves us to will and act well, in the other way as a divinely given dispositional quality (*habituale donum*) . . ."[10] (*Summa Theologica*, i–ii, 111, 2). Since both substances in question are personal, existing as mind and will (grace as a gift is a "habit" of *willing* the good), this ineluctably sets the problem of the cooperation between the graceful God and the—supposedly in *this* fashion—graced creature. The problem has been the crux of all Western theology.

The nature, profundity, and ultimate insolubility of the cooperation problem can all be displayed at once by citing the best solution yet offered, that of Aquinas. Grace, as a quality of God and as a quality of the faithful *taken together*, is divided by a crossing distinction

> according to the one who operates and the one who cooperates. The operation of any effect is not attributed to the one who is moved but to the one who moves. In that . . . our soul is only a moved reality and not a mover, only God being the mover, operation is attributed to God; in this respect, it is called "operating grace." But in that . . . our mind moves as well as being moved, operation is not solely attributed to God but also to the soul; in this respect, it is called "cooperating grace." (Ibid.)

When Aquinas' problem is the problem set, one must surely speak exactly as Aquinas does: God is the sole agent of salvation, but there is no way a *will* can be authentically "moved" except by itself co-willing. The difficulty is in pastoral practice. "Our grace-renewed souls cooperate with God's grace." "Must I cooperate?" "Yes." "All right, what do I have to do?" To the last question, at the end of that sequence, all answers are equally destructive of faith—even the biblical answer to an only superficially similar question: "Believe and be baptized."

Second, when the saving relation between God and believers is understood as the causality of one substance on another, salvation is necessarily understood as a *process*, in Aquinas' formulation, a "movement (*motus*) by which the human mind is moved by God from a state of sin to a state of righteousness" (ibid., i–ii, 113, 5). That is, grace is understood as the primary cause of a sequence of events, each of which must occur for the next to be possible. Thus, for example, early scholasticism defined a sequence with the following steps: first, impact of the church's mission, then appropriate response (*meritum de congruo*), sacramental infusion of love, "justification," authentically altered life (*meritum de condigno*), eternal reward.[11] Or, for another instance, pietist Puritan divines specified a sequence of modes of experience, each of which must occur before the next can: consciousness of sin, and struggle for righteousness in the terms of the law, defeat in this endeavor and acknowledgment that only God can save, a period of waiting for grace, experience of the goodness of God.[12]

Whatever may be the virtues of such descriptions as phenomenology of religion, they are theological catastrophes. For if salvation is thus understood as a stepped process between two agents, then unless I am to be a mere spectator of my own life, there must be points in the process when the move is up to me and where the next stage will not occur unless I make the move. It is in the transfer from third-person description to first-person and second-person teaching and preaching that this reveals itself as an evil. Thus, for example, in the Puritan scheme, when the preacher—with descriptive truth—says, "God freely forgives those who sincerely repent," I must then discover in myself whether I do indeed sincerely repent to know if God's forgiveness intends me in particular; and then it is my work of repentance and not the gospel which is the experientially decisive condition of my hope.

Indeed, it is in general the third-person descriptive modality of the doctrine of grace that is its flaw. For one thing, it may well be doubted that there is any vantage from which thus to observe the entities God and creature, so as to be able to describe the process between them. And be that as it may, the attempt to think from such a vantage has created in Western theology an alienation of the third article, a transformation of the biblical discourse about God's Spirit into a stipulation of method for our spirituality. That is, the traditional doctrine of "grace" is a works-righteous *structure* lodged at the heart of the chief theological concern and achievement of the Western church.

Justification by Faith

It was precisely this perversion that necessitated the Reformation. We will understand little about the Reformation if we understand it only as a protest against specific abuses or as a theological quarrel adjustable by dialectical reconciliation of opposed formulations.[13] The Reformation was a protest against a whole way of thinking about and proclaiming the faith, and against corresponding structures of the medieval Western liturgies of penance and the Supper—which came first, the theology or the liturgy, we need not settle here. There are two ways in which the reform occurred theologically.

It is a cliché that Luther radicalized the Western desire for the grace of God into desire for the graceful God. He was concerned no longer for God's effect on us but for God's own presence among us. Rather, he was concerned for God as *God's* effect on us—that is, precisely for God the Spirit. Thus an immediate consequence of Luther's insight was recovery of the biblical and pre-Augustinian discourse about the Spirit, an almost uncanny ability simply to speak and write biblical and patristic Spirit-language.[14]

Merely to talk of "the work of the Holy Spirit"[15] instead of "grace," as the theologians who followed Luther then regularly did, is not, however, a guarantee that the ancient perversion has been overcome. The Lutheran theologians of the sixteenth and seventeenth centuries conducted a careful analysis of the biblical testimony to the Spirit's work, taking Luther's catechetical "calls, gathers, enlightens, sanctifies, and preserves" as a model. As the later among them systematized the analysis, the Spirit "calls, illumines, convicts, justifies, renovates, unites with Christ, and sanctifies."[16] They called the sequence "the order of salvation," meaning a *logical* order; the Spirit does not, they thought, perform a mere collection of works in our lives, but one structured work. Each of the verbs—"calls," "illumines," and so on—represented a whole field for analysis of God's one act, within which the concern of these theologians was always the same: to display the nature and character of spiritual life precisely under the rule that we do *not* "cooperate" with God's grace. But this did not prevent Lutheran pietism, without formal contradiction of any individual item of orthodox Lutheran teaching, from turning the analysis into a traditional stipulation of a normal sequence of Christian experience.

Already the great Johann Arndt, starting with the descriptively orthodox proposition that only to "unfeigned repentance" is the "imputation of Christ's righteousness" promised (*True Christianity*, i, iv, 13), established a sequence: "Remission of sins immediately follows true repentance" (ibid., viii, 24). Whereupon he is promptly lost in advice for how to discover whether such true repentance is indeed present (ibid., xvi, 49; iii; xviii, 410) and maxims for promoting it (ibid., iii; vi, 382; xvi, 408). The disaster is then complete with someone like August Hermann Francke,[17] who for all his proper Lutheran insistence that the gospel is always decisive, nevertheless flatly stipulated that until the "repentance struggle" is over, the gospel simply cannot be heard, and made the completion of the struggle depend on the sincerity and persistence of the penitent. Around this essential step Francke then constructed the same experience order we saw in the Puritans—which is no accident, since continental pietists and English Puritans made one network.

What is needed over against the whole traditional doctrine of grace is a complete shift of pneumatological discourse from this third-person vantage, from attempted description of a process between God and creature, to a location *within* the carrying-out of first- and second-person proclamation and teaching. Precisely as a doctrine of the work of the *Spirit*—of which work "calls, illumines, converts, justifies, renovates, unites with Christ, and sanctifies" is a perfectly good list—theology must be done from the location of the preacher, liturgical president, and adviser, and the recipient of these ministrations. To use recent jargon, pneumatology must become hermeneutical reflection, reflection about Christian discourse done in the course thereof, as part of that discourse's accomplishment, reflection about how to speak the gospel done internally to the speaking—which brings us to the Reformation's second theological mode: the proposed dogma of "justification by faith alone."

The Reformation doctrine of justification is not a new attempted description of a process of grace—and when it has been taken for such, sometimes also by would-be champions, the difference between the Reformation and the standard tradition has always promptly become obscure. The doctrine is rather an *hermeneutical instruction* to preachers, teachers, and confessors: so speak of Christ and of the life of your community that the justification for that life which your words open is the kind grasped by faith rather than the kind constituted in works.

That this is the character of the Reformation's dogmatic proposal can perhaps best be seen from the first, and for many Protestants the dogmatically authoritative, commentary on the proposal, Article IV of Melanchthon's Apology of the Augsburg Confession. Article IV of the Augsburg Confession itself said: "Furthermore it is taught, that we cannot obtain forgiveness and righteousness before God by our own power, merit, or works, but rather that we are justified by grace for Christ's sake, through faith." The papal response, the Papal Confutation,[18] was a flat contradiction: For example, "That . . . they attribute justification to faith alone is directly opposite to evangelical truth. . . . However much one may believe, if he does not do good, he is no friend of God" (Confutation, 6); when it is said "of good works that they do not merit the remission of sins . . . , this is . . . disapproved" (ibid., 20).

Melanchthon's Apology is mostly a long defense of the Augsburg Confession's fourth article, against this rejection. At the start of Article IV, he specifies the difference between the Reformers and their "adversaries" as that between "two kinds of teaching," two modes of churchly proclamation and practice, with the theories that sustain them. Of each, he proposes to discover and state the generating starting point (Apology IV, 4). He formulates the starting point of reforming teaching: "The whole Scripture can be sorted into two principal modes of discourse, law and promises" (ibid., 5). Thus the starting point of reforming teaching is hermeneutical: a conviction about the duality of ways in which churchly discourse functions or ought to function. The starting point of the adversaries' teaching is thus also an hermeneutical conviction, or rather the lack of this one: a failure to practice the distinction of law and promise (ibid., 7). The adversaries themselves would not distinguish the two theologies in these terms but just that is the difference between them and the Reformers.

Melanchthon proceeds to exposition of the Reformers' hermeneutic, with a metalinguistic description of "promise" (ibid., 7). The biblical promise has narrative content; it is "about Christ." This discourse about Christ, as a live act of communication, has a triply statable existential function: It "promises remission of sins, justification, and eternal life." As becomes apparent throughout the treatise (ibid., e.g., 44, 120, 292–93), the promise of remission of sins is not a statement that hearers will in the future be forgiven; the promise is rather a grant of forgiveness, an absolution, and is promise as absolution itself is promise, namely, of the restored life that ensues. Neither is justification promised as only future; it is rather the restoration just named (ibid., e.g., 40, 117, 161). The future content of the promise is eternal life, the content of blessing won by Christ. How narrative about Christ can have this existential function, Melanchthon does not say in the Apology. An answer to that question would be a doctrine of atonement, beyond the scope of the Apology and this *locus*.

To describe the *law* hermeneutically, Melanchthon needs two antithetical specifications of function, reflecting in their dialectic the ambiguity of fallen human life. In its own terms, the existential character of "law" discourse is precisely that it does not penetrate to the heart, that it works at the level of our mutual relations without engaging the original fear and hope by which these are for each of us *our* relations, or, what is the same thing, without engaging our relation to God (ibid., 214–17). The law's immediate sphere is "external and civil works," the "second table" of the decalogue (ibid., 34). And the level of judgment and motivation at which law operates is "reason" (ibid., e.g., 7, 34), by which Melanchthon does not understand a neutral "faculty" of the soul, but the entire activity of humanity's effort to order our own life, in its historical reality and continuity, insofar as this activity has not been effected by the gospel: "Nor does reason see another justice than the justice of law understood as civil order. Therefore there will always be those in the world who teach only a carnal justice, the justice of faith having been repressed" (ibid., 394). Reason's judgment is simply the judgment "of the world" (ibid., 212); "the righteousness of reason" and "civil works" are synonyms (ibid., e.g., 9, 288).

But law, since it is God's law, does speak *about* matters of the heart: "For the decalogue requires not only external and civil works . . . , but works located far beyond the power of reason, such as truly to fear God" (ibid., 8). Therefore it can gain access to the heart; and when it does, it has an existential function that is the opposite of promise. Those who hear the law in their hearts find that "law always accuses" (ibid., e.g., 38, 285), that is, it pronounces guilt instead of remission, creates enmity instead of justice, and promises hell instead of heaven (ibid., e.g., 36–38, 117, 128, 295).

We should not have difficulty with Melanchthon's concept of law. "Law" is human discourse as we daily and ordinarily practice and understand it: as a means of transferring information, as a regulation of common or opposing needs and interests—and with the potential of suddenly breaking all these quotidianities open, at which point the gospel must be at hand as pure promise, or all is lost.

The starting point of the adversaries is (from this point of view) that they assimilate these two modes of discourse to one (from their own point of view, of course, that they refuse to impose a dubious distinction) and determine the existential functions of the amalgam by the characteristics proper to "law." "From these, the adversaries take law . . . , and then seek by law remission of sins and justification" (ibid., 7). Remission and justification are still sought and Christ spoken of, because this intends, after all, to be Christian teaching (ibid., 17). But remission and justification now enter the church's discourse *as if* they were matters of controllable conditions and rewards, *as if* they were "external and civil works" (ibid., e.g., 9, 22–23, 34, 130–31). The conditions are then those named by biblical law as God's will for the saints (ibid., 122ff.): love of God, and so on. "Truly, works stick in humankind's eye. Human reason is naturally impressed with them; and since it only perceives works, and not faith . . . , supposes that these works must . . . justify" (ibid., 265). And discourse about Christ, when assimilated to the logic of law, becomes merely "historical" speech about him, lacking existential power of any peculiar sort (ibid., 7), a transfer from one head to another of the sort of information about Christ possessed also by devils and the damned (ibid., e.g., 48, 249, 303).

When Melanchthon is pressed to the minimum of his complaint about the dominant theology and its practice, it is always a simple lack he adduces (ibid., e.g., 121, 377). Given what we have seen, the issue is the sheer presence or absence, in what claims to be church, of "promise," of that radical proclamation of Christ that by its *non*legal character, by its *un*conditional bestowing of forgiveness and *un*conditional assuring of final salvation, is itself God's act to make all humanity right.

Melanchthon's demand for the doctrine of faith is both a demand that promise in fact occur in the church and a demand that the church's theological enterprise be the reflective support of the occurrence. There is a kind of theology that must occur in the church if promise—at least in the long run—is to occur: a reflection that takes the actual proclamation, and the logical and existential situation of the speaker and the hearer, as both its object and its reflective location. Where those committed to the Lutheran reform proposal see only other modes of theological reflection, perhaps the third-person process-describing that Melanchthon called "scholastic," there they must be pessimistic about prospects for unconditional proclamation. Where the *sort* of thinking we find in the Apology is absent, there we must eventually expect promise to be absent also.

We have called the Reformation doctrine of justification a "dogmatic proposal."[19] Were we to describe the Augsburg Confessions central contention, justification by faith alone, simply as dogma, we would thereby read out of the true church the bulk of Western Christendom, which has not accepted the contention. This neither the confessors at Augsburg nor we have wished to do.[20] Yet the contention of the Augsburg Confession was clearly proposed as a regulation of teaching that is decisive for the authenticity of the gospel, that must be binding on the whole church, and that is definitely potentially divisive of the church.[21] Thus "dogmatic proposal" is the precise description of the Reformation justification-doctrine's status to date. As we have noted, the papal representatives at Augsburg rejected justification by faith alone. And subsequent apparent rapprochement in the Committee of Fourteen was illusory.[22] But the action of the papal delegates was confirmed by no higher papal authority, and it is now generally agreed that the condemnations pronounced at Trent, though aimed at the Lutheran doctrine, do not in fact touch it.[23] The doctrine of Trent itself, to be sure, represents the traditional doctrine of grace at its most dubious.[24]

Within a hermeneutical mode of description, the classical descriptions of the Spirit's work (that the Spirit "calls," "illumines," and so on) will function very differently than in pietism or in standard contemporary Protestantism, which descends from the pietists. First the negative. None of these terms rightly names an experience or a modification of the habits of a substance, "the soul." All descriptions of how "conversion" (for example) works or feels are equally false, since conversion is not a process and has no feelings. This is not to say that processes and feelings in plenty do not fill believers' lives, only that no set of them is the Spirit's work of converting—and similarly for the other verbs on the traditional lists.

Rather, verbs specifying the Spirit's work must be understood as instructions to preachers, liturgical leaders, teachers, and advisers. For example, "The Spirit illumines" should mean "So speak of Christ and the lives of your hearers, that our lives' meaning in Christ is made visible." Nor do these instructions stipulate an experience or process in the hearer, which gospel-speaking is to strive to *produce*. We are not to exhort to or describe or even promise illumination. We are verbally to illumine—illumination is a work of the prophetic Spirit, that is, it is an aspect of the spiritedness of the preacher's words.

Returning to our first example, the instruction is not to induce, or manipulate, conversion by our discourse; the hearers' conversion is to be accomplished as the act of gospel-speaking itself. Conversion is a change in the communication situation within which every person lives; a proper sermon or baptism liturgy or penance liturgy just *is* that change. Using penance as the simplest paradigm, when the confessor says, "You have confessed cheating and coveting. Now I forgive all your sins, in Jesus' name," these words do not seek to stimulate conversion as an event external to their being said. Rather, this utterance *is* a conversion of the penitent's life, from a situation in which the word he or she hears and must live by is "You are a cheat and a coveter," to one in which the word he or she hears and must live by is "You are Jesus' beloved."

Predestination

Once the hermeneutic character of pneumatology is firmly established, we can flip back again to more direct discussion of God and God's work. When we do, we are in the doctrine of predestination. Predestination is simply the doctrine of justification stated in the active voice.[25] If we change "We are justified by God alone" from passive to active we get "God alone justifies us." That God's promise to us is unconditional or that God's will for us is final and externally unmotivated obviously come to the same thing. The need thus to consider the doctrine of justification in the active voice is given with the circumstance that we are dealing with the reality of God and the Spirit and must remind ourselves that God is indeed *God* the Spirit, lest even yet all turn into a fascination with our own spirituality. Conversely, we must remember that the doctrine of predestination is then itself hermeneutic, that it is instruction to speakers of the gospel, and not an attempt at third-person description of God's ways with humanity.

That the logic thus leads us to the Spirit as the predestining God[26] is untraditional and somewhat surprising. Predestination, like creation, redemption, and so on, is of course a work of the one triune God, in traditional trinitarian theory a "work directed externally" and therefore not to be parceled out to the identities. But the very word "*pre*destination" suggests, as what traditional trinitarianism called an "appropriation," a reference to the Father, to God as the prior given to all history. And this appropriation has worked out in the context in which traditional theology has set discussion of predestination: a context determined by the notions of prevenience and origin. Thus Aquinas defined predestination as "a division of providence,"[27] of God's total antecedent effective intention for all creatures. Calvinist theologians located the matter no differently: The decrees of general providence and predestination are one event in pretemporal eternity, differing only as this one divine decision determines, generally, the history of all creatures and, more narrowly, the history of intelligent creatures, in the ways appropriate to each sort.[28] For the modern period, Schleiermacher merely assimilated predestination and providence more simply even than before.[29]

Location of predestination doctrine primarily in the context of God's general rule of creation—crudely, in the first article of a standard creed—fits the general way the traditional doctrine of grace understands divine effectiveness among us, as supernatural causality. Readers will perceive that a shift of this location is proposed. Predestination discourse is fundamentally just assertion of the gospel's character as pure and unconditional promise. The assertion of predestination is fundamentally: "Since God says your life will be fulfilled with Christ for Christ's sake, it will be—because God says it, come or be what else may." Thus the primary location of predestination doctrine should be the second or third creedal article, and this must come out in the language and logic of the doctrine.

But there was a reason for the doctrine's traditional casting in the language of prevenience and origin, and the *problem* of the doctrine appears only when we reckon with this reason. The absoluteness of God's will, primarily asserted of God's will as proclaimed in the gospel, must be interpreted as universal, and it has been to that end that predestination has been coordinated to creation. For if the gospel promise of our ultimate fulfillment is indeed unconditional, the will that acts in this promising must encompass all events whatsoever. If God's will is not determining at any moment of reality's history, there will sometimes be valid responses to the gospel that begin "Yes but." It is a strict corollary of the Reformation doctrine of justification: All things happen by God's will.[30]

Our practical atheism finds such propositions mortally offensive. We can at most tolerate God as a supernatural helper for occasions when we autonomously decide our powers do not suffice. That we should be truly and pervasively dependent, that our destiny should not be in our final control, we take as a denigration. And indeed, the doctrine of predestination does set us down from self-vaunting as gods or beasts, to our precise status as human creatures.[31] For if we interpret God as indeed God, so that we are not God, we thereby posit some mode of predestination. The word "God," after all, marks the point where the metaphysical buck stops. Any serious religious interpretation of reality will therefore display some analogue of the biblical notion of predestination; and if, with the Bible, we apprehend reality temporally and historically, the metaphysical buck stops with a last *word*, a decisive *choice*, that is, with the precise notion of pre*destination*.[32]

Thus no even distantly Christian thought can avoid a doctrine of predestination. Fear of the doctrine is merely—or profoundly—fear of God. Nor can this fear validly argue, as it regularly does, that it is human freedom that must be defended against the notion of a truly final God. For the absoluteness of God's will is in no way inconsistent with the reality of our freedom. On the contrary, if we think of God and ourselves as competitors for control of our mutual affairs, so that to whatever extent God determines my destiny I do not, then increased assignment of determination to God must indeed mean lessened freedom for me. But the very point of the doctrine of predestination is to deny any such competition, any such appearance of God and creatures on the same level of decision. Precisely because God is absolute, we are in no competition with God's freedom to choose—and just so God's absolute freedom does not diminish our creaturely freedom. Medieval theologians worked this point out with beautiful precision and subtlety. Whatever God wills, they said, must indeed happen, and exactly as God wills it. Thus, if God wills some things to happen as acts of free choice, they will happen, and happen in that way.[33]

If there is the God of the Bible, there can be no such thing as the free will (*liberum arbitrium*) of traditional discussion.[34] But this classical posit of free will is much more than the simple posit that human acts are—some more, some less—freely done. The posit of free will is a metaphysical claim that this practical freedom manifests a core of indetermination over against all external choices. The free will most theology has worried about does not denote the actual freedom of our actions; it *explains* them, by a pseudodivine capacity that is supposed to belong to human substantiality.[35] This claim is inconsistent with the reality of the God of the unconditional gospel, who is in person, the explanation of our freedom. And it has no necessary relation to the actual freedom or unfreedom of our actions.

But while assertion of the unconditionality of God's will is not the problem of determinism versus freedom that it is often taken to be, there is a grave theological problem that opens just when one sees this. If all things happen within the choice of God, then the will of God becomes morally dubious, precisely by the light of that gospel for the sake of which we posited the absoluteness of God's will in the first place. If God wills all things, God in *some* way wills Auschwitz and the torture of the child in Ivan Karamazov's fable, and the damnation of the damned if God chooses. How is that to be reconciled with the revelation of God's will in the gospel as a "fountain of sheer love?"

Two absolute wills of God appear in our reflection, not easily interpreted as the same. Indeed, the two are absolute in different ways. The will of God proclaimed in the gospel is absolute by the immutability of its known content: God's gospel-affirmation of us is independent of all conditions. The will of God posited as the prius of all events, on the other hand, is absolute precisely by the absence of known content: Whatever happens, God wills it.

It is this threatening split in our image of God which is the true religious occasion of theological history's many attempts to mitigate the assertion of predestination. These run from the semi-Pelagianism with which Augustine's first powerful analysis of the doctrine was promptly met,[36] through such devices as the teaching (shared by Jesuits and most Lutherans from 1600 on) that God eternally preordains to salvation those who God foresees will by free choice believe the gospel when it is preached to them,[37] through Arminian Calvinism, to current benign neglect in hope that the whole question—and any real God with it—will go away.

Instead of such evasions, what is needed is the insight that God's general rule of creation is not the appropriate primary context in which to interpret the particular absoluteness of the gospel's God. The necessary step from the dominant tradition is recognition that our predestination is not the act of a God-the-Father abstracted from the triune relations, sorting fates in a pretemporal eternity. It occurs rather as the act in time of Christ's death and resurrection and of the proclamation of the gospel. When someone speaks to me the promises made by Christ's resurrection, that event *is* the event of God's choice about me. Such a christological and hermeneutic understanding of predestination first emerged in early Lutheranism,[38] but it was carried to systematic reflection only by Karl Barth: "Precisely Jesus Christ is himself God's act of election, and therefore God's word, decision and beginning." Since Jesus Christ is a personal reality, it is only an alternate formulation: "Jesus Christ is the electing God."[39]

Although a christological interpretation of election is the first necessary step from the traditional position, it cannot be the last one. The logic that led to the traditional position remains and must be dealt with: God not only absolutely ordains my salvation in the christological word to me; God as Creator absolutely ordains all events. The early Lutherans tried merely to evade this logic;[40] the result was that also their new insight slipped away from them. Barth moved more drastically.[41] He reversed the traditional pattern altogether, incorporating God's general rule of creation *within* his choice of grace. This move set the structure of Barth's entire systematic theology. Barth's system is "supralapsarian": in all eternity, God has chosen to join the divine self to fallen creatures in Christ; therefore God chose that there should be creatures and to permit them to fall. And Barth's system has as its heart his notorious doctrine of the preexistence of the man Jesus Christ: the event in which there is God *and* something other than God is the life of Jesus Christ, and all temporal history is the consequence of this event. But Barth's systematics will not quite suffice.

Barth unites God's rule in Christ and God's rule of all history by making the Christ-event itself to be the reality of eternity, and he does this by bringing the trinitarian dialectic to new life. These are indeed what must be done. But Barth unites the two wills of God by the relation of only the Father and the Son. Correspondingly, the eternity that Christ fills is defined as pretemporality, thus remaining within the traditional interpretation. This creates the peculiar ambiguity that pervades Barth's theology: Has the abstract, pretemporally eternal, divine choosing come down to time to be Jesus' choice about us? Or has Jesus himself been taken from us into pretemporal distance? One can read Barth either way. The christological reality of predestination is not, after all, unambiguous in Barth's doctrine.

It can be no secret where we are heading. We will be able rightly to interpret the unity of God's absolute will only if we make *Spirit*-discourse—rather than Father-discourse or Son-discourse—the primary *locus* of our interpretation. It is indeed the human Christ's temporal address to us that is the event of God's eternal choosing about us, as the Lutherans and Barth have said. But the eternity of this moment must be established not by the prefix "pre-" but by the prefix "post-": It is in that the man Christ *will* be the agent and center of the final community, that his will for us is the eternal determination of our lives. The trinitarian dialectics can be the appropriate conceptual scheme of predestination only if the whole scheme—of Father, Son, *and* Spirit—is used and only if the Spirit's metaphysical priority ("God is Spirit") is affirmed. The speaking of the gospel is the event of predestination in that the gospel gives what it speaks about, but this eschatological efficacy of the gospel is the Spirit.[42] We must parody Barth: The Holy Spirit is the choosing God.

The deep offense posed by all legitimately predestinarian reflection is the split between God revealed in the gospel as absolute love and God revealed in all history as merely absolute. So long as only the first two articles are the context of our reflection, we must seek the unity of God in the past and present, and then we must seek a conceptual synthesis of the two images of God, a grasp of how they now are one. We must seek to *explain* how the God revealed in the gospel can consistently choose as God does in history; we must create a theodicy. But if we interpret predestination as the work of the Spirit, the Power of the future, we will leave off such synthesis. How the God of the gospel and the Will behind all events can be one is—we will say—the one truth about God reserved for the End, when we shall see God face-to-face. Luther, as always, is blunt:

Faith is "of things that do not appear." Therefore in order that there be room for faith, whatever is believed must be hidden.... Thus [God] hides his eternal mercy ... under eternal wrath, his justice under inequity. This is true faith, to believe that he is merciful who saves so few and damns so many, who indeed makes us damnable by his own choice; so that he seems ... to delight in the tortures of the wretched and to be more worthy of hate than of love. If therefore we could by any reasoning comprehend how that God is merciful and just who displays such wrath and inequity, there would be no need of faith.[43]

If we thus abandon the attempt now to know how God's will is one, how indeed God is one God, faith becomes what it is in

Reformation discourse—a desperate conflict within an encompassing hope: "For Christ's sake, I trust the God who rules *this*
world." From a third-person viewpoint, there is, in the case of
any believer, no guarantee that the conflict will not burst the
hope, that the hiddenness of God's goodness, which makes
room for faith, will not also one day defeat faith. But for faith
and proclamation themselves, recognition of the Spirit as the
postdestining God does provide an appropriate conceptuality with which to carry on the struggle. As seen in the gospel,
God's will is absolute because it is immutably determined, as
love; as seen in the total course of events, God's will is absolute
in that it is absolutely undetermined—whatever happens, God
has willed. Precisely the synthesis of these two determinations is
the notion of spirit: a determinate reality that just by the actual
character of its particular determination is utterly free. The Holy
Spirit is the freedom of Jesus' future to transform and renew
all previous events whatever. Short of the end, we cannot conceive how Auschwitz can fit into the will of Jesus' Father, but
we can conceive—in hope against hope—that triune structure
of God's reality by which this unimaginable transformation will
be accomplished. An isolated "God the Father" would have no
such structure; of this God's goodness, Auschwitz is conclusive
refutation.

   To return to the main point, "God alone ordains your salvation" is a necessary form of the gospel, and "God alone ordains
all" is a necessary corollary of it. Rightly understood as pneumatological statements, these are assurances and solicitations
from the last future, promises of the encompassing sovereignty
of the transformation to come: The winds that sweep through
history and your life are but eddies and currents of the breath
of new creation.

CHAPTER THREE

Spirit-Discourse as the Church's Self-Interpretation

The Spirit is the presence of the risen Christ. Since the church is essentially Christ's community, the church interprets the problems of its own life by doctrine about the Spirit. The problems of community arise in all communities; what is distinctive to the church is not the problems, but the answers imposed by the church community's specific character, that is, by the gospel.

Ecclesial Christology

The church's self-understanding is intrinsically, and to a great extent historically, accomplished as pneumatology, which here functions as a sort of ecclesial christology.[1] Our first task in this chapter is to trace this logic.

Every community has spirit. To whatever extent you and I share a common life, to that extent you pose human possibilities that are new to me, simply by the ways in which you differ from what I already am. If these possibilities are at once surprising and fulfilling, that is, if they are liberating, you are present in my life as spirit. And just so my life also is itself spirit. If the possibilities you pose to me are in no way liberating, if you are not spirit in my life, we make no community, for the group we are has thus no space of freedom in which to conduct a moral life of its own.

Indeed, every community has *a* spirit. For nothing in the previous paragraph changes if the "you" in it is plural; the described event is not additive. If you are two, to make with me a community of three, it is still *one* spirit as which I encounter you and to which I respond as spirit. And it is the *same* spirit to which each of you responds, when the other of you and I are the two. It is *we* who are spirit for each of us. These last assertions would perhaps be impossible to prove, but they must be assumed, for if they are false, if we are so shut into individuality that each of us, necessarily facing a different set of people than any other of us, thereby encounters a different spirit, there can be no community at all—which is the dismal analysis of many. "The spirit of America," "the team spirit," "the spirit of our family" are—we will therefore assume—individual realities.

Moreover, it is not strange for the spirit of a community to be identifiable also as the spirit of an individual, in case the existence of the community depends on the presence of the individual. Thus the spirit of an academic seminar that has so developed as to make a community will not be identifiably separable from the spirit of its teacher; in earlier times no one would have been embarrassed to speak of "a master and his disciples" in such a case.

We may therefore go some way in understanding the church's "possession" of Jesus' spirit without saying anything esoteric. The church, like any community, has a spirit. The risen Jesus, like any living person, has a spirit. And since the church simply *is* Jesus' disciples, its spirit and Jesus' spirit are identical.

But now, Jesus' community and the reality of its spirit differ in one decisive structure from that of other communities of master and disciples: To state the church's situation we had to insert "risen." The individual whose presence makes the church is not present in the church as its other members are. He has died; and though he nevertheless lives, by his liveliness to create the community of the church, it belongs to the very point of the proclamation "He is risen" that he is not merely resuscitated, that he has not returned to die again, that is, that he is not now an item of this age as his disciples still are.

The endings of all three synoptic Gospels (taking Mark's long ending), as well as Acts' preliminary repetition of the ascension story, show the paradox (Matt. 28:16–20; Mark 16:9–20; Luke 24:44–53; Acts 1:4–14). In Luke's ascension stories and in Mark,

Jesus explicitly leaves this age, to be with God elsewhere; but also Matthew's concluding story is definitely of a farewell manifestation. The gloriously blunt Markan description must be quoted: "Then the Lord Jesus . . . was taken up into heaven, and sat down at the right hand of God" (Mark 16:19). The risen Lord is not present in the gatherings of the church as are the other members thereof; we cannot look about and discover, "Oh. *There* he is." Yet precisely the motif of presence is a chief point of all these accounts; classically in Matthew: "And lo, I am with you always" (Matt. 28:20). And in all four accounts, precisely at the crux of this paradox, the coming of the Spirit is promised, materially in the power and signs language of Matthew and Mark, explicitly by Luke. It is this complex—nobody's invention but simply given in the actual situation of the primal church—of which John finally makes a whole theological scene and discourse (John 16:5–15).

It is definitive of the church that we are Jesus' community. Therefore, as the church encounters decisions and problems that make it reflect on its own purpose and character, it must reflect christologically, it must interpret itself by the fact and identity of the risen Jesus; the church necessarily develops a sort of ecclesial christology. But the risen Jesus is not an item of our age and so is not in the community as others are.

When we speak of the risen Christ simply as such, we rightly use the whole complex of whatever language we have for discourse about living people. But when we speak of the risen Christ as the *church's* determining person, we cannot but reckon with the oddity of his churchly personhood. Given the "spirit" phenomenon and language, it is this language that will inevitably and rightly serve the purpose.

Paul could write to the Corinthians: "For though absent in body I am present in spirit" (1 Cor. 5:3), describing a situation in which the Corinthians had to reckon with Paul's initiative and freedom, even though when they in turn intended him they had to do so at a distance, intending a person located somewhere else. In such a situation, as opposed to when Paul is "in body" present in Corinth preaching and advising, it is not that first Paul is personally present to the Corinthians and that then his being spirit is the future-opening aspect and reality of his presence; that he challenges and surprises them is in this case the whole evidence and truth of his being present. The Corinthians do not in this instance first discover Paul among them and second experience that he is spirit; they first encounter future-creating spirit, in being addressed by Paul's letter, and so, having also by way of the letter identified this spirit as Paul's, can say, "Paul is among us." This time of Paul present simply is the spirit of his presence. But after the end of the resurrection appearances, Jesus' presence *always* has this structure. Therefore Paul says, "The Lord is the Spirit" (2 Cor. 3:17).

The analogy between Paul's presence from a distance and the risen Jesus' presence from a distance is not perfect; the kinds of distances are not the same. If a Corinthian journeyed to find Paul "in body," he could; not so with Jesus. But just this difference gives the notion that Jesus is spiritually present in the church great ontological weight, such as the notion of our spiritual presence to one another cannot have. Jesus is someplace else from the church, not because he is in another place but because he is of the coming eon. He must *come* to us not merely incidentally to spatial separation but because coming, advent, is in this age his proper mode of being. But that is to say that spirit is his mode of being. And so, while for Paul presence "in spirit" is a deficient mode, lacking presence "in the body," Jesus' spiritual presence is intensified presence—which can in appropriate contexts even be described as more unavoidably embodied than Paul or we ever are.[2]

We can now introduce the following material sections of this chapter. There are certain problems that arise in the life of every community simply because it is a community. Thus these problems arise, in appropriately particular form, also in the church. If a community is self-conscious about its spiritedness, its effort to deal with such problems will occur as discourse about its spirit. Such effort by the church occurs, therefore, as pneumatology. Each of the following sections discusses one such problem in the church's pneumatological self-understanding. Each section first introduces a pneumatological choice that every community must make, then states the decision incumbent on the church, by criteria developed in the previous chapters, and finally analyzes a sample of historical instances in which this choice has, or has not, been carried out. The four choices posed do not make a system; they rather display the choices posited in the chief pneumatological problems that have become historically important for the church.

The Spirit and God

Every community has spirit, indeed *a* spirit. And every community has some god. The community's god may be the one *whose* spirit the community has. But more usually a community's god is its defense *against* its own spirit, for the normal function of religion is to provide stability. Conversely, a community's spirit is either the spirit of its god, or threatening and uncanny—perhaps demonic—dynamism.

The communal reality of spirit itself demands the posit of God or the gods in one of these ways or the other, for life in a spirit transcends the merely ethical. The status quo that the spirit challenges will not always be only our inadequate obedience to the values by which our community now coheres. In actual fallen history, a community's spirit will sometimes challenge the community's own legitimacy over against some or all of those values. Then the new creation toward which its spirit moves will include new value. When it is not merely my behavior that is challenged by the community's commitments, but the adequacy of the communal commitment itself, moral *creativity* is required.

When, for example, Americans in the last decades increasingly have come to the point of doubting that casting a ballot between the offerings of two manifestly conniving parties is a good thing, since we have been taught precisely by the ideology of representative government that casting a ballot between two slates submitted by one party is an evil, fervent reiteration of republican ideology will not halt political alienation. Only drastic institutional innovation will restore governmental legitimacy, and that innovation will involve the discovery of new value. Many, for example, now think that representative democracy in the nation can be saved only if it is paired with new institutions of direct democracy in the localities, and if these institutions have powers of decision encompassing much of what the representative government now decides. But to say such things involves affirming values that are not unprecedented but do not now belong to our communal commitment.

When a community must thus posit new good, we enter a space of freedom that we cannot independently inhabit. We turn dizzily in our own not-yet-being. When a community is called to posit new good, more must be present than the imperative that we should carry on, for it is the sense of "should" and "on" that is then undone. Thus the community confronts transcendence, and transcendence will appear either as the community's defense against the spirit that thus disorients it or as the very disorientation.

The first is the more likely event, and it has many forms. A community may freeze, exclude the moral challenge that brought it to crisis, and live by willingly unexamined tradition indefinitely—as America may go on voting more and more and meaning it less and less. A community may commit spiritual suicide, violating its own commitments—as a newly self-aware urban neighborhood may deny ethnic encroachers the very justice in the campaign for which it organized itself. In the modern West a fully nihilist relativity of all values may yet be achieved, in a public sphere ruled by a completely mechanist state and a private sphere lived only in the present tense. And if any of this is done, religious practices and institutions will be the main bulwark against the future, and God or the gods will be the status quo's chief justification; the transcendence of God's presumed timeless eternity will be set *against* the transcendence of spirit.

Or challenging spirit may be recognized as the spirit *of* God, as threat to what is, made by what more encompassingly and surely is. It is in a community's knowledge that good will come to pass despite all, because the future is God's, that the community can risk the vertigo of freedom, can allow its moral life to lead where we fear to go. It is in the knowledge of what surely will be that a community may be at once open and confident about what should be.

Only if, somehow, there is freedom not merely in the community, but also for the community from beyond it, is community a tolerable venture over the long run. Only if promises are made and relied on whose guarantor is none of the community's members or any combination of them can ethical community be sustained. In the kingdom of God, love will doubtless be greater than faith and hope (1 Cor. 13:13); in the meantime, love (i.e., the acceptance of strange possibility) is utterly dependent on faith and hope.

In Israel, the decision between positing God as defense against spirit and identifying spirit as God's own was made clearly and was a main event and determinant of its history. There are historical traces of a demonic experience of spirit. But the outcome of Israel's history is unequivocal identification of the breath of Israel's future with God.

The church claims to be established as a community by fulfillment of Israel's final hope for the Spirit. Thus the identity of God and Spirit is mandated also for the church. Only one further determinant must be recalled: In the church there is a middle term. The Spirit is the Spirit of Jesus; the Father is the Father of Jesus; and *so* the Father and the Spirit are one God. The unity of God and Spirit is trinitarian. In the church, the Father is the *givenness* of God and the Spirit the *futurity* of God; and these stand against each other only by the different ways in which each is the one and the same God.

While the entire catholic tradition agrees in the above, a particular Western attempt to emphasize it has occasioned a great deal of dogmatic controversy.[3] In Western trinitarian teaching, Augustine made it customary to speak of the Spirit's procession from the Father "and the Son," emphasizing both the Spirit's immediacy to the Father, the "source of deity,"[4] and the christological determination of the Spirit. Eastern tradition uses a variety of expressions, perhaps best represented by the second council of Nicaea's "from the Father through the Son"; none has creedal status. From the fifth century, the practice of inserting "and the Son" into the Nicene-Constantinopolitan Creed grew in the West, with Charlemagne giving the decisive impetus, and Pope Benedict VIII, in 1014, finally stipulating it for the text to be said at mass. The insertion caused continual great offense in the East, partly on the strong ground that insertions should not unilaterally be made into conciliar creeds, and partly on the ground that there is a substantive theological difference between "and the Son" and "through the Son"—a much more dubious contention, which either chops logic very fine or betrays a residual hankering to arrange the three trinitarian identities in an Arian-style descending hierarchy of deity. Despite recurrent agreement that the difference, if any, between "and . . ." and "through . . ." should not be church-divisive, most notably at the Council of Florence in 1439, the *filioque* remains an offense between the Eastern and Western branches of the church. On the theology, the West is surely right; on the proper creedal text, the East is right.

Returning to the point itself, there can be in the church no transcendence and therefore, for example, no final authority, that is other than Spirit: the church's God *is* its Spirit. This norm has wide application in the church's life: This section's earlier discussion of representative polity can be directly applied. We will mention two matters in which the application has been actually struggled for. In the first, the historical struggle achieved enduring dogmatic significance.

The tension between leadership as office and leadership as gift of the Spirit is permanent in the church, as in every living community.[5] It is the very function of offices to be institutions of continuity and stability, to guard against disruption of a community's self-identity through time. Spirit, on the other hand, is the impetus of transformation given with the lead each of us has in some however tiny human possibility over the rest of us, and which will obviously blow more strongly from some than from others, whether these hold office or not. In the church, just *because* its spirit is God's Spirit, so that charismatic leadership is seen as divinely given, official leadership and charismatic leadership can never legitimately be more than dialectically opposed.

The church's initial chief ministry, the apostolate, was the perfect union of office and charism. As witnesses of the resurrection, the apostles embodied continuity with the church's beginning. As proclaimers of the gospel, they had pneumatic immediacy that could not be challenged; what they proclaimed was the right gospel just because they proclaimed it. And each of these authorities depended on the other. When the apostles died, the only ministry fully appropriate to the church ceased. Since then the imperative unity of office and charism must always be reachieved, and it has found its chief reality not so much in institutional characteristics of particular forms of leadership as in a sacrament of such unity: ordination.

Ordination claims to install in an office and grant a charism, by the same act.[6] It is the necessary audible and visible word of the gospel to those caught in the impossible tension of postapostolic ministry: the promise of the Spirit "for the work of a minister in the church of God," given not by uncontrollable experience but by institutionalized succession and procedure.

The unity of office and charism can never, after the apostles, be taken as settled; it is and must be repeatedly fought for. But one classic struggle established dogmatic principle. The North African church was disturbed from the closing decades of the second century through the whole of the fourth by pneumatological-ecclesiological controversy, which went through several periods but always involved a coherent complex of issues. Several of these issues will occupy us in this chapter. Our present concern is with the pair of issues agitated after the Decianic persecutions of 250–251, and in the Donatist controversy of the following century.

After the Decianic persecution,[7] charismatic authority clashed with the official authority of the bishops, over control of readmission to fellowship of those who had denied the faith under pressure. On the one hand, the continuation of an older charismatic movement, the "new prophecy" of the turn of the century, opposed all readmission of the lapsed, to maintain the church's eschatological rigor; on the other hand, heroes of the persecution claimed unchallengeable charismatic freedom to readmit. Against both, Bishop Cyprian of Carthage claimed that there is indeed a charismatic freedom over discipline, and that it belongs to the office of bishop. At synods in Carthage and Rome, Cyprian's position became the standard of the Western church.

In the subsequent Donatist controversy,[8] the converse question was posed: whether such charism of office depends on other charisms that are not granted by office, that is, whether the ministrations of an otherwise religiously unworthy bishop or priest can nevertheless be relied on. The anti-Donatist doctrine that the reliability of ministry does not depend on other spiritual gifts in the minister was finally established, though not so much by particular councils or synods as by the founding significance for all Western Christianity of the theology of Augustine, the chief anti-Donatist polemicist.[9]

This historical preemption of charismatic ministry by "ordained" ministry carries an explosive consequence for the ordained.[10] Over against whatever other official leadership the church may from time to time have, and even more over against the commitment to the status quo given with their own official position, ordained ministers must be responsible to the free Spirit that they claim. The very *office* of the ordained ministry is to speak and enact the gospel with *charismatic* immediacy, without worrying about its possible alarming effects on the institution, for example, about whether conventional members—whose contributions and influence are needed—will be offended, or about whether the unconditionality of the gospel will lead to laxity in well-doing. The church must worry also about such things, and there may be officials charged to do it, but ordination is the grant of freedom not to.

We will discuss a second consequence of the church's spirit-deity coincidence yet more briefly, though it is not less important. As an existing community, the church will usually live in situations where it weighs on other communities to which its members also belong, most notably the political community. To the extent, usually great, to which a political community separates spirit and deity, its permanent chief political division will be between the demand for permanence and the demand for change, and the church will be a factor in this conflict. Calls for the church to keep out of politics are always but dissimulating attempts to enroll it on the side of permanence. Since Constantine first recognized that the church had acquired political potential, the church has had over and over to choose. No choice has yet been so principled as to acquire dogmatic authority for following generations; perhaps we are now being compelled to choose principle.

Over against the polity's permanent conflict between change and the status quo, the church must refuse to accept that stability and change are in fact incompatible: The Father and the Spirit are one God. But this very identity must put the church decisively on the side of the future, which in a world that separates deity and spirit means that the church must expect often to favor change. Since the church's inevitable interpretation by society as a religious group means that the church will be expected—also by its own uninstructed members—to be a support of the status quo, the openness of the church to change will itself be a fundamental choice by the church and a political act in the polity.

Also, current "theology of liberation" may sometimes betray the Spirit's creativity, by making of exodus and resurrection a timeless idea which we endlessly imitate[11]—and which, moreover, can be as comfortingly imitated by Afrikaner "freedom-fighters" as by the blacks they in turn oppress. What, after all, did not Israel do to the Canaanites? But that the church's message and demeanor, in its christological specificity (to which we will come), may and must be at all times *liberation*[12] is something of which no part of the church should ever have needed to be reminded. The status quo does in fact sometimes need defending; and if the church, as an available group of pious people, is then used by Providence for that purpose, well and good. But *as* the church, as the community of the Spirit that is God, the church can never acknowledge a status quo as norm. For the church, encompassing reality is yet to come, and it is the Wind of the future that expresses the Creator.

The Spirit and the Letter

For any community, identification of its spirit over against other spirits is a continuing necessity. The American nation has an entire sovereign presbytery, the Supreme Court, continuously deciding what is in the spirit of the national community and what is not. On the most notable occasion when they and others similarly charged manifestly failed, only a civil war could settle the matter.

In the primal church, the problem appeared with urgent simplicity. In the daily governance and liturgy of the congregations, interventions claiming to be by the Spirit, and manifestly agitated by some spirit or other, clashed. Since, for example, the advice "Listen to Paul" and the advice "Ignore Paul" could not be of the same spirit, how could one tell which opened the community's true future? Said Paul, "I want you to understand that . . . no one can say 'Jesus is Lord' except by the Holy Spirit" (1 Cor. 12:3). That is, he provided a means of identification, which every community must have.

In a community for which its spirit is the Spirit of God, the identification of its spirit and the identification of God go together. Israel's identification of God is clear. Asked "Who or which do you mean, 'God'?" Israel answered, "Whoever got us out of Egypt." But while this identification was in itself straightforward, its strictly past tense had to make it ambiguous for the future-laden Spirit; the ambiguity appeared as the persistent problem of discerning true prophecy from false prophecy.[13] One could, of course, say that true prophecy had to be appropriate to exodus, for example, "liberating." But quandaries had still to appear.

Within the span of the Hebrew Scriptures, the problem became more pressing as Israel's faith became more decisively eschatological. What finally happened was that the problem dialectically became its own solution. The exilic and postexilic prophets joined free future to established past by prophesying as content of the future the past's decisive repetition. When the Spirit in which the prophets opened Israel's future came to be evoked as itself the eschatological gift of that future, then the exodus or the deliverance by David, appropriateness to which is the self-identity of the prophet's Spirit, became itself the promised future: There will be a "new exodus" (e.g., Isa. 40:3–5), a "new" exodic "covenant" (e.g., Jer. 31:31–34), a new David (e.g., Zech. 9:9–10).

"New exodus" and the rest are, of course, metaphors. But that classification gets us only a little way. In the "new exodus" and its like, history is decisively to repeat itself. Merely as such, the repetition of saving events is the main intuition of all mythic religion, but there its function is precisely to keep history from being decisive, to anchor possessed blessings in an eternal beginning.[14] The prophetic promise of *decisive* repetition, in contrast, does not mean reiteration of a timeless archetype, but faithfulness to a task begun and now to be finished. And it was as "faithfulness" that Israel conceived her God's eternity. But now we must note the kind of language we have just been compelled to use: The historical continuity posited by exilic prophecy is that of a personal life. The problem of true and false prophecy can finally be mastered only if the unity of Spirit-opened future and God-identifying past history is the historical self-identity of a person.

That is, the Spirit can be identifiable only if we can speak of him as the Spirit of so-and-so. Nor will it do merely to say he is the Spirit of God, and then characterize God as "personal," nor yet to say he is Israel's Spirit, and "personify" Israel, for both moves would be vacuously circular. The Spirit can only be identified as the Spirit "of" a person *otherwise* identified. The church's identification of the Spirit as the Spirit of Jesus is the dialectically necessary next step—though it is also contingent and possibly false.

The church's prophecy—"the gospel"—is "Jesus will triumph." The word "Jesus" identifies a single person, by his particular life and particular death, as does any proper name. The future, says the gospel prophecy, is *his*. The spirit of the church is identifiable as the spirit of this historically identified man; yet since this man nevertheless lives, the Spirit is not thereby inappropriately pinned to a merely past event or its historical deposit.

What is the true spirit of the church-community? That which can also be identified as the spirit of Jesus. This answer by itself does not solve a single practical problem. The church has still to labor as mightily as ever the Supreme Court. But identification of the Spirit by Jesus does shape the labor and eliminate certain possibilities.

If the Spirit is identifiable by Jesus, he is identifiable by an historical figure and so by the means of historical memory; that is, the identification of the Spirit is an *hermeneutical* labor. We thus come to Scripture. All the church is agreed that the self-identity of the gospel through its history, and therefore the identifiability of the Spirit, depend on Scripture.[15] In the Spirit, we can speak only the same message—in some sense of "same"—as the apostles, and are thus, after their death, dependent on the documents of their proclamation: on their texts (the Hebrew Scriptures) and on the sparse relics (the New Testament) of their actual activity. That is, we are dependent for the gospel's self-identity on recorded words. But how can such identify the Spirit? Are we not back with Israel's old problem? The whole history of the church could be written under the rubric of so many controversies "on the Spirit and the letter."[16]

Again and again we have so attempted to identify the Spirit by the letter of Scripture that little Spirit has been left. All doctrines of inerrancy and so forth fall under this verdict, and so, ironically, does what is usually now meant by "the inspiration of Scripture." If by this we meant that these texts belong to and have a special and necessary role in the Spirit's impelling of the church toward the End, the doctrine would be biblical. But what is nearly always meant is the opposite: an attempt to deify the letter. Nor yet does anything change in principle if Scripture is conceived as the document of a great religious movement or teacher and leader, and authority of some sort is attributed to the movement or leader, or if we make Scripture a field for the detection of subtextual primal archetypes. So long as we in any way deal with Scripture as a document of the past, from which we by some method or ideology have to extract a contemporary significance, we are dealing by the letter against the Spirit.

It is arguable that the church has survived at all only by the outbursts which so dead a hand of the past had to provoke: Montanism, various medieval movements, the Reformation-era spiritists, current theology that begins and ends in "the theologian's" freed-up experience, and so on. Nevertheless, such outbursts for the Spirit against the letter are if anything even less appropriate to the church's mission than the letter-bondage they react to. We come to the excluded possibilities customarily lumped together as "enthusiasm." The historically classic struggle was that between Martin Luther and those he called the *Schwärmer*. Luther's position was dogmatically asserted by the Augsburg Confession: "We condemn the anabaptists and others, who think that the Holy Spirit comes to us without the external speaking of the gospel."[17]

The spirit that is independent of the letter by which the Lord is identified is not in the church identifiable at all. And when the church becomes a field for the sweep and clash of unidentifiable spirit, the wise will depart. In such a church, we may by chance be called to the now so much admired peasant revolution, or to the splendid works and austerities of some early English spiritist movements. But we may equally be called to slaughter the innocents: When an outburst of "spiritual freedom" swept a medieval district, it was time for the Jews to seek refuge in the castles of the no more friendly, but letter-obeying, bishops.[18]

The great second- and third-century struggle with Montanism[19] displayed all the factors of the many subsequent such struggles, and its resolution has been authoritative ever after. "Montanism" is a later name for the extreme form of a widespread reaction against the cooling of eschatological expectation in the second century, and with it of prophecy and ethical rigor—against, that is, a church which had acknowledged that the Lord's return would not necessarily be chronologically soon and that it had to settle in for a longer haul. Montanus and his two prophetesses announced the imminent time and place of the millennium and dictated rules of church discipline far harsher than any previously contemplated. On the readmission of the lapsed, they decreed: "The church *can* indeed remit guilt; but I will not do it, lest they commit more sin."[20] That neither such eschatological information nor such disciplinary rigor could be supported by apostolic witness did not bother the prophets, since they spoke directly for God. The spirit speaking through them said, "Neither an angel nor an elder, but I, the Lord, God the Father have come."[21] The prophecy of the "Paraclete" was a new and therefore higher revelation than that of the earlier prophets or of the evangelists and apostles.[22]

The Montanist movement was quickly expelled from the just then rapidly organizing church. In its home territory of Asia Minor, the church's very first synods were to combat it; in its second great territory, North Africa, the break was already sealed in 207 by a synod at Carthage. The chief point of separation was precisely the claim of a revelation by the Spirit that was not subject to control by the biblical witness to Christ; conversely, the anti-Montanist reaction was a chief impetus to the development of a definite New Testament canon.[23] Somehow the church's Spirit must be subject to the letter *about* Christ, and just so be the free Spirit *of* Christ. Understanding and practicing this dialectic is a chief and permanent pneumatological task of the church.

The Spirit and the Word

Israel's and the church's identification of God and Spirit and of Christ and Spirit is simultaneous with and dependent on identification of word and Spirit. This brings us to a third area.

The life of any community is above all shaped by whether in it word and spirit are one or two. Not to cast unnecessarily far afield for an extrachurchly example, the American community is now being perturbed precisely by confusion at this point. Democratic theory, which settlement of a new continent unexpectedly allowed to be put into practice, harbored two incompatible doctrines of communal spirit. America has tried to follow both.

One, in the line of Rousseau,[24] locates the community's spirit in prelinguistic shared impulse, in a "common will" that antecedes all joint attempts to reach consensus, which may be better divined by one inspired leader than by the assembled community. This theory has justified all modernity's totalitarian democracies, from Robespierre on; the leader is the one who "just knows" what the people want. But it also justified the American Constitution, Mr. Madison's Newtonian machine-polity of representation and balances.[25] For, as Madison well knew and made plainer than we have since admitted, it is only interests, never moral convictions, that can be represented, or checked and balanced as if they were masses in motion. What our constitutional machinery is designed to produce is not a consensus about what is believed to be good, but a balance of what is premorally wanted. This balance can then be presented as the common good only on Rousseau's principle, only because the community's grasp of its own future good is presumed to subsist with or without joint moral reflection, that is, discussion and argument, and to express itself best in sheer joint want.

The other theory of democracy, given in Puritan theology of covenant, locates the community's spirit in face-to-face moral discourse.[26] The community's spirit is not just there, to be discovered by whatever means of divination; it comes into being by actual common discourse about the future of the community. In that we *argue* our common good, there is one spirit.

It is the polity of such discourse that Madison called "democracy" and rejected, because of its alarming spiritedness and because of its limitation, under the technology of the time, to small communities. But although the spirit of the word was thus shut out from our state machinery, it persisted, so long as Puritanism persisted, in a second informal public sphere.[27] In Athenaeums and Chautauquas, in the congregations of great preachers, in societies and clubs for one reform after another, there occurred the actual American ethical community, which civilized the frontier, established our education, fought slavery, campaigned for women's suffrage and industrial justice, promoted just wars and opposed unjust ones, and tried to outlaw liquor.

So long as both public spheres lived, our nation flourished as a community. For whenever matters become serious, Mr. Madison's mechanistic polity could call on the informal Puritan ethical community for spiritual succor. But in the ethical community's isolation from the state, it was unable to assimilate the great nineteenth-century immigrations of people who came for reasons of necessity rather than of religious or political conviction, and it never tried to recruit the great existing spirit of the black community. It was thus too weak to counter the post–Civil War rise of corporate capitalism, which creates a collective that depends not at all on discourse and demands that moral individuals merely set themselves over against this collective. The very existence of an American community is now threatened thereby.

Where there is community, there is communication. And the word is either itself spirit, or resistance to spirit; conversely, spirit is either word or subverts word. If we detach spirit from the word, it will attach itself instead to the world, and turn reactionary. The word is in any case the reality of our relation to each other and so to the future; it is by language that we have a world, so as possibly to come together in it. Just so, we have the world as an interpreted world, and therefore as an interpretable world, as a world that might have been and so might be different. The question is, do we *open* possibility by our mutual addresses, so that our mutual presence in the word is spirit, or do we by our addresses *close* possibility, so that spirit is driven off to become a prerelational collective self?

In Israel, it is settled: There is no spirit that is not word, and there is to be no word that is not spirit. The word in any case is power; in the church and the rest of Israel, because of the content of its word, that power is spirit.

Most of the church's problems and controversies about its mission to the world, on the one hand, and about its internal liturgical life, on the other hand, have been and are centered on the relation of its word to the Spirit. There is a plain scriptural direction: The Spirit *is* the spirit of the Word about Christ. That this direction has historically often had little effect may be attributed to the extreme difficulty of holding on to it in daily churchly practice.

Sent into the world as a conspiracy on behalf of the world's own future, as the community of the spirit that is God the Spirit, how is the church to discern God's future? The question here is not of the criterion, as in the previous section, but of the nature of the activity of discerning. Throughout the church's history, many have turned from discourse as the way of such discernment, to one or another sort of divination or, in the modern world, to one or another ecclesiastical-bureaucratic analogue of Madison's need-averaging machine.

Often these two errors now combine, by virtue of their common basis. For example, "situation ethics," however qualified by scholarly advocates, have in churchly practice usually meant that the church—because it is so loving—just *knows* what in each situation has to be done. Argument is no longer required, or even tolerated. Install such diviners in a bureaucracy, as those that now administer "social concern," and what the church then *divines* always turns out to be what the world, years before, has discovered it *wants*: for example, most Protestant bodies' capitulation to abortion by free choice.

We are neither merely to accept the world's hopes as the world interprets them, nor merely to cast a contrary vision from the church population's own given impulses. The church's mission can be discovered only in an act of language, of interpretation. The one pole of interpretation is the church's constant claim that Jesus is risen, so that his particular human intention, defined by his particular life and death, must finally triumph. The other is the antecedent hopes and fears by which the people of a time and place are somehow related to the future. The outcome of such interpretation is on the one hand an eschatological metaphor, and on the other hand a founded ethic—the interpreting itself is the actuality of the Spirit.

For instance—an instance chosen for its reciprocal relevance to the principle under discussion—it is already a banality that Americans feel shut out from their governing. If we ask our fellow citizens, "What do you want?" they answer, "We want some say about our lives." This need can interpret and be interpreted by the assertion of Jesus' resurrection. As the claim of Jesus' liveliness is interpreted by the hope for participation, we will say, "In that Jesus lived wholly by his hope for his fellows, and in that he will triumph, there *will be* a polity in which none is excluded from final decision. In the kingdom, the last will be first." Thus appears an eschatological vision. As the hope for participation is interpreted by the claims of Jesus' aliveness, we will say, "What will happen can happen. Therefore a mutual polity is not a human impossibility; it is worth working for. And your hope for participation, since it is a look forward to Jesus' triumph, need not elbow your neighbor aside. In fact, your neighbor's sovereignty and yours can only grow together." Thus appears a founded ethic.

Turning to the church's inward life, all the great and trivial liturgical disputes that have torn the church have been about the relation of Spirit and word. Is it possible so to receive the Spirit, feathers and all, as to need no external verbal authority? If the recitation of the words of institution consecrates, do we need a subsequent epiclesis of the Spirit? Can I receive "water baptism" and still lack "Spirit baptism"? If baptized infants have the Spirit, can they be made to wait for first communion?

From the welter of cases in point, we choose one that is now actual in much of the church and seems likely to continue for some time: speaking in tongues.[28] Modern glossolalia can be described so: It is articulated speech that lacks one kind of articulation, that by which sounds and sequences of sounds are correlated to items of the world. It is articulated speech; it has rhetoric, melody, and, at least sometimes, rudimentary syntax.[29] But it does not have semantic articulation: rules correlating speech to the world's items and structures. Why would someone want to speak so? Precisely in order to speak without having to judge and shape one's utterance to the world and its ways.

But if one no longer speaks about the world, why speak at all? And why especially attribute such speech to the Spirit? As we have seen, all believing discourse, whether proclamation or prayer, has a quality of prophecy. Prophecy is the word that opens the future. But integral prophecy does so precisely in responsibility to the world that already is: It is the children of Abraham, in all their historical specificity, that will inherit the land, an historical figure, Jesus, who will judge all people in love. Glossolalia is prophecy that has cast off this bond to be nothing but sheer experience of how the prophetic word frees us from the way things are, sheer evocation of the possibility of transformation.

But just there is the difficulty. For Christ is an item of the world, and the Holy Spirit is his Spirit and the Spirit of the word that specifically tells about him, that is, of a word that does have the kinds of articulation that let it be about things in the world. The problem with tongue-speaking is the same as the problem with purely instrumental music in the services of the church. Music is undoubtedly the most powerful speech we have, except that it does not by itself say anything specific, whereas the gospel is specific. One could well say that instrumental music is the sophisticated church's equivalent of speaking in tongues. And that suggests the discrimination and test we need: It has long been understood that the proper churchly function of instrumental music is to release and vivify texts; a proper organ piece is a hymn prelude or an accompaniment of the gospel procession, or the like. Just so, proper glossolalia would release and vivify the prayers and proclamations in mundane language. If glossolalia is the natural and appropriate accompaniment and vivification of what others in the congregation are saying mundanely, and is recognized by them as such, it is a good thing. If not, it may not be permitted in the congregation at all, for then the spirit that moves is not the Holy Spirit, be it ever so religious and comforting to those who experience it. This spirit is again a dumb spirit, an urge from the premoral, precommunal needs of the mere collective group.

Finally in this line, one more phenomenon of the contemporary church must be mentioned, to avoid misunderstanding of the foregoing and for its own sake. Language and gestures can be used, not for communication, not for the word, but for the sort of exchange that is currently called "sharing." The *word* is discussion, argument, and proclamation and distinct affirmation or rejection; communication creates a common objective world and consensual purposes in it. "Sharing" refrains from all this; it is the mutual display and cosseting of preexisting individual needs and attitudes. That is, "sharing" is an actualization of

Rousseauean premoral collectivity. All affirmations in this section are about the word; none are to be taken of "sharing."

"Sharing" can only occur between relatively few people at one time, since emotional intensity—real or fictive—is its necessary medium. The word, on the other hand, can occur between "two or three" or between two or three thousand. Thus "sharing" has a natural affinity for small groups. The point that must be made is: Where it is supposed that the Spirit blows more freely in small groups than in larger liturgical or deliberative groups, there the church's mandated identity of Spirit and word has been betrayed. The error here noted is now pervasive in the church, appearing impartially among charismatics, "facilitators," social activists, devotees of touching-and-feeling, and the soberest of the faithful. Wherever it appears, it is destructive of faith.

The Spirit and History

It is decisive for every community whether it understands possession of its spirit as a free event in the life of the community or its members, or as a natural endowment. The case that both makes the issue utterly clear and shows its importance is that of Nazi Germany, where the possession of true German *Geist* was exclusively a matter of "blood and soil," of genetics and geography. That Jews were some of the greatest adepts of German art, philosophy, literature, and communal tradition could not qualify them.

Our example shows where we think the danger of the one choice lies, but it should not be supposed that we think the spirit of no community should be given by nature. The choice discussed in this section differs from those of previous sections in that the same choice would not be best for all communities. The family is an obvious case of a community whose spirit must and should be given by blood. Moreover, there are a variety of combinations that may be right for various communities. The spirit of a community may be given naturally to some members and historically to some, as in a family with adopted members, or given naturally but liable to be lost historically, and so forth.

Insofar as the spirit of a community is a natural endowment, the community will display a characteristic important for our concern: Since any natural endowment varies quantitatively between individuals, and since this variation is only within limits alterable by history, such a community will have some who simply *are* more endowed with its spirit than others. Doubtless the classic extreme and self-conscious case was the gnostic[30] religious communities of late antiquity. In consequence of the transcendental history by which, according to gnostic lore, the world came into existence, there are three immutable human kinds: "matter-persons," incapable of virtue or religion; "soul-persons," capable only of culture and virtue; and "spirit-persons," whose culture and virtue are turned into saving religious knowledge by predetermined inner openness to transformation from beyond the world. If the middle, "soul-person" group is at all admitted to the community, then leadership is the sole prerogative of the pneumatics.

The church's choice can be in no doubt. One does not enter the church or receive its spirit save by baptism,[31] that is, historically, by an event *in* one's life. Even the practice of infant baptism does not change this; it only recognizes that birth into a home already under the church's discipline can be a claim on initiation. But just thereby birth into a disciplined home is itself conceived in historical categories, so that the claim it constitutes is not valid apart from the promise of the parents to teach the child and their tested ability to fulfill the promise.

A vital consequence of the church's mandated decision is that in the church there can be no spiritual aristocracy. This fundamental point was established in the church's first great struggle against alienation, the struggle in which the institution we call "church" was created. We need not here decide the much controverted question whether gnosticism was a movement that invaded or originated within the nascent Christian movement. Whichever, it was the most comprehensive threat of alienation that Christianity has yet experienced.[32] And one decisive point of the church's achievement of self-awareness in difference from the gnostics was over against the gnostic conception of spirit as natural endowment, with its aristocratic consequences.

The key antignostic polemicist was Irenaeus.[33] And the basis of his polemic, against both naturalism and aristocracy, is a strictly christological understanding of pneumatic endowment: "[God] promised to pour out [the Spirit] in the last days. . . . Therefore the Spirit descended on the Son of God who had become a son of man, with him becoming accustomed to dwell in the human race . . . and renewing humans . . . into the newness of Christ."[34] The Spirit is for all believers; just so, his coming depends on God's free choice and so is not given by nature.

But although the church overcame the explicit gnostic temptation, a closely related naturalistic conception was, nearly contemporaneously, accepted into the conceptual structure of standard theology, so that the church has ever since been ill-defended against misunderstandings analogous to gnosticism. Spirit is life, insofar as life is elusive and unpredictable. As patristic theology adopted modes of interpretation provided by the tradition of Greek reflection, it analyzed spirit's elusiveness in terms of certain characteristics of some realities, by which these realities evade our perception: invisibility, intangibility, inaudibility, and so on. The result is a version of the classic Greek two-level ontology, with a new Christian name, "spirit,"[35] for the upper level: There are "material" beings possessed of characteristics by which they are subject to our sense-bound apprehension; and there are "spiritual" beings, defined by the negation of all such characteristics. In Aquinas' definition, "a spirit is an invisible entity . . . ; thus we attribute this name to all immaterial and invisible substances."[36]

If we once accept that such terms as "immateriality," "invisibility," and the like define a kind of being, it is difficult to deny that these terms have some natural application to human being and that therefore human being must, at least in part, be of this kind; it is this that has led to the idea of "the soul." Therefore this metaphysics makes the Spirit a natural endowment of our race, however theology that works with this metaphysics may maneuver to deny the consequence. Thus there has been a tendency given in the conceptual structure of traditional theology which, in our view, runs counter to the pneumatological decisions of Scripture. It is our proposal to eliminate this item of metaphysics from theology; indeed, that has been an agenda item of this whole *locus*.

The first great theologian to break decisively with the identification of spirit with an incorporeal kind of being was Martin Luther. This break was the true crux of his controversy with the sacramentarians, and even of the sacramental and christological differences between him and John Calvin.

It is clear that the spirit/matter ontology must make the central gospel-assertion about the sacraments, of Christ's authentic and complete human presence in the Supper and in the church's life generally, into a conceptually difficult problem. For by such an ontology, the Lord who "*is* the Spirit" among us will just therefore *not* be a body among us. Thus the classical Western formulation of the Lord's bodily presence in the Supper, the doctrine of transubstantiation, accepting the spirit/matter opposition, can affirm the presence of Christ in the body only as the occurrence of a conceptual impossibility brought to pass by God's sheer omnipotence.[37] So Aquinas: The presence of the body of Christ cannot be discussed in terms of location, since a body can be only one place at a time (*Summa Theologica*, iii, 75, 1–2); therefore the presence of the body of Christ can come to pass only by a "conversion of the bread's substance into it," which is a sheer miracle, "wholly supernatural" (ibid., 4). But if the Supper is to function as sacrament, this miracle must be predictable: We must be able to know that at particular occasions of eating bread and wine it in fact happens. That is, there must be authorized secondary agents of the miracle. So Aquinas: The "power of consecration" resides in a formula of consecration, "This is my body," and in ordination's authorization to certain people to speak the formula truly (e.g., ibid., 82, 1). Therewith at a stroke the medieval doctrine of priesthood and, built up around this, of the church.

But what if, as by all the Reformers, such institutionalized miracle-working is denied? Then there are but two possible outcomes. One is that the support is simply removed from under the ancient affirmations of Christ's bodily presence in the

Supper, that the spirit/matter ontology is freed to produce its natural consequences. The presence of Christ in the Supper will then be understood as Spirit—which can be anyway presence-at-a-distance and causes no problem—and just so as not-body. Then the bread and the cup, which are manifestly bodies, can be presented not as the presence of Christ but only as means— reminders, symbols, or whatever—of an event that itself occurs in the realm of immateriality. Thus Calvin begins by defining: "Flesh must therefore be flesh and spirit spirit, each in the rule and condition in which God created it. And this is the condition of flesh, that it holds to its one particular place, and to its dimensions and its shape" (*Institutes* [1536], 123). Consequently, the presence of Christ's body in the sacrament must be construed as the gift to faith of the benefits Christ won in the body (ibid.), the function of the bread and cup being to remind us of Christ's body and its benefits (ibid., 120); insofar as the elements fulfill this function, they lead us away from their own reality as bodily objects "to spiritual realities" (ibid., 120), for "the sacrament is a spiritual thing, by which God feeds our souls, not our bellies" (ibid., 121).

The other possible outcome is that the spirit/matter ontology is broken through, and "spirit" recaptured for its biblical uses. This is what happened with Luther. He mocked the "enthusiasts" for supposing that "spirit is nothing more than a substance that has no flesh and blood." On the contrary, Christ's "very flesh . . . is sheer spirit [because it is] holiness and purity. For what can holiness and purity and innocence be except spirit, sheer spirit?"[38] Thus Luther's doctrine of Christ's presence in the Supper is created by abandoning the opposition of "body" and "spirit" as ontological kinds and relating them instead as moral—what we now call existential—categories. Luther is able to maintain the classic affirmations about Christ's reality in the Supper, without resting them on the medieval doctrine of the ministry, by locating them in a conceptuality utterly different from the standard Western metaphysics.

Further development of this matter would take us beyond this *locus*. It will be seen that our agreement, on the precise point, is with Luther. The objective, however, cannot now be to adjudicate the old controversy, but rather to carry on the conceptual revolution inaugurated by Luther, in the hope that thereby possibilities of interpretation will emerge in which Calvinists and Lutherans and Roman Catholics can join. In any case and in the meantime, one Lutheran affirmation must stand: "Spirit" is not a kind of being specifiable by its differences from "matter."

The Spirit is Jesus' unlimited, resurrection-liberated freedom. What people do in their freedom is history. So also with Jesus: The Spirit is Jesus' freedom to effect historical reality. The Spirit is the very opposite of a liberation from history, or of a realm of being beyond history. The Spirit is precisely Jesus' freedom to be bread and wine, to live in our historically actual congregations.

CHAPTER FOUR

Cosmic Spirit

Despite the perils of the enterprise, the Hebrew Scriptures and the doctrine of the Trinity compel us to describe a cosmic reality and work of the Spirit. In the often esoteric tradition, we find cosmic Spirit identified as the freedom of history, the spontaneity of nature, and the beauty of all things. The dogmatic task is to reclaim these insights by discovering what it must mean that this Spirit is the specific Spirit of Jesus and his Father.

The Logic of Cosmic Pneumatology

In the previous two chapters, we have discussed the work of the Spirit mostly as a work only within the believing community. That is as it should be; it is the Spirit of Israel's particular God and of Jesus and of the church that is our object. Yet we cannot entirely confine ourselves to this analysis, for Israel's God is creator of all things. Thus if the Holy Spirit is God, this Spirit's wind must blow on and through all things. In the New Testament, the creator Spirit is almost exclusively proclaimed as the creator of the new life of God's particular people; but the very meaningfulness of this New Testament discourse depends on the Hebrew Scriptures, which evoke the Spirit as a universal creativity.

The enterprise of cosmic pneumatology is thus necessary; indeed, it is dogmatically mandated by the Trinity doctrine's assertion of the unity of Father and Spirit. But the enterprise is also perilous, for it must be the particular Spirit of Jesus and of the church to whom we attribute cosmic efficacy; that is, we must assert the universal potency of events in one little religious group. Such an assertion strains the Western intellectual tradition to breaking. As we will see, those who have ventured cosmic pneumatology have not always been able to avoid producing nonsense or myth. And conversely, the enterprise exposes theology to powerful temptation: to mitigate the offense by relaxing the restriction by "of Jesus and the church" a little, to fudge the particularity of the Spirit.

If a cosmic pneumatology faithful to the gospel is possible, its function will be double, and exactly match with respect to creation the function of the previous chapter's analyses with respect to community. First, we hope by interpreting the gospel's proclamation and invocation of the Spirit over against the world—as before over against the church-community—to display part of the sense of this proclamation and invocation, and so further their vitality and accuracy. Second, we hope to obtain true statements about the world, which are valuable for their own sake, just as we hope that the previous chapter is valuable truth about the church-community.

There are two great differences between analyzing the pneumatic reality of community and analyzing that of the world. First, there are not merely in possibility but in fact many communities, each with its spirit and its different pneumatic structure; thus our method could be to analyze the abstract pneumatic choices before "any community," and then state the church-community's proper actual decisions. But there is only one world; therefore our cosmic pneumatology must be concrete and specific from the start. Second, the church, whose Spirit we are discussing, is already a community but is not yet the world. Therefore in cosmic pneumatology we are one eschatological step back from the previous chapter, which is doubtless the prime cause of the undertaking's difficulty and peril.

We will derive our proposals by a simple device. We will note powerful cosmic pneumatologies from the tradition, and then try to save their insights by restoring whatever they may have lost of the offensive claim that it is *Jesus'* individual spirit of whom the insights are true. In the tradition, there seem to be three themes: The Spirit is the freedom of universal history; the Spirit is the spontaneity of natural process; the Spirit is the beauty of creation. We will consider each. In the very first cosmic pneumatologists, Theophilus of Antioch and Irenaeus, all three themes are already present.

Theophilus of Antioch was eccentric among the mid-second-century apologists in that he appropriated the biblical predicate and figure of "Wisdom" to the Spirit rather than to the Son (*To Autolycus*, ii, 15);[1] this characteristic will recur in later cosmic pneumatologists.[2] It is then consistent with the biblical traditions about Wisdom that knowledge of creation is attributed to inspiration by this Spirit-Wisdom (ibid., ii, 9) and that the Spirit-Wisdom is seen determinative in creation. The Spirit is God's "breath," by which he "begets life" in and "nourishes" all things (ibid., i, 7; ii, 3). Nor is the activity of the Spirit only exterior to creation; but just here, Theophilus can make his point only by reviving the crudest kind of myth: The Spirit of Genesis 1:2 "nourishes" the waters and then together they nourish creation (ibid., ii, 3); creation is "surrounded" by the Spirit, and these together are surrounded by God's hand (ibid., i, 5).

This Spirit-Wisdom tradition, with its attribution of the biblical Wisdom's cosmic function to the Spirit, was continued by Irenaeus[3] on a less mythic basis[4] and with greater specification of the Spirit's role. By the Word, God grants sheer existence; by the Spirit, he makes what exists a "cosmos," an ordered whole whose order is fundamentally one of mutual appropriateness and adaptation:[5]

> Since God is "logical," by his Logos he created all that is created; and since he is spiritual, by his Spirit he made a cosmos of all things. . . . Since then the Logos . . . grants the fact of being, and the Spirit grants order and shape the Logos is rightly . . . called God's Son and the Spirit God's Wisdom.[6]

It is Plato's aesthetic cosmology that Irenaeus draws on: The world is one and is God's world in that it is internally harmonious. This cosmology will in later theologians become a chief structure of theology, and in that role prove a doubtful blessing, but this story belongs in another *locus*, and in Irenaeus we are anyway dealing with a less principled adaptation. In that the Spirit has thus wisely shaped creation, the Spirit is able also to reshape it from within, "mingling . . . with the creature shaped by God that man might be in the image of God."[7]

The Freedom of History

In the Western tradition, one thinker above all others has taken the biblical evocation of the Spirit as a key to reality: Georg W. F. Hegel.[8] It is, in Hegel's interpretation, a central insight of the Western tradition that reality is at its heart conscious. All our knowledge of reality is just that—knowledge; and this tautology itself is both the chief puzzle posed by and to our attempt at knowledge and the chief clue to the puzzle. The puzzle: How *can* we know anything? What bridges the disjunction of knowing subject and to-be-known object? The clue: Perhaps *to be* anything at all, and so to be a possible object, is intrinsically *to be known*, so that there is no gap. The world is not first a mere given, and then subsequently and mysteriously the object of a consciousness, yours or mine; it is a given in that and only in that it is the object of a universal Consciousness. Reality is thus Consciousness—with that object that is given with itself.

But here a disjunction appears. In our self-consciousness, we know consciousness sometimes as *mind*, registering and leaving the object as it is, and sometimes as *spirit*, grasping the object precisely by intruding transformingly on it. Which experience shall we let lead our interpretation of universal Consciousness?

The Greeks said: "God is Mind—or something more like Mind than any mind is."[9] Hegel made the opposite, philosophically revolutionary choice: Universal Consciousness is Spirit.[10] If the world subsisted as the object of Mind, of Consciousness that leaves its object as it is, then the world would always remain as it is. Then the world would best be understood with the Greeks as a cosmos, a changeless structure encompassing the processes of history as a machine encompasses its own workings without itself being changed thereby. But it was exactly the sheer reality of historical change—the French Revolution—that burdened

Hegel and that he needed to explain, not explain away, and therefore he instead interpreted universal Consciousness by the biblical intuition of consciousness as primarily spirit. The world subsists in that it is transformed, by a God who is—far from static Mind—lively Spirit.

Therefore historical change does not have its sense only in something else, the structure of a changeless cosmos within which it occurs. Historical change has its *own* kind of sense, the sense that spirit finds in its object: the sense of a community's lively debate or of creative process in the arts or of lifelong love.

Hegel formalized the logic of this sense by his famous three-step dialectic. Precisely what seems to prohibit that history make sense, the frequent occurrence of historic conflict so extreme that when conceptualized it amounts to contradiction, is the very location of historical meaning. Every historic reality sooner or later acquires, or rather evokes, its own negation; history is made of "thesis" and "antithesis." Thus, for example, the French revolutionary posit of "liberty, equality, and fraternity" evoked the Terror. History makes sense in that precisely from such contradiction a new thesis emerges, a "synthesis" embracing the contradiction in a larger meaning, as does the resolution of a good play's dramatic conflict. Thus Napoleon synthesized the Revolution and the Terror to create Europe's first popular state.

In that the world has *this* sort of sense for the Consciousness as whose object it subsists, neither can the world and this Consciousness merely lie over against each other; their relation too must have the three-step dialectic. Universal Consciousness evokes the world, the mere unconscious object, as its own opposite. But just so Consciousness finds its own meaning— and meaning is the very self of consciousness—in this object, by this transforming action to fulfill itself as Spirit and not mere Mind, and to fulfill the world as history and not mere cosmos. Thus the Spirit not only creates but involves the world; the Spirit is the freedom *of* universal history. The Spirit is the act in which God as Consciousness overcomes history's apparently static standoffs, by creative discovery of the meaning of the contradictions. The Spirit is the freedom of whatever merely is, and just so is involved in some contradiction, for the new synthesis that will come of that conflict.

This reflection's debt to the gospel is obvious, but so is its alienation therefrom. The quickest stipulation of the alienation is dogmatic: The last paragraph's doctrine of God is clearly and intentionally trinitarian, but with the world where Christ ought to be, as the Object in whom the Father finds himself. To reclaim Hegel's truth for the gospel, we need only a small but drastic amendment: Absolute Consciousness finds its own meaning and self in the *one* historical object, Jesus, and *so* posits Jesus' fellows as its fellows and Jesus' world as its world. What we thereby provide a theory for is the assertion of the risen Jesus' universal lordship.

If the risen Jesus is Lord, not only is he Lord of the church, but his will determines the history not only of believers but also of all nations (e.g., Eph. 1:20–23).[11] Theology has had great difficulty stating so brash a claim, and when it has dared, it has regularly emptied it in the very attempt, disingenuously making Jesus Lord of the world by baptizing whatever the world anyway wants, as "really" Jesus' will. Throughout the theological recent past, we have been exhorted to let "the world determine the agenda," to "listen to what Christ is saying from outside the church," and so on. The exhortation is in fact nearly as old as the church; noting that its greatest triumph was the now decried "Constantinian era" may suggest how dubious it is. We must make the exact opposite move: We know who the Freedom of history is, because he is Jesus' Spirit and we know Jesus historically; and we thus can and must proclaim the world's agenda to it.

The Spirit of Jesus is the freedom in which universal history occurs. Here is our thesis. We will unpack it both ways, as an interpretation of the Spirit of Jesus and as an interpretation of history.

The specific Lordship of Christ outside the church occurs when and where the miracle of Hegelian "synthetic" creativity actually occurs. We must speak of "miracle" because that

is what Hegel in fact described, whether or not he adequately
so conceptualized it. Hegel, his vision guided by Christian
proclamation, doubtless saw history at least insofar rightly: Its
process has meaning only in the free appearance of reconciliation between antithetical historical powers. We need not here
decide the controverted question[12] whether or not Hegel's own
system allows this reconciliation to be truly free transformation—to be eschatological—or compels it to be what we more
usually mean by "synthesis," mere result, mere product. We
will unambiguously posit the former, by identifying historical
synthesis as *Jesus'* action, as what is possible only to a resurrected one.

We do not by this identification acquire criteria by which to
look through history, identifying true reconciliations in order
then to attribute these events especially to Christ. We do state a
hope: Living in the actuality of historical contradiction, we recognize therein the very sort of situation appropriate to the action
of one whose freedom is that he is risen from the dead. In an
historical confrontation, where we might otherwise see hopeless
impasse, we therefore perceive instead the possibility of a new
initiative of Jesus' love. And we do also acquire the right to an
after-the-fact application of this hope: the believer's ineradicable
penchant to look back and say, "The situation was hopeless; but
then the Lord. . . ."

Conversely, when Hegelian synthesis truly occurs, when
new love freely appears out of historic contradiction, there some
pieces of history are gathered for the kingdom of God. At the
End, all history will be harvested as an inexhaustible complex
of opportunity for the love of Christ. But if that were all that
could be said, if there were no penultimate gatherings *in* history,
then all temporal events would be equivalently grist for the End,
and then all temporal events would lack point, since it would not
matter what happens before the End. The assertion that Christ's
Spirit is the very inner-historical freedom of history, that where
events unpredictably triumph over impasse this is the act of his
lordship, says instead that history is available to the final triumph of Christ's love by its own structure—recurring to Hegel,

by the recurrent miracle of freedom at the juncture of synthesis with thesis-antithesis.

We must give at least one example. For all that it is now fashionable to deride an earlier American understanding of the appearance of this new nation as a creative act of God, and for all the harm such American self-consciousness doubtless has done, might not the proposition yet be true?[13] The antithesis of the Enlightenment to pietist Christianity, of "life, liberty, and the pursuit of happiness" to eschatological vision and commitment to the brothers and sisters, was synthesized in the local institutions equally of Massachusetts or Virginia and in the thought of someone like John Adams. May we not regard this as an act of Christ's Lordship? That this new thesis soon provoked a new contradiction, which perhaps still awaits its synthesis, need not inhibit our praise for what has been given.

The Spontaneity of Natural Process

If the sort of biblical apprehension exploited by Hegel is true, all reality is historic and the traditional disjunction of "history" and "nature" is only preliminary. But, as preliminary, the distinction doubtless marks a real difference: between the uniqueness and final unpredictability of some events, those we call history, and the regularity and predictability of natural processes. Has the Spirit any role in the latter?

The most theologically influential of modern Anglo-American philosophies, "process" philosophy, has taken natural process as its paradigm of reality, and Christian theologians among the process-thinkers have devoted some attention to the role of Spirit in reality so conceived. According to process-thinkers, reality is composed not of things but of events, or, as they prefer to say, of "actual occasions." An enduring entity, a thing, is but a chain of such occasions, linked by shared characteristics and certain kinds of causal relations.

Each actual occasion is what it is as an integration of its antecedent occasions; for example, a speech is an integration of the experience of the speaker, the events that led up to the assembly addressed and the choice of speaker, and so forth. If each actual occasion's character were without remainder determined by the antecedent occasions it integrates, there would be no novelty in temporal process. But this does not seem to be the case. Anyway, assert process-thinkers, that integration occurs cannot itself be determined by the antecedent occasions; thus temporal process necessarily involves a factor of "event-spontaneity." And sometimes this event-spontaneity does seem to bring with it also a "character-spontaneity," so that the new actual occasion displays novel characteristics not explicable by its antecedents. The suggestion of some process-thinkers is that this spontaneity of temporal process is the referent of Christianity's discourse about the Spirit.[14]

There are several problems with this process-pneumatology.[15] The very choice of natural process as the paradigm of reality, so that history is understood merely as a subclass of process in general, surely prohibits complete faithfulness to the biblical witness to the free Spirit. And by making the spontaneity of cosmic process the chief validation of discourse about the Spirit, process theology shares Hegel's trinitarian alienation; also in this thinking, the world is the trinitarian Son.

Yet here too there is a claim we cannot abandon. Insofar as natural process is, even penultimately, distinguishable from history, it must not by that distinction be made a realm in which Jesus' Spirit is ineffective. Our task is the same as throughout this chapter: here to reclaim natural spiritedness as *Jesus'* Spirit. And it must be a spontaneity of natural process in which we have to locate a natural reality of the Spirit. Our thesis must be: The Spirit of Jesus is the spontaneity of natural process.

But is there any spontaneity in natural process? The attitude toward nature usually fostered by the scientific enterprise is still a cause-and-effect determinism: We suppose that if we knew the total state of the world at any moment, we could predict its entire future. We are here doing dogmatics, not apologetics; this is not the place for a full-scale attack on determinism. But so much must and may be said: If we knew all there is to be known about the world at any moment, we could still not predict the future behavior of all parts of the world, because of an essential character of knowledge about the world.

All scientific knowledge, it now seems, is fundamentally statistical.[16] Its hypotheses about the world's behavior apply to populations—of gas molecules in a space, neutrons released by a fusion, planets in a galaxy, people in a theater, or whatever—and have the form "Of this population, x% will do f under conditions F, G. . . ." Interpreted of individual molecules, neutrons, or theater-goers, such hypotheses become statement of odds: "It is x to y, that any one member of this population will do f under conditions F, G. . . ." And here it is vital to remember what every gambler must, that odds exert no pressure on individual events: When we know the odds are ten to one against, say, filling a particular poker hand with two draws, this knowledge enables no prediction about the actual event other than repetition of the odds. It must therefore be said that there is a factor in natural process which can be interpreted as spontaneous and that it is the one process-thinkers point to, the actual individual occasion. Whether we should so interpret is another matter and does not seem determinable by the content or nature of our scientific knowledge. Believing that the Spirit is the freedom of all realms of created reality, we so interpret.

So to our thesis. Its consequences are shocking. First, if nature's spontaneity is Jesus' Spirit, nature does not subsist apart from personality. Apprehending an actual occasion, we confront someone's communicative freedom; we are in someone's intrusive presence. And we know that someone; the Gospels tell of him. Apprehending any actual occasion, we are involved in conversation with Christ and so in his conversation with his Father.

Our side of this conversation is prayer. If the freedom of natural process is someone's spirit, that someone can be addressed. We can meaningfully and reasonably ask, "Make it rain," because the rain will or will not occur in freedom that is someone's freedom. And if the spirit of natural process is the Spirit of Jesus and his Father, he can be addressed in trust and joy, by petition and praise.

Natural process is usually still understood as a network of causal determinism. Then prayer, if taken seriously, must be understood as appeal to an agent exterior to this network, to intervene in it. Prayer so understood is vulnerable to the old rationalist question: What kind of God would in the first place have made a world which that God has then constantly to adjust? In the contemporary church, such questions have extensively undone the practice of prayer, which is interpreted and phrased not as actual conversation with someone who can and does act but as self-help and self-exhortation: "Lord, make us feel right about the poor," instead of "Lord, feed the poor." Nor is it only petitionary prayer that succumbs. If God can do nothing about the crops or an election, for example, neither *has* God done anything about such matters, and there is also no basis for praise.

In fact, however, the one to whom we pray is not an agent merely exterior to natural process. All actual occasions occur not mechanistically determined but in freedom, and this freedom is the freedom not of mere chance but of a spirit. It is the freedom of the risen Lord's freedom, of the Holy Spirit, of the very Spirit we address in both petition and praise. The arrow of time is Jesus' breath.

Petition and praise are response to challenge and blessing. These then are what all occasions say to us. By every actual occasion, the risen Lord says: "There are possibilities. Ask," and "There are marvels. Praise." That believers are able to hear these addresses, that we are able so to interpret natural spontaneity, depends on the gospel, on our knowledge of the risen Christ. Thus the foregoing propositions about natural spontaneity provide no basis for an independent natural theology. Yet neither is there any reason Christ should not make himself heard in natural spontaneity also by unbelievers. Their ability to hear must then depend on guides other than the gospel—but if they hear, they hear.

On the present line, one other matter must be mentioned, and within this *locus* only mentioned. If the spontaneity of natural process is by a spirit, natural process has not merely a direction but a goal. And since we know whose spirit it is—that it is Jesus'—we know the goal: unconditional love. That is, we know the tendency of cosmic evolution: toward a world apt for love. With this assertion, we touch a long tradition of Christian speculation, of which Teilhard de Chardin[17] is the most recent notable representative. Consideration of the achievements and dangers of this tradition belongs in other parts of this work.

The Beauty of All Things

Readers will have noted how skimpy the previous two sections are compared to other discussions in this *locus*, and how often we have to say that full treatment of some matter would transgress the bounds of dogmatics. Perhaps this has been merely evasive of problems. But there is another preferable explanation: Insofar as the universal role of the Spirit is describable in books, these should be books of faithful speculation, making no strong claim to be the teaching of the churches. The dogmatic substance of what must here be said belongs not so much in books as in liturgies.

All liturgy is sacramental, for merely by its communal character and by the formalization of discourse this imposes, the gospel in liturgy becomes a visible and not merely audible word, elements of the natural world (gestures, cups, books, etc.) are made to speak. And Jewish and Christian liturgy brings also history out of its sheer dumb givenness and makes it speak. Does it say anything to us that, for example, some Aramaean tribes escaped oppression in Egypt and founded a little state in Canaan? Outside liturgy, it can become extremely doubtful that it does; the past can lapse into silent brute fact. But in liturgy the exodus says liberation and unconditional love. In liturgy, nature and history are brought into the proclamation of the gospel and into answering prayer and praise. That is, liturgy says with manifest sense that nature and history belong to the community in which Jesus' Spirit lives.

At the great thanksgiving of the eucharist, the great traditional orders are not content that only those gathered around a particular table should thank God for his divine works. That departed saints and absent saints join is almost obvious. But then even in restrained Western orders appear "angels and archangels." And more exuberant orders, as that of the Apostolic Constitution,[18] go on from the angels and archangels to catalogs of natural phenomena and historic events, not quite making these subjects who directly sing the praises, but also not quite leaving them as only occasions of our praising. In liturgy, natural and historical events appear with spirit; and this seems— there—to make sense.

What about liturgy enables such discourse to have a sense that it would not have as mere propositions on a page? The suggestion emerges from bits of the tradition and from experience of liturgy: It is in that liturgy is *art* that angels and archangels and streams and stars are spirited in it. Sung, "with angels and archangels," seems perfectly natural. Even in a said service, if the language of the great thanksgiving has poetic dignity, all is well. But when liturgical experimenters have tried to make the prayers relevant by reducing them to prose, the presiding minister feels foolish at such passages.

That beauty is thus a third cosmic reality of the Spirit perhaps gains some plausibility from the circumstance that this claim can be interpreted as a Hegelian synthesis of the two previous. On the one hand, beauty is obviously in some sense in the eye of the perceiver; it is a phenomenon of the life of people which we here have called history. Yet not only the products of our eyes, works of art, are beautiful, but also occasions of nature. And their beauty cannot be plausibly interpreted as merely subjective in us; it is somehow a real character of the beautiful occasions. Without solving the great philosophical problem thereby posed,[19] we simply observe what all have observed who have seriously pondered the matter: Beauty at once is a real character of certain objects, whether only natural or also historic, and is in those objects only for personal subjects. Beauty is not only both natural and historic; it transcends the distinction.

Identification of beauty as a cosmic reality of the Spirit appears already in Irenaeus, but thereafter it is a decidedly esoteric tradition. Perhaps the most noteworthy more recent instance of this tradition is the sophiology of Sergius Bulgakov.[20] As a Russian, Bulgakov was heir of the Palamitic-sophiological tradition of

Russian-Byzantine thought;[21] but he was greatly influenced by
German idealism and spent most of his career in Western Europe.

According to Bulgakov, the Spirit lives in the cosmos as
an aspect of *Sophia*,[22] the divine Wisdom by which the Lord
created all things according to Proverbs 3:19. Divine Wisdom
is the nature of God, insofar as this nature is love, and so must
be also outside itself, to be an *object* of love, insofar, that is, as it
is God's nature to reveal himself. Creation is an act of sacrifice
by God, in that God by creation gives up self-sufficiency; and just
so creation is an act of love, a revelation of God's nature, an actuality of Wisdom. And in that God loves the created cosmos—
which God must, since it exists only for love—God sacrifices
also his exclusive possession of Wisdom, so that she is not only
God's Wisdom but the creature's, a created Wisdom that is
the immanent meaning of the cosmos. Thus Wisdom is both the
nature of God and the meaning of the creature.

Since Wisdom is God's self-revelation, the Son and the Spirit—
the "persons" who in trinitarian theology reveal the Father—are
in this scheme, at least with respect to creation, mere aspects of
Wisdom. The Son, as God's rationality, is the content of Wisdom;
within created Wisdom, he is the abstract plan of the cosmos. The
Spirit is the life of Wisdom; in created Wisdom; the Spirit is
the actual appearing and triumph of the cosmos' purpose, the joy
of the cosmos—in a word, its beauty. "Through the Third hypostasis, God not only knows himself as the Truth . . . , but *lives* the
Truth, *senses* the Truth. And the reality of sensed truth is beauty."[23]

To understand fully the Sophia-Spirit's association with
beauty, we must know that Sophia is not primarily an intellectual construct but an *image* of visionary and iconic experience.
She (and in the accounts it is "she"[24]) *appears*, as the Wisdom
figure of the Proverbs, to those seeking the knowledge of God
in visionary experience. In Western Europe, the chief tradition
of such appearances is in German mysticism, where the vision
also produced intellectual constructions strikingly like Bulgakov's.[25] In Russia, much of the impulse for Wisdom speculation
is an esoteric iconographic tradition, in which Wisdom and the
Mother of God blend.[26]

The alienation of this sort of experience and construction from the gospel is obvious. Sophia is a myth on the verge either of nonsense or of polytheism. And Sophia—not a trinitarian hypostasis—has explicitly reduced the Son and the Spirit to aspects of herself, meanwhile acquiring exactly the role attributed by pre-Nicene theology to its "Logos"; thus the Nicene achievement is undone. In this system, we are introduced to the world's Beauty not by an experience of the gospel about Christ, but by private vision. Where claims then follow about this Beauty such as those made by sophiology, this is surely an actual heresy. Yet once again this alienation may be that of an authentic Christian insight come loose from its proper object. We will again make our reclamation experiment.

Insofar as a proposition can here function as our thesis, it must be: The beauty of the world, natural or historic, is the cosmic actuality of *Jesus'* Spirit, is the world's occurring openness to the final triumph of his love. But the meaningfulness of such a proposition is clearly fragile: What can one do with it? The proposition could perhaps achieve reliable form in a speculative analysis of beauty, but that cannot be our task here. Dogmatically, we suggest, the reclamation of the world's beauty for Jesus' particular Spirit can be asserted only liturgically; the propositional form of our thesis is only an instruction to do this.

The Beauty we here wish to acknowledge, the one that Jesus' Spirit is, does not introduce herself in private visionary or aesthetic experience. She introduces herself through the public liturgy of the congregation, where the gospel about Jesus is communally spoken, and just so necessarily spoken dramatically and by formalized and therefore heightened audible and visible words. The claim that the world's beauty is Christ's Spirit is thus appropriately made only by celebrating christological liturgy beautifully.

A liturgy is in any case a work of art, and a liturgical order (the rubrics and texts for liturgy which can appear in books and pamphlets) is instructions for works of art, like a musical score or a playbook. Liturgical experimenters of the sort who suppose that "relevance" or "communication" is achieved by imposing the language, tunes, and ceremonies of "everyday" do not succeed in making liturgies that are not works of art; they make only bad works of art, dispirited works of art, prisons for Jesus' Beauty. Therefore the beauty of a liturgy is not, as generally supposed in the contemporary church, a nice extra, adventitious to the essential function of the liturgy. By its beauty, liturgy says one of the things it must say to be an event of the gospel. By its beauty, liturgy reveals Jesus' Spirit as Beauty, and so as a wind blowing through all the world to open it to final transformation.

If we thus by liturgical beauty claim the world's beauty for Jesus' Spirit, much follows for the world's beauty. We will close by naming two areas of such consequences.

Ethically, Christians may not regard the world's beauty as a secondary value. In our bureaucratic capitalist and socialist societies, it is generally acknowledged that beauty is a good thing. But in the crunch, if, for example, conventional techniques will not allow a new apartment building to be both profitable and in appropriate scale with its neighbors, neither will there be much question which value is to be sacrificed, nor will much effort be invested in seeking new techniques. Believers may not share this attitude. For it would be the new building's appropriate scale that would be the building's present openness to the final human Habitation.

Aesthetically, identification of the world's beauty as Jesus' Spirit provides the axiom of a specific Christian aesthetic: The world is beautiful in that it will be Jesus' stage, in that it will make a "unitive work of all arts"[27] of liturgical praise to the one "that sits on the throne and the Lamb." We here have space to suggest the character of such an aesthetic by only one example: Since beauty is the Spirit of the Crucified and Risen One, mere suffering is never beautiful (e.g., the "theater of cruelty" is perverse), but neither is any suffering irredeemable (e.g., there are no limits to the suffering that the theater may appropriately embody and transform).

One closing remark to the whole *locus*: An entire theology could, as Karl Barth once observed,[28] be done as doctrine about the Spirit. Readers will have noted how each chapter of this *locus* approaches some other *locus* or *loci* of this work and must restrain itself lest approach become trespass. As "grace," the Spirit has been the chief theological impetus of the Latin church; as a trinitarian identity, the Spirit's reality has been the chief theological impetus of the trinitarian and christological dogmatics of the Greek church. The Spirit is in fact discussed throughout dogmatics. Our decision to make "The Holy Spirit" a *locus* of its own, contrary to the tradition, was more a decision to explicate a point of view than a decision to explicate a subject matter.

As to the particularity of this point of view, readers will by now perhaps not be put off if we say the particularity is hermeneutic. Pneumatology is the attempt to explicate the whole work of God as a communal reality among *us*. Pneumatology is the attempt to make Luther's insistence on "for *us*," as the condition of all meaningful discourse about God, be itself the vantage of that discourse. Whether this attempt can succeed, we must judge together—as a decision by the Spirit!

Notes

Part I

Introduction

1 Karl Barth made this clear. Karl Barth, *Kirchliche Dogmatik* (Zurich: Zollikon, 1932–67), 1/1:313–20.

2 Most notably represented by Peter Lombard, Bonaventure, and Barth.

3 Gustaf Aulén, *The Faith of the Christian Church* (Philadelphia: Fortress Press, 1948), pp. 245–49.

4 E.g., Regin Prenter, *Creation and Redemption*, trans. Theodore I. Jensen (Philadelphia: Fortress Press, 1967); Helmut Thielicke, *The Evangelical Faith*, trans. G. W. Bromiley (Grand Rapids: Wm. B. Eerdmans, 1967), 2:124–83.

5 Leonard Hodgson, *The Doctrine of the Trinity* (New York: Charles Scribner's Sons, 1944); Claude Welch, *In This Name* (New York: Charles Scribner's Sons, 1952); Karl Rahner, *The Trinity*, trans. J. Donceel (New York: Herder & Herder, 1970).

Chapter 1: The Triune Name of God

1 Brackets around "Yahweh" (Hebrew: YHWH or JHWH) are used throughout this *locus* in quotations from the Revised Standard Version of the Bible. The RSV follows the Jewish custom of avoiding the proper name of God and substituting "the Lord," but in this *locus* we are speaking precisely of God's proper name and thus use the name "Yahweh."

2. Gerhard von Rad, *Old Testament Theology*, trans. D. M. G. Stalker, 2 vols. (New York: Harper & Row, 1962–65), 1:10–11.

3. On the exegesis, Walther Zimmerli, *Old Testament Theology in Outline*, trans. D. E. Green (Atlanta: John Knox Press, 1978), pp. 19–20.

4. Von Rad, *Old Testament Theology*, 2:180ff.

5. E.g., Zimmerli, *Old Testament Theology*, pp. 21–27.

6. Von Rad, *Old Testament Theology*, 1:121ff.

7. From the third century BC *RGG*³, s.v. "Namenglaube," by K. Baltzer.

8. The most convenient recent marshaling of the evidence is by Peter Stuhlmacher, "Das Bekenntnis zur Auferweckung Jesu von den Toten und die biblische Theologie," *ZThK* 70 (1973): 377ff., 389ff.

9. Cf. Rom. 4:24 with Rom. 8:11; 1 Cor. 15:15; 2 Cor. 1:9; 4:14; Gal. 1:1; Col. 2:12; 1 Pet. 1:21.

10. As a name, *Kyrios* appears only in Scripture references, e.g., Matt. 4:10; 22:37. Otherwise, referring to God, it is only an alternate to *theos*.

11. For less hasty observation, see Josef A. Jungmann, *The Place of Christ in Christian Liturgical Prayer*, trans. A. Peeler (New York: Alba House, 1965).

12. Ignatius, *To the Magnesians*, xiii, 1, 2; Clement, *To the Corinthians*, xlii, 3; xlvi, 6; lviii, 2; *2 Clement*, xx, 5; *Martyrdom of Polycarp*, xiv, 3.

13. Georg Kretschmar, *Studien zur frühchristlichen Trinitätstheologie* (Tübingen: J. C. B. Mohr [Paul Siebeck], 1956), pp. 182–216.

14. As posited by Henry A. Wolfson, *The Philosophy of the Church Fathers* (Cambridge, Mass.: Harvard University Press, 1956), 1:147–54. See also Hans von Campenhausen, "Taufen auf den Namen Jesu," *VigChr* 25 (1971): 1–16.

15. So also J. N. D. Kelly, *Early Christian Creeds* (New York and London: Longmans, Green & Co., 1950), pp. 23ff.

16. For the second and third centuries, Kretschmar, *Studien*, pp. 196–216.

17. The passages in Acts that describe baptism "in Jesus' name" (2:38; 8:16; 10:48; 19:15) are all theological descriptions, not rubrics.

18. E.g., Günther Bornkamm, *Jesus of Nazareth*, trans. I. and F. McLuskey (New York: Harper & Row, 1960), pp. 124–29.

19. Martin Hengel, *The Son of God*, trans. J. Bowden (Philadelphia: Fortress Press, 1976).

20. Von Rad, *Old Testament Theology*, 1:24ff., 62ff.

21. Robert W. Jenson, *Visible Words* (Philadelphia: Fortress Press, 1978), pp. 6–11.

22. For an account of the spread of the baptismal formula into the rest of the primal church's worship, see Kretschmar, *Studien*, pp. 182–216.

23. The ancient church laid great stress on this point. See Basil the Great, *On the Holy Spirit*, 26, in *PG* 32:67–218: "For if baptism was the beginning of life for me . . . , clearly the address spoken to me in the grace of my adoption is for me the foremost of utterances." According to

Gregory of Nyssa, *Refutation of Eunomius' Confession*, in his *Opera*, ed. W. Jaeger (Leiden: E. J. Brill, 1952), 2:313: "For we have learned once for all from the Lord to whom we must attend . . . : to 'the Father and the Son and the Holy Spirit.' Therefore we say that it is a fearful and evil thing, to contemn . . . these divine sounds."

24 This is not only our after-the-fact interpretation. The ancient trinitarian theologians who created the developed doctrine worked out this logic explicitly; e.g., Gregory of Nyssa, *Refutation*, pp. 314–15.

Chapter 2: The Trinitarian Logic and Rhetoric

1 See *2 Clement*, i, 1–2.

2 Thus Ignatius, who has the Greek diction, a Logos concept, and treats the ascription of deity and temporality to one subject as a paradox, nevertheless refers to Jesus simply as God, quite without noting a problem: *To the Ephesians*, viii, 2; *To the Smyrneans*, i, 1; *To the Romans*, viii, 2; *Ephesians*, xix, 2; xvii, 2.

3 Thus "Clement" does exegesis on his own dictum in *2 Clement*, i, 1–2: ". . . as about the Judge of the living and the dead."

4 On the following about Israel, see Walther Zimmerli, *Old Testament Theology in Outline*, trans. D. E. Green (Atlanta: John Knox Press, 1978), pp. 21–32. On the general pattern of ancient religion, see Mircea Eliade, *Cosmos and History*, trans. W. R. Trask (New York: Harper & Row, 1959), the classic study.

5 Zimmerli, *Old Testament Theology*, pp. 43ff.

6 Ibid., pp. 27–32, 64–65.

7 Walther Zimmerli, "Die Bedeutung der grossen Schriftprophetie fur das alttestamentliche Reden von Gott," *VT.S* (1972): pp. 63–64.

8 I.e., in what Jean Daniélou, *The Theology of Jewish Christianity*, trans. J. A. Baker (Chicago: Henry Regnery Co.; London: Darton, Longman & Todd, 1964), somewhat misleadingly calls "Jewish Christianity."

9 Klaus Wengst, *Christologische Eormeln und Lieder des Urchristentums*, StNT 7 (Gütersloh: Gerd Mohn, 1972).

10 See Wolfgang Schrage, "Theologie und Christologie bei Paulus und Jesus," *EvTh* 36 (1976): 123–35.

11 Ibid., pp. 124–25.

12 Ibid., p. 125.

13 Ibid., pp. 127–28.

14 Wilhelm Bousset, *Die Religion des Judentums*, ed. Hugo Gressman, 3d ed. (Tübingen: J. C. B. Mohr [Paul Siebeck], 1966), pp. 302–57; Robert L. Wilken, ed., *Aspects of Wisdom in Judaism and Early Christianity* (Notre Dame, Ind.: Notre Dame University Press, 1975), pp. 1–31, 103–41; Martin Hengel, *Judaism and Christianity*, trans. J. Bowden (London: SCM Press, 1974), 1:153–75.

15 From the "angel of the Lord" in the patriarchal narratives (e.g., Gen. 22:9–19) to the great eschatological figure of Dan. 7:13–14.

16 E.g., Ferdinand Hahn, *The Titles of Jesus in Christology*, trans. H. Knight and G. Ogg (Cleveland: World Publishing, 1969), s.v. "Lord."

17 In Paul the list of such uses is long, e.g., Rom. 14:17–18; 15:30; 1 Cor. 2:2–5; 12:4–6; 2 Cor. 3:3; Phil. 3:3; 1 Thess. 5:18–20.

18 Elsewhere in this literature: Eph. 1:11–14; 1:17; 2:18–22; 3:2–7, 14–17; 4:4–6; 5:18–20; Col. 1:6–8; Titus 3:4–6.

19 It is regularly "Spirit" that is omitted as a word but present in substance; e.g., 1 Pet. 1:3.

20 Daniélou, *Theology*.

21 *2 Clement*, i, 2.

22 On these images, see Daniélou, *Theology*, pp. 146–66; Aloys Grillmeier, *Christ in Christian Tradition*, trans. J. S. Bowden (New York: Sheed & Ward, 1965), 2:41–53; Jaroslav Pelikan, *The Christian Tradition: A History of the Development of Doctrine*, vol. 1, *The Emergence of the Catholic Tradition (100–600)* (Chicago: University of Chicago Press, 1971), pp. 176ff., 184ff.; Georg Kretschmar, *Studien zur frühchristlichen Trinitätstheologie* (Tübingen: J. C. B. Mohr [Paul Siebeck], 1956), pp. 20–22.

23 Daniélou, *Theology*, pp. 117–47, esp. pp. 128ff.; Johannes Barbel, *Christos Angelos* (Bonn: Hauslein, 1941), pp. 181–311; Martin Werner, *The Formation of Christian Doctrine* (New York: Harper & Row, 1957), pp. 120–61; Grillmeier, *Christ*, pp. 46ff.

24 *Ascension of Isaiah*, xi, 32–35. For other documentation, Kretschmar, *Studien*, pp. 71–124.

25 E.g., Origen, *Commentary on Isaiah*, 1, 2; 15; 41; *Commentary on Ezekiel*, 14, 2; *On First Principles*, i, 3, 4; iv, 3, 14. See Kretschmar, *Studien*, pp. 220–23.

26 Or we may be gleeful if we oppose the later doctrines of true godhead and believe ourselves now to discover that the earliest church contradicted them. This is Martin Werner's blunder, which invalidates all the arguments of his otherwise admirable investigations.

27 Daniélou, *Theology*, pp. 117ff.

28 E.g., Hermas, *Similitudes*, viii, 1–2.

29 Ibid., ix, 12, 7–8; *Ascension of Isaiah*, viii, 16–18.

30 The standard presentation is by J. N. D. Kelly, *Early Christian Creeds* (New York and London: Longmans, Green & Co., 1950), pp. 6–29.

31 Ibid., pp. 17ff.

32 See ibid., pp. 40–49.

33 Hippolytus, *Apostolic Tradition*, 21.

34 Kelly, *Creeds*, pp. 40ff.

35 Ibid., pp. 30–130.

36 Ibid., 119ff.

Chapter 3: The Nicene-Constantinopolitan Dogma

1 The following depends on the standard histories: Jane Ellen Harrison, *Prolegomena to the Study of Greek Religion* (Cambridge: At the University Press, 1903), chaps. 1, 6, 7; Martin P. Nilsson, *A History of Greek Religion*, trans. E. J. Fielden (Oxford: At the Clarendon Press, 1923); Martin P. Nilsson, "Die Griechen," in *Lehrbuch der Dogmengeschichte*, ed. Chantepie de la Saussaye (Tübingen: J. C. B. Mohr [Paul Siebeck], 1925), 2:281–417; Ulrich von Wilamowitz-Moellendorf, *Der Glaube der Hellenen* (Berlin: Weidmann, 1932). The interpretation is heavily influenced by Ulrich Mann, *Vorspiel des Heils* (Stuttgart: Klett, 1962).

2 Mann, *Vorspiel*, pp. 62ff.

3 Sophocles, *Oedipus the King*, ii, 1528–30.

4 Aristotle, *Metaphysics*, 1051b, 29–30.

5 Werner Jaeger, *The Theology of the Early Greek Philosophers* (Oxford: At the Clarendon Press, 1947).

6 Aristotle, *Physics*, 4, 203b7.

7 See Eberhard Jüngel, *Zum Ursprung der Analogie bei Parmenides und Heraklit* (Berlin: Walter de Gruyter, 1964).

8 K. von Fritz, "The Function of *Nous*" *CP* 38 (1943): 79–93; 40 (1945): 223–42; 41 (1946): 12–34; Werner Marx, *The Meaning of Aristotle's "Ontology"* (The Hague: Nijhoff, 1954), pp. 8–29.

9 See Hans Jonas, *Gnosis und spätantiker Geist* (Göttingen: Vandenhoeck & Ruprecht, 1954); Hans Jonas, "Gnosis und Moderner Nihilismus," *KuD* (1960): pp. 155–71. On the *Corpus Hermeticum*, which preserves the best witness of the crisis, see André M. J. Festugière, *La Révélation de l'Hermes Trismégiste* (Paris: Lecattre, 1944–54), vol. 4.

10 E.g., Hal Koch, *Pronoia und Paideusis* (Berlin: Walter de Gruyter, 1932), pp. 180–314; Nilsson, "Die Griechen," pp. 394–417.

11 Plato, *Symposium*, 101A–212B.

12 See Wolfhart Pannenberg, "Die Aufnahme des philosophischen Gottesbegriffs als dogmatisches Problem der frühchristlichen Theologie," *ZKG* 70 (1959): 1–45; Yehoshua Amir, "Die Begegnung des biblischen und des philosophischen Monotheismus," *EvTh* 38 (1978): 2–19.

13 E.g., Theophilus of Antioch, *Apology to Autolycus*, i, 2, 5; Melito of Sardis, *Address to Antonius Caesar*, 6–8.

14 Jaroslav Pelikan, *The Christian Tradition*, vol. 1, *The Emergence of the Catholic Tradition (100–600)* (Chicago: University of Chicago Press, 1971), pp. 52ff.; René Braun, *Deus Christianorum: Recherches sur le vocabulaire doctrinal de Tertullian* (Paris: Presses Universitaires, 1962), pp. 62ff.

15 Justin Martyr, *Apology*, i, 12, 13, 25; Melito of Sardis, *Address to Antonius Caesar*, 2; Theophilus of Antioch, *Apology to Autolycus*, i, 3;

Athenagoras, *Supplication for the Christians*, 10. On the standard middle-Platonist theology of Justin, see L. W. Barnard, *Justin Martyr: His Life and Thought* (Cambridge: At the University Press, 1967), pp. 79ff.

16 Barnard, *Justin Martyr*, pp. 77ff.; Braun, *Deus Christianorum*, p. 74.

17 On the failure of creative synthesis, see Pannenberg, "Die Aufnahme," pp. 312–46.

18 Pelikan, *Emergence*, pp. 136–82; *RGG*³, s.v. "Trinität," by F. H. Kettler.

19 The first great antimodalist work was Tertullian's *Against Praxeas*, shortly after A.D. 207. At the theoretical level, another had never been needed.

20 Aloys Grillmeier, *Christ in Christian Tradition*, trans. J. S. Bowden (New York: Sheed & Ward, 1965), 1:190–206.

21 See *TDNT*, s.v. "Word," by H. Kleinknecht.

22 E.g., *Theologia Graeca*, 16; "Hermes is the Logos, whom the gods sent to us from heaven, to make man rational (*logikos*) . . . but even more to save us."

23 Justin Martyr, *Apology*, i, 32.

24 Ibid., 13, 62–63; see also Justin Martyr, *Dialogue with Trypho*, 10, 126–28; Theophilus of Antioch, *Apology*, ii, 22.

25 Justin Martyr, *Dialogue*, 55–62; *Apology*, ii, 6, 13.

26 E.g., Athenagoras, *Supplication*, 10; Theophilus, *Apology*, ii, 22; Justin Martyr, *Dialogue*, 61.

27 E.g., Justin Martyr, *Apology*, i, 5.

28 See Braun, *Deus Christianorum*, pp. 287–91.

29 Justin Martyr, *Dialogue*, 62, 128.

30 Georg Kretschmar, *Studien zur frühchristlichen Trinitätstheologie* (Tübingen: J. C. B. Mohr [Paul Siebeck], 1956), pp. 1–15.

31 E.g., Tatian, *Address to the Greeks*, 7. See Kretschmar, *Studien*, pp. 40–61; Pelikan, *Emergence*, pp. 185–86.

32 On the first, see Justin Martyr, *Apology*, i, 13; on the second, see J. Armitage Robinson, ed., "Introduction," in Irenaeus, *The Demonstration of the Apostolic Preaching* (London: SPCK, 1920).

33 Novatian, *On the Trinity*, is entirely concerned for the Logos' mediatorial function but appends a piece on the Spirit (xxx–xxxi) because, he says, "the authority of the baptismal confession reminds us . . . that we also believe in the Spirit" (xxix).

34 E.g., Irenaeus, *Against All Heresies*, ii, i–ii; ii, vi; ii, xvii, 3; ii, vii, 6; ii, xiii, 4–6.

35 On this and the following, see Braun, *Deus Christianorum*.

36 Ibid., pp. 71–72.

37 Ibid., pp. 158–67.

38 On the following, see ibid., pp. 207–32.

39 Ibid., pp. 228–32. On the following, see ibid., pp. 235–36.

40 Ibid., pp. 173–94.

41 On Origen, see Robert W. Jenson, *The Knowledge of Things Hoped For* (New York: Oxford University Press, 1969), pp. 26ff.; there further bibliography.

42 The most typical representation of the left was Eusebius of Caesarea, *Demonstration of the Gospel*, iv, v. For the right, we may name the young Athanasius, *Discourse on the Incarnation of the Word*.

43 On Lucian and the Lucianists, see Gustave Bardy, *Recherches sur Saint Lucien d'Antioch et son École* (Paris: Gabriel Beauchesne, 1936); here the remaining Lucianist texts are collected. On the following theological history, see Louis Duchesne, *Early History of the Christian Church* (New York and London: Longmans, Green & Co., 1912), 2:98ff; Grillmeier, *Christ*, 218ff.; J. N. D. Kelly, *Early Christian Doctrines* (New York: Harper & Row, 1960), pp. 223–71.

44 See, e.g., Kelly, *Doctrines*, p. 231.

45 Arius, *To Eusebius*, in Bardy, *Recherches*, p. 227: "We do not agree with those who daily cry, 'always God, always Son.'"

46 Ibid., p. 227.

47 Asterius the Sophist, chief publicist for the Arians in the ensuing controversy, formulated the principle: "ageneton . . . to me poiethen . . ." (frag. vii, in Bardy, *Recherches*). The great leader of later Arianism, Aetius, made the whole doctrine of God a mere abstract dialectic on *agennetos/gennetos*; *Syntagmata*, in *PG* 42:533–45.

48 Arius, *Thalia*, in Bardy, *Recherches*, p. 286: ". . . he monas en, he duas de ouk en prin hyparxe."

49 Arius, *To Alexander*, in Bardy, *Recherches*, pp. 236–37.

50 Arius, *To Eusebius*, in ibid., p. 228.

51 Arius, cited by Athanasius, *Discourse against the Arians* (in *PG* 26:321–407), iii, 28.

52 Arius, *To Alexander*, in Bardy, *Recherches*, p. 237.

53 Arius, *Thalia*, in ibid., p. 261.

54 Ibid., 267: "Nor is the Logos true God. He is, to be sure, called 'God' . . . , but by participation granted by grace."

55 Eunomius, cited by Gregory of Nyssa, *Against Eunomius*, in his *Opera*, vols. 1–2, ed. W. Jaeger (Leiden: E. J. Brill, 1960), iii/viii, 14.

56 The text of the relevant part of the second article and of the appended anathemas: "And in one Lord, Jesus Christ, the Son of God; born of the Father (*ek tou patros*) uniquely, i.e., out of the being of the Father (*ek tes ousias tou patros*); God of God; light of light; true God of true God; born, not made; of one being with the Father (*homoousion to patri*). . . ." "The catholic church condemns those who say, 'There was when he was not' and 'Before he was born he was not' and 'He originated from what is not,' calling him either 'of another hypostasis.' or 'of another being' (*ousia*), so that he would be a changeable and mutable 'Son of God.'"

57 Heinz Kraft, "OMOOUSIOS," *ZKG* 66 (1954–55): 1–24; Adolf M. Ritter, *Das Konzil von Konstantinopel und sein Symbol* (Göttingen: Vandenhoeck & Ruprecht, 1965), pp. 270–93.

58 Origen, fragment 540, as collected by M. J. Rouët de Journal, *EnchP*, 1965.

59 Arius, *Thalia*, in Bardy, *Recherches*, p. 256.

60 If Marcellus was not a modalist (as Grillmeier, *Christ*, pp. 275–96, labors to show), he fooled everyone at the time.

61 See Duchesne, *Early History*, pp. 125–200, 218ff. For the best brief account of the theology, see Michel Meslin, *Les Ariens d'Occident* (Paris: Servil, 1967), pp. 253–99.

62 Athanasius, *Discourse I against the Arians*, 18. Athanasius explains that *homoousios* is the logical product of "possessed of identical characteristics (*homoiousios*)" and "from the being (*ek tes physeos*)" (*Epistle on the Councils of Ariminum and Seleucia*, 41–42).

63 See Ritter, *Konzil*, pp. 64–85.

64 Duchesne, *Early History*, pp. 276–77.

65 Ritter, *Konzil*, pp. 68–85.

66 On this paragraph, see ibid., pp. 21–40, 132–204, 293–307.

67 Meslin, *Ariens*, pp. 325–435; Ritter, *Konzil*, pp. 68–85.

68 Ritter, *Konzil*, pp. 133–51, 172–75, 204–8.

Chapter 4: The One and the Three

1 Origen, *Commentary of Romans*, in *EnchP*, 1965, 502:7, 13: "naturam Trinitätis et substantiam unam." Origen, *Commentary on John*, 2, 10, 75: "treis hypostaseis . . . tyganein."

2 *COD*, 1973, 28: There is one "deity and power and being (*ousia*) . . . in three perfect hypostases."

3 In Athanasius, e.g., *Discourse III against the Arians*, 65.

4 See, e.g., the "Creed of Lucian," in *Creeds of Christendom*, ed. P. Schaff (New York: Harper, 1889), 2:27.

5 The Greeks occasionally used *prosopon* instead of or with *hypostasis*. *Prosopon* and *persona* should be close translations of each other. But *prosopon* was never of any trinitarian conceptual importance in the East. And the Latins did not adopt *persona* as its translation, but for its own sake. See Rene Braun, *Deus Christianorum: Recherches sur le vocabulaire doctrinal de Tertullian* (Paris: Presses Universitaires, 1962), pp. 240–47.

6 On *ousia*: Joseph Ownes, *The Doctrine of Being in the Aristotelian Metaphysics* (Toronto: Pontifical Institute, 1951); Werner Marx, *The Meaning of Aristotle's "Ontology"* (The Hague: Nijhoff, 1954). On *hypostasis*: *ThWNT*, s.v. "Hypostasis," by H. Koester.

7 Basil the Great, *Letters*, ccxiv, 4: "As a common noun is related to a proper name, so is the *ousia* related to the *hypostasis*."

8 Ibid.
9 E.g., Gregory of Nazianzus, *Oration XXXI*, in *The Five Theological Orations*, ed. A. J. Mason (1899), 9; Gregory of Nyssa, *Against Eunomius*, in his *Opera*, vols. 1–2, ed. W. Jaeger (Leiden: E. J. Brill, 1960), 1:278–80.
10 Posed by Gregory of Nyssa, *To Abablius: That There Are Not Three Gods*, in his *Opera*, vol. 2/1, ed. F. Mueller (Leiden: E. J. Brill, 1958), p. 117.
11 E.g., Gregory of Nazianzus, *Oration XXXI*, 15–16.
12 E.g., Basil the Great, *Against Eunomius*, ii, 22; Gregory of Nazianzus, *Oration XXXIV*, 10.
13 According to Gregory of Nyssa, *To Ablabius*, 135, there are three ontological questions: "Whether [it] is," "What [it] is," "How [it] is." The distinction of the three hypostases is relative to the third question only.
14 E.g., Gregory of Nazianzus, *Oration XXIX*, 11: "If it is a great thing for the Father to have no source, it is no less great for the Son to have the Father as source."
15 Or alternatively, the incarnation and not the Logos as such is the mediation. So Gregory of Nyssa, *Refutation of Eunomius' Second Book*, in his *Opera*, 2:144.
16 E.g., Gregory of Nazianzus, *Oration XXXI*, 8.
17 This is Karl Barth's language.
18 This is now so thoroughly researched that there is no point in passage-listing here; Ekkehard Muehlenberg, *Die Unendlichkeit Gottes bei Gregor von Nyssa* (Göttingen: Vandenhoeck & Ruprecht, 1966). For earlier theological use of "infinite," see Werner Elert, *Der Ausgang der altkirchlichen Christologie* (Berlin: Luthcrisches Verlagshaus, 1957), pp. 118–32.
19 This too is now thoroughly analyzed; Jean Daniélou, *L'Être et des Temps chez Grégoire de Nysse* (Leiden: E. J. Brill, 1970).
20 Augustine, *On the Trinity*, v, 10.
21 So much at least is proven by Olivier du Roy, *L'intelligence de la Foi en la Trinité selon Saint Augustine* (Paris: Études Augustiniennes, 1966); his conclusions are summarized on pp. 413–14, 435–56.
22 Thus in Aquinas, *Summa Theologica*, i, 2–26, the existence, simplicity, perfection, goodness, infinity, etc., of God are all discussed before there is any reference to his triunity. And note which of these comes first.
23 Augustine, *Commentary on John*, 38, 10.
24 Aquinas, *Summa Theologica*, i, 43, 2. On Augustine himself, see Alfred Schindler, *Wort und Analogie in Augustin's Trinitätslehre* (Tübingen: J. C. B. Mohr [Paul Siebeck], 1965), pp. 160–62; Jean-Louis Maier, *Les Missions Divines selon Saint Augustin* (Freiburg: Presses Universitaires, 1960), pp. 7–98. Lombard, at the foundation

of medieval discussion, develops the distinction at great length in *Sentences*, i, 14–16.

25 Augustine, *On the Trinity*, iv, 28.

26 Michael Schmaus, *Die psychologische Trinitätslehre des heiligen Augustinus* (Münster, 1927), pp. 125–26, lists the texts.

27 As, e.g., again in Athanasius, *Letter to Serapion*, iv, 3.

28 Augustine, *On the Trinity*, i, 12–15; iv, 30; i, 7–10.

29 Schindler, *Wort*, lays all this out; there is a summary on p. 233.

30 Ibid., e.g., p. 180.

31 Augustine, *On the Trinity*, iv, 1: "Let the reader strive to use those things which are made, to know him by whom they are made; so we will arrive at that image that man himself is, in that . . . which is called 'mind' or 'soul.'"

32 Du Roy, *L'intelligence*, esp. pp. 420–28, 447–50. In *On the Trinity*, it is the argument of book 8 that makes this pivot.

33 Ibid., pp. 447ff; there abundant citations.

34 Pervasive in *City of God*.

35 Maier, *Missions*, p. 187.

36 If we line up Augustine's main soul-analogies in columns, so:

being	knowledge	will
lover	loved	love
mind	knowledge	love
memory	knowledge	will

The posited equivalence of the terms in the first column gives the proposition: The being of mind as subject is immediate self-consciousness. Therewith the whole of Western philosophy to come.

37 On the following technical history, *DThC*, s.v. "Trinite" and "Relations Divines," by A. Michel.

38 Council of Florence, "Decree for the Copts," *COD*, 1973, pp. 57–58.

39 Aquinas, *Summa Theologica*, i, 27–28; Bonaventura, *Sentences*, xiii, 1.

40 Aquinas, *Summa Theologica*, i, 27, 1.

41 E.g., ibid., i, 28, 1.

42 In all these formalities, I will follow Aquinas' version; here, ibid., i, 28, 4.

43 Ibid., i, 32, 3.

44 Ibid., i, 40.

45 Ibid., i, 28, 2–4; Bonaventura, *Sentences*, xix/ii, 1, 2. This is the main medieval line; *DThC*, s.v. "Relations Divine," 2147ff. It was denied by a line of thinkers from Gilbert de la Porrée to Joachim of Flores; see ibid., 2145ff.; *DThC*, s.v. "Trinité," 1715–32.

46 E.g., Bonaventura, *Sentences*, xxiii, 1, 1; 1, 2; xxv, 1, 1–2.

47 Aquinas, *Summa Theologica*, i, 29, 4.

48 Lombard, *Sentences*, i, xxvi, 2–3.

49 E.g., Georg W. F. Hegel, *Phänomenologie des Geistes*, 1952, ed. in *PhB*. 313ff.

50 The critical text is in J. N. D. Kelly, *The Athanasian Creed* (New York and London: Longmans, Green & Co., 1964), pp. 76ff., which see also on the following.

51 Ibid., pp. 53–69, 109–14.

52 Emanuel Hirsch, *Geschichte der neuern evangelischen Theologie* (Giitersloh: Bertelsmann, 1951), 2:114–20, 186–93.

53 John Locke, *The Reasonableness of Christianity as Delivered in the Scriptures*, 1695.

54 *RGG³*, s.v. "Servet" by H. Bornkamm; and "Sozinianer," by H. R. Guggisberg.

55 Ibid., s.v. "Unitarier," by M. Schmidt.

56 Hirsch, *Geschichte*, 4:1–119.

57 Cyril C. Richardson, *The Doctrine of the Trinity* (Nashville: Abingdon Press, 1958).

58 G. W. H. Lampe, *God as Spirit* (New York and London: Oxford University Press, 1977).

59 C. F. D. Moule, *The Holy Spirit* (Oxford: Mowbray, 1978), pp. 43–51.

60 The classical document of Enlightenment religion is Immanuel Kant's *Religion within the Limits of Reason Alone* (1783). On this, see Hirsch, *Geschichte*, 4:271–76, 320–29.

61 Quotations from Friedrich Schleiermacher's *The Christian Faith* are from the 7th edition (Berlin: Walter De Gruyter, 1960).

62 Hegel, *Phänomenologie* iv, A; vii, C; Georg W. F. Hegel, *Vorlesung über die Philosophic der Religion*, introd.; pts. 1, 3; *Encyclopädie der philosophischen Wissenschaften*, 1840 ed., vol. 6; Hirsch, *Geschichte*, 5:231–68; Robert W. Jenson, *God after God* (Indianapolis: Bobbs-Merrill, 1969), pp. 33–35.

63 John Macquarrie, *Principles of Christian Theology* (New York: Charles Scribner's Sons, 1966), pp. 94–110, 174–93; Paul Tillich, *Systematic Theology*, 3 vols. (Chicago: University of Chicago Press, 1951–63), 3:283–94.

64 On Barth's trinitarianism, see Eberhard Jüngel, *The Doctrine of the Trinity* (Grand Rapids: Wm. B. Eerdmans, 1976); Colin Gunton, *Becoming and Being* (New York and London: Oxford University Press, 1978), pp. 117–85.

65 For fuller analysis, and on the following, see Jenson, *God after God*, pp. 95–156.

66 Karl Barth, *Church Dogmatics*, vol. 1/1, trans. G. T. Thomson (Edinburgh: T. & T. Clark, 1936), pp. 32, 329.

67 Ibid., pp. 311–52.

68 Ibid., p. 312.

69 Ibid., pp. 321–22.

70 On this and the following, see ibid., pp. 101–8; there also citations.

71 Eberhard Jungel, "Das Verhältnis von 'ökonomischer' und 'immanenter' Trinität," *ZThK* 72 (1975): 363: "The concept of the divine

essence can no longer be thought in abstraction from the event of God's triune existence." This demand, nearly universal in contemporary theology, is variously met, most ambitiously by Karl Barth and "process theology."

72 Karl Rahner, *The Trinity*, trans. J. Donceel (New York: Herder & Herder, 1970), pp. 21–22; Jüngel, "Verhältnis."

73 Bluntly stated, e.g., by Tertullian, *Against Praxeas*, ix, 2–3.

74 E.g., Bonaventura, *Sentences*, vii, 1, ii.

75 Franz K. Mayr, "Trinitätstheologie und theologische Anthropologie," *ZThK* 68 (1971): 427–77.

Chapter 5: The Being of God

1 As in Altizer's use; Thomas J. J. Altizer, *The Gospel of Christian Atheism* (Philadelphia: Westminster Press, 1966).

2 E.g., Plato, *Phaedo*.

3 Wolfhart Pannenberg, "Die Aufnahme des philosophischen Gottesbegriffs als dogmatisches Problem der fruhchristlichen Theologie," *ZThK* 70 (1959): 1–45.

4 E.g., Aristotle, *Metaphysics*, 1028a, 13–15.

5 E.g., ibid., 1026a, 15–19.

6 John Gerhard, *Loci communes theologici*, ii, 93. Aquinas, *Summa Theologica*, i, 3, 3. Since Boethius, *essentia* was the standard theological equivalent for *ousia*, instead of *substantia*, which is more natural and used elsewhere. To compound confusion, translating *essentia*, where it stands for *ousia*, into English, we are compelled to revert to the anglicization of *substantia*.

7 See, e.g., Werner Marx, *The Meaning of Aristotle's "Ontology"* (The Hague: Nijhoff, 1954).

8 In Aristotle, see *Metaphysics*, bk. lambda.

9 Leslie Dewart, *The Future of Belief* (New York: Herder & Herder, 1966), pp. 134–43.

10 Peter Brunner, "Die Freiheit des Menschen in Gottes Heilsgeschichte," in *Pro Ecclesia*, vol. 1 (Berlin: Lutherisches Verlagshaus, 1962), p. 110.

11 Karl Barth, *Kirchliche Dogmatik* (Zürich: Zollikon, 1932–69), 2/1:288–305.

12 Ibid., p. 284.

13 Ibid., p. 300.

14 Ibid., pp. 306–61. On this, see Colin Gunton, *Becoming and Being* (New York and London: Oxford University Press, 1978), pp. 17–214; Robert W. Jenson, *God after God* (Indianapolis: Bobbs-Merrill, 1969).

15 E.g., John Cobb, *A Christian Natural Theology* (Philadelphia: Westminster Press; London: Lutterworth Press, 1965); Ralph E. James, *The Concrete God* (Indianapolis: Bobbs-Merrill, 1967); Schubert Ogden, *The Reality of God* (New York: Harper & Row, 1966).

16 I will be heavily dependent on Gunton, *Becoming and Being*, pp. 11–114.

17 E.g., Charles Hartshorne, *The Logic of Perfection* (La Salle, Ill.: Open Court Publishing Co., 1962), pp. 216ff.

18 On this paragraph, see, e.g., Charles Hartshorne, *A Natural Theology for Our Time* (La Salle, Ill.: Open Court Publishing Co., 1967), pp. 6–28; Charles Hartshorne, *The Divine Relativity: A Social Conception of God* (New Haven: Yale University Press, 1948), pp. 30–47, 67–75, 88–94.

19 P. F. Strawson, *Individuals: An Essay in Descriptive Metaphysics* (Garden City, N.Y.: Doubleday & Co.; London: Methuen, 1959).

20 *RGG*[3], s.v. "Person," by Wolfhart Pannenberg.

21 *RGG*[3], s.v. "Gott," by E. Würthwein.

22 Sten Konow, "Die Inder," in *Lehrbuch der Religionsgeschichte*, ed. Chantepie de la Saussaye (Tübingen: J. C. B. Mohr [Paul Siebeck], 1925), 2:1–88; Radakrishnan, *Indian Philosophy* (New York: Macmillan Co., 1923–27), 1:63–267; and vol. 2.

23 On the following, Emanuel Hirsch, *Geschichte der neuern evangelischen Theologie* (Gütersloh: Bertelsmann, 1949–54), 4:345–75. Also *RGG*[3], s.v. "Person," 232.

24 It is worth noting that this is the same dialectic by which Paul Tillich argued Jesus' qualification to be "final revelation": *Systematic Theology*, 3 vols. (Chicago: University of Chicago Press, 1951–63), 2:135–37.

25 For a change of reference, Johannes Pedersen, *Israel*, trans. A. J. Fausboll (London: Oxford University Press, 1926–40), 2:611–69.

26 Brunner, "Freiheit," pp. 109–10. This article is the best single investigation of the matter here at issue.

27 Aquinas, *Summa Theologica*, i, 78, introd.

28 Friedrich Schleiermacher, *Speeches on Religion to Its Cultured Despisers*, ii.

29 *Critique of Pure Reason* (1781), *Critique of Practical Reason* (1788), *Critique of Judgment* (1790).

30 Arthur Schopenhauer, *The World as Will and Idea*, ii, 19.

31 The first Protestant systematic theologian, Philip Melanchthon, built his entire systematics around the disconnection of mind and will in the fallen creature; *Loci communes* (1521) (T. Koldeed, 1890), pp. 68ff.

32 Neatly summarized in *RGG*[3], s.v. "Voluntarismus," by H. Blankhertz.

33 Martin Luther, *On the Bondage of the Will* (1525), hereafter cited in the text by pagination of *WA* 18. See Gerhard Forde, "Bound to Be Free: Luther on the Gospel and Human Freedom," *Bulletin of the Lutheran Theological Seminary, Gettysburg* 57 (Winter 1977): 3–16; Eberhard Jüngel, "Quae supra nos, nihil ad nos," *EvTh* 32 (1972): 197–240.

34 For more extensive analysis, especially on soteriological import, see Robert W. Jenson, *Visible Words* (Philadelphia: Fortress Press, 1978), pp. 120–39.

35 Ibid., pp. 34ff.

36 On this paragraph, see, e.g., G. van der Leeuw, *Religion in Essence and Manifestation*, trans. J. E. Turner (London: George Allen & Unwin, 1938), p. 21.

37 Cited from Evelyn Underhill, *Mysticism* (1910; repr., New York: Noonday, 1955), p. 320.

38 For further analysis, see Jenson, *Visible Words*.

39 Read Martin Luther's *Confession Concerning Christ's Supper* (1528), *LW* 37:151–372.

40 Ibid. One great Lutheran thinker, Johannes Brenz, developed a profound speculative understanding of space from this position of Luther; e.g., *Von der Mayestet unsers lieben Herrn und etnigen Heilands Jesu Christi* (1562).

Chapter 6: The Attributes of God

1 Martin Luther, *Theses for the Heidelberg Disputation*, WA 1:350–74, theses 19–20. English translations of these theses have not successfully dealt with the ingenious chiasmus of *conspicere* and *intelligere* and therefore miss most of the point.

2 The following is modeled on Aquinas, on whom see Ralph McInerny, *The Logic of Analogy* (The Hague: Nijhoff, 1961); George P. Klubertanz, *St. Thomas Aquinas on Analogy* (Chicago: Loyola University Press, 1960); Robert W. Jenson, *The Knowledge of Things Hoped For* (New York: Oxford University Press, 1969), pp. 67–85. That classic Protestantism followed the same general method can be seen from, e.g., John William Baier, *Compendium theologiae positivae* (1686–94), i, i, 4ff.

3 This "intellectual perception," *nous*, is the deepest and most original ideal of Greek theology; here it dominates the methodology of theology as elsewhere it dominates the matter. See Werner Marx, *The Meaning of Aristotle's "Ontology"* (The Hague: Nijhoff, 1954), pp. 11–16.

4 Behind this amendment lies that broad methodological movement in recent theology that can be represented in one of its aspects by Wolfhart Pannenberg, ed., *Revelation as History*, trans. D. Granskou (New York: Macmillan Co., 1968); and in another by Jenson, *Knowledge*.

5 For the intellectually most vigorous instance of this interpretation, see the work of James Cone, e.g., *A Black Theology of Liberation* (Philadelphia: J. B. Lippincott Co., 1970).

6 Aquinas, *Summa Theologica*, x; John Gerhard, *Loci communes theologici*, i, 137; and for an example from the Calvinist tradition, the

textbook of colonial American theology, William Ames, *The Marrow of Theology*, i, iv.

7 Aquinas, *Summa Theologica*, ix; Gerhard, *Loci communes theologici*, ii, 150; Ames, *Marrow of Theology*, i, iv.

8 Aristotle, *On Poesy*, 1452a, 1–11; 1554a, 33–36.

9 Standard Protestantism is materially identical; e.g., Gerhard, *Loci communes theologici*, ii, 171ff.

10 Pioneeringly analyzed by Thomas F. Torrance, *Time, Space, and Incarnation* (New York and London: Oxford University Press, 1969).

11 Gerhard, *Loci communes theologici*, ii, 172.

12 Martin Luther, *Confession Concerning Christ's Supper* (1528), WA 26:327ff.

13 Gerhard, *Loci communes theologici*, ii, 113.

14 *On the Bondage of the Will*, WA 18:619.

15 On this paragraph, J. N. D. Kelly, *Early Christian Creeds* (New York and London: Longmans, Green & Co., 1950), pp. 136ff.

16 Melito of Sardis, fragments xxxi, xvi.

17 On this, see Werner Elert, *Der Ausgang der altkirchlichen Christologie* (Berlin: Lutherisches Verlagshaus, 1957), pp. 71–169.

18 Ibid., pp. 105–9.

19 Ibid., pp. 165ff. The council's decree reads: "If someone does not confess that the one crucified in the flesh, the Lord Jesus Christ, is the true God and the Lord of Glory, and one of the Holy Trinity, let him be condemned" (*Sacrorum conciliorum nova et amplissima collectio*, ed. J. D. Mansi [Firenze, 1759–1827], 9:375).

20 Jaroslav Pelikan, *The Emergence of the Catholic Tradition* (Chicago: University of Chicago Press, 1971), pp. 176–82.

21 Aquinas, *Summa Theologica*, vi; Gerhard, *Loci communes theologici*, ii, 208–15.

Part II

Introduction

1 For our purposes, we need not concern ourselves with the history-of-religions background of the biblical use of "Spirit," since the same notion appears generally, so that where it comes from in a particular case is of purely historical interest.

2 For the Greek, a compendious presentation of the historical-linguistic facts is by Hermann Kleinknecht, in *TDNT* 6:332–59. For the Hebrew, anyone may check the passages in just the one book of Genesis: 1:2; 6:3, 17; 7:15, 22; 8:1; 26:35; 41:38; 45:17.

3 The classic study, which made clear that idealist pneumatology is a perversion, is Erich Schaeder, *Das Geistproblem in der Theologie*

(Leipzig: Deichert, 1924). Schaeder remained, however, method-
ologically within idealism, as he himself insisted; see, e.g., ibid.,
pp. 1–3. A complete break with idealism was first made by Karl Barth
in his writings in the 1920s. The most prominent recent work within
the idealist tradition (but attempting not very successfully to reckon
with biblical critique) is Paul Tillich, *Systematic Theology*, 3 vols.
(Chicago: University of Chicago Press, 1951–63), 3:11–30, 111–61.

Chapter 1: The Spirit That Spoke by the Prophets

1 See, e.g., Sigmund Mowinckel, *He That Cometh*, trans. G. Anderson
   (Oxford: Basil Blackwell, 1956).
2 Heinrich Kraft, "Die Anfänge des geistlichen Amts," *ThLz* 100
   (1975): 81–98.
3 Job 33:4; 34:14; Ps. 104:29–30.
4 We will mention only passages where the Spirit is explicitly named,
   to avoid all possible false extrapolations. This also enables us to
   avoid the dispute over the origin of archaic prophecy—on which see,
   for the bibliography and the position least favorable to our enterprise, Hans-Christoph Schmidt, "Prophetie und Tradition," *ZThK*
   74 (1977): 255–72.
5 Gerhard von Rad, *Old Testament Theology*, trans. D. M. G. Stalker,
   2 vols. (New York: Harper & Row, 1962–65), 1:310–11.
6 Ibid., 2:86–87.
7 E.g., ibid., 2:84–162. The extent to which primeval magical conceptions of the word's power are still alive in Mark is beside the point.
8 Ibid., 2:91–92.
9 Also Isa. 11:1–19; 28:5–6.
10 See Claus Westermann, *Isaiah 40–66*, trans. D. M. G. Stalker (Phila-
    delphia: Westminster Press, 1969), ad loc. "Servant Songs."
11 How seriously one should take the words of Moses in Num. 11:29 is
    difficult to judge: "Would that all the Lord's people were prophets,
    that the Lord would put his Spirit upon them."
12 The obvious conclusion of Westermann's exegesis in *Isaiah 40–66*,
    which Westermann will not draw, is that the servant is a prophet
    whose personal memory encompasses the whole history of prophecy
    (i.e., in patristic language, in whom the logos is incarnate) and who
    dies and rises again.
13 At least in Mark; see, e.g., Kraft, "Die Anfänge des geistlichen Amts,"
    cols. 91ff.
14 The point we make here is independent of what John may have meant.
15 This is the unanimous exegesis of the fathers, and a foundation of
    their ecclesiology.
16 For a quick survey of the New Testament, see Ernst Käsemann, in
    RGG[3] 2:1272–79.

17 E.g., Acts 11:27–28. On their importance, see Ernst Käsemann, "Sentences of Holy Law in the New Testament," in *New Testament Questions of Today*, trans. W. Montague (Philadelphia: Fortress Press, 1969), pp. 61–81.

18 Robert W. Jenson, *Visible Words* (Philadelphia: Fortress Press, 1978), pp. 191–94; there literature.

19 Georg Kretschmar, *Die Geschichte des Taufgottesdienstes in der Alten Kirche*, in *Leiturgia*, ed. K. F. Mueller and W. Blankenberg, vol. 4 (Kassel: Stauda, 1954).

20 1 Pet. 1:11–12; Acts 7:51–52; Heb. 3:9; 9:8; 10:15; Acts 28:25; 2 Pet. 1:21.

21 Rom. 9:1; 15:18–19; 1 Cor. 2:4; 7:40; Phil. 1:19; 1 Thess. 1:5.

22 Acts 4:31; 5:32; 6:3, 5, 10; 7:55–56; 13:4; 15:28; 19:21; 20:22–23.

23 Acts 8:29; 10:19–20; 11:12; 13:2, 4; 16:6–7; 21:4.

24 See, above all, the great Pauline argument, Rom. 8:1–27, exegeted below.

25 On the following, see Jenson, *Visible Words*, pp. 126–51; there literature and citations.

26 E.g., from various branches of the church, Heb. 6:4; Acts 2:38; 19:2–6; 1 Cor. 6:11; 12:13; 1 Pet. 3:18–21; Titus 3:5.

27 Throughout the Pauline corpus and John. Elsewhere, e.g., 1 Pet. 1:2; Heb. 6:4; Rev. 19:10–11; Eph. 1:13; 2:2.

28 See the order of the lists in 1 Corinthians and Romans, and the whole of 1 Corinthians 14, esp. v. 39. Paul can even return to simple identification of Spirit and prophecy; 2 Thess. 5:19–20.

29 On Paul's pneumatology in general, see Kurt Stalder, *Das Werk des Geistes in der Heiligung bei Paulus* (Zurich: Erziehungsverein, 1962), pp. 19–69.

30 The themes of this argument are by no means found only here in Paul. Practically the whole of it could be put together from other writings: 2 Cor. 1:22; 3:6, 8, 17–18; 5:5; Gal. 3:2–5; 4:6–7; 5:5, 16–25; 6:8. On the exegesis of this passage, see ibid., pp. 387–487.

31 This is clearly what *nomos* means here; v. 2.

32 ... *Apo tou nomou teshamartias kai ton thanatou* ... is subjective *and* objective genitive; v. 2.

33 *Ho ... nomos tou pneumatos tes zoes ... eleutherosen* ... is the same construction; v. 2.

34 *Hina* carries over both this immediately following clause and the subordinated phrase; v. 4.

35 Eduard Schweizer, in *TDNT* 7:124–44.

36 Note the string of sentences with *gar* from v. 3 through v. 8.

37 For the same opposition: Rom. 7:6; 2 Cor. 3:6.

38 Thus in Gal. 3:2–3, "hearing with faith" and "beginning with the Spirit" are the same.

39 *Dia tou enoikountes autou pneumatos en hymin.*

40 *En ho.*

41 *Stenazomen.*
42 *Hosautos.*
43 *Ten aparchen tou pneumatos.*
44 On this paragraph, see Hans-Jochen Jaschke, *Der Heilige Geist im Bekenntnis der Kirche* (Münster: Aschendorff, 1976), pp. 8–147.
45 G. W. H. Lampe's naivete about his own mild-Platonist presuppositions makes his *God as Spirit* (Oxford: At the Clarendon Press, *1977*) historically useless.
46 Ignatius, *To the Philadelphians*, viii; *To the Smyrneans*, introd.; x, 2; *To the Ephesians*, xviii, 1; *To the Magnesians*, introd.
47 On Irenaeus in general, see Gustaf Wingren, *Man and the Incarnation*, trans. Ross Mackenzie (Philadelphia: Fortress Press; Edinburgh: T. & T. Clark, 1959). There is now a monograph on Irenaeus' pneumatology and its historical location; Jaschke, *Der Heilige Geist*, which see on the following.
48 The opinion of some earlier scholarship that the third articles are merely composites of original third, fourth, fifth, etc., articles consolidated to fit the later trinitarian dogma is untenable; e.g., Jaschke, *Der Heilige Geist*, pp. 135ff.
49 The fourth-century but pre-Constantinople creed of Jerusalem, e.g., had exactly this set; text in J. N. D. Kelly, *Early Christian Creeds* (New York and London: Longmans, Green & Co., 1960), pp. 183–84, which see on this whole paragraph: pp. 82–94, 111–13, 155–66, 188–96. The epithets of the "Nicene," actually the Constantinopolitan, Creed, "the Lord, the giver of life," do not belong to this history. They were inserted by the fathers of Constantinople as functional equivalents for Nicaea's "of one being" of the Son, and belong to the dialectics of trinitarian theology, with "proceeds from the Father" and "with the Father the Son is worshiped and glorified."
50 In the Apostles' Creed "the forgiveness of sin" means the same as, e.g., "one baptism for the forgiveness of sins" in the "Nicene" Creed; ibid., pp. 160–61.
51 In the Apostles' Creed "communion of saints" is disputed, but probably means fellowship with past heroes of faith; thus it specifies that the extension of the church, just confessed, is not only in space ("catholic") but also in time; ibid., pp. 388–97.

Chapter 2: Pneumatological Soteriology

1 Tertullian, *On Penitence*, 6, 4.
2 Conveniently, E. Kahler in *RGG*³ 3:1639–40; there literature.
3 Above all in the antitheses of Rom. 3–5 and in the charism-doctrine.
4 That this correlative use of the language of substantiality and causality to both God and creatures is, as the scholastics said, by "analogy" does not affect the present point.

5 Conveniently, R. Lorenz in *RGG*³ 1:743–48.

6 In *Sacrorum conciliorum nova et amplissima collectio*, ed. J. D. Mansi (Venice, 1759ff.), 8:712ff, appended affirmations.

7 The *locus classicus* is Rom. 5:15–21. On the exegesis of this passage, and on Paul's general use of *charis, charisma,* and *dorea tou charitos,* see Kurt Stalder, *Das Werk des Geistes in der Heiligung bei Paulus* (Zurich: Erziehungsverein, 1962), pp. 363–87.

8 Gotthard Nygren, *The Augustinian Conception of Grace,* 71/64 (1957): 257–69; Etienne Gilson, *Christian Philosophy of Saint Augustine,* trans. S. Lynch (New York: Random House, 1960), pp. 143–64.

9 Aquinas, *Summa Theologica,* i–ii, 110, 3: "And so the gift of grace is a certain *quality.*"

10 The late-scholastic doctrine of "uncreated grace" and "created grace" is both the faithful formulation of this standard Western teaching and its *reductio ad heresiam.*

11 Johann Auer, *Die Entwicklung der Gnadmlehre in der Hochscholastik* (Freiburg, 1942–51), vol. 1.

12 An illuminating document of this conception is a work interesting and important in itself: Jonathan Edwards, "A Faithful Narrative of the Surprising Work of God" in Jonathan Edwards, *Works,* 6 vols. to date, ed. John Smith (New Haven: Yale University Press, 1957–), 4:144–211.

13 More fully, Robert W. Jenson, "On Recognizing the Augsburg Confession," in *The Role of the Augsburg Confession,* ed. Joseph A. Burgess (Philadelphia: Fortress Press, 1980), pp. 151–66.

14 The classic study is Regin Prenter, *Spiritus Creator,* trans. J. Jensen (Philadelphia: Fortress [Muhlenberg] Press, 1953).

15 From Quenstedt on, Lutheran dogmaticians have a major section with some such heading.

16 Pending the completion of more critical compendia, see Heinrich Schmid, *The Doctrinal Theology of the Evangelical Lutheran Church,* trans. Charles A. Hay and Henry E. Jacobs (Philadelphia: Lutheran Publication Society, 1889), pp. 413ff.

17 On the following, Erhard Peschke, *Studien zur Theologie August Hermann Franckes* (Berlin: Evangelical Press, 1964), pp. 28–42, 61–78.

18 Available in English translation in *The Augsburg Confession: A Collection of Sources,* ed. J. M. Reu (St. Louis: Concordia Seminary Press, n.d.), pp. 348ff. The Latin text is in *CR,* ed. C. C. Bretschneider (Braunschweig, 1859), 28:92–95.

19 For fuller discussion of this notion, see Eric Gritsch and Robert W. Jenson, *Lutheranism* (Philadelphia: Fortress Press, 1976), esp. pp. 2–7.

20 Indeed, the confessors asked only that the bishops "tolerate" them; Augsburg Confession, XVI, 2.

21 Against recent doubts on this score, see Jenson, "On Recognizing the Augsburg Confession."
22 For this and other viewpoints, see *The Role of the Augsburg Confession*, ed. Burgess; there also literature.
23 Vinzenz Pfnür, "Zur Verurteilung der reformatorischen Rechtfertigungslehre auf dem Konzil von Trient," *AHC* 8 (1976): 407–28.
24 E.g., *Canons and Decrees of the Council of Trent*, ninth session, V and VI, where we read such statements as that the grace of God works on sinners "so that they . . . may be disposed by [God's] energizing and helping grace to convert themselves to their own justification, freely assenting to and co-operating with that grace."
25 See, e.g., the scope set for the doctrine of predestination by the Lutheran Formula of Concord, Solid Declaration, XI, 13: The entire doctrine is to be considered as "the counsel, decision and determination of God in Christ Jesus, who is the real 'book of life,' is revealed to us through the Word."
26 That it does so was pointed out to the author by Jonathan Jenkins, research assistant in this work.
27 Aquinas, *Summa Theologica*, i, 23, 1.
28 Heinrich Heppe, ed., *Reformed Dogmatics Set Out and Illustrated from the Sources*, rev. ed., trans. G. Thomson (London: George Allen & Unwin, 1950), vii, 14.
29 Friedrich Schleiermacher, *The Christian Faith* (1830), ed. H. R. Mackintosh and J. S. Stewart (Edinburgh: T. & T. Clark, 1928), pp. 116–20.
30 Martin Luther, *On the Bondage of the Will*, WA 18:619: "For if you doubt . . . that God foreknows and wills all things, not contingently but necessarily and immutably, how will you be able . . . to rely on his promises?"
31 Ibid., p. 632: "Two things mandate the preaching of predestination; the first is the humiliation of our pride and the recognition of God's grace."
32 On the Hebrew Scriptures, in convenient summary, see Walther Zimmerli, *Old Testament Theology in Outline*, trans. D. E. Green (Atlanta: John Knox Press, 1978), pp. 21–58. The big notion is "covenant," which never means a "mutual" arrangement between Yahweh and Israel; see *THAT*, s.v. On the New Testament, see Erich Dinkier in *RGG*.³ 5:481–83.
33 Aquinas' analysis is summarized, with all necessary references, by Harry J. McSorley, *Luther: Right or Wrong?* (New York: Newman Press, 1969), pp. 148–54.
34 Aquinas, *Summa Theologica*, i, 83, 1, defines the notion: "Free will is a cause of its own process (*motus*), in that man by free will moves (*movet*) himself to action." That Aquinas then tries to make this cause theologically harmless by making it inefficacious without God's grace helps not at all, for either, at the level of actual preaching

and liturgy, this qualification is meaningless, or the posit of free will becomes itself meaningless, as Luther remarks in *Bondage of the Will, WA* 18:636: "What is an 'inefficacious' *power* except simply no power?"

35 Aquinas, *Summa Theologica*, i, 83, 1: "Although 'free will' can characterize an act . . . , according to its standard use it devotes rather a principle of the act, that by which man chooses freely. The principle of an act in us is a potentiality and a habit."

36 Karl Rahner, "Augustin und der Semipelagianismus," *ZKTh* 62 (1938): 171–96.

37 This is the doctrine of *intuitu fidei* or *praevisa fide.* John Gerhard, *Loci communes theologici* (1610), ii, ix, 14: "We say, therefore, that those are elected by God from eternity for salvation; whom . . . he foresees will truly believe and persevere in faith to the end of life." See Hans Emil Weber, *Reformation, Orthodoxie und Rationalismus* (Gütersloh: Gerd Mohn, 1940), 1/2:93–104; 2:166–75.

38 E.g., Formula of Concord, Solid Declaration, XI. See Werner Elert, *The Structure of Lutheranism*, trans. Walter A. Hansen, 2 vols. (St. Louis: Concordia Publishing House, 1962), 1:10–11.

39 Karl Barth, *Kirchliche Dogmatik* (Zurich: Zollikon, 1932–67), 2/2:1–563, which is cited here from this German original (pp. 102, 111) because the English translation is unreliable. On Barth's doctrine of election, see Robert W. Jenson, *Alpha and Omega* (New York: Thomas Nelson & Sons, 1963).

40 See the logically doomed struggles of the Formula of Concord, Solid Declaration, IX, 41ff.

41 On the following, see Jenson, *Alpha and Omega*; there references.

42 Also this is anticipated in the Formula of Concord, Solid Declaration, XI, 29–30, 73–75.

43 Luther, *Bondage of the Will, WA* 18:633.

Chapter 3: Spirit-Discourse as the Church's Self-Interpretation

1 The epochal presentation of pneumatology as eccelesial christology is Schleiermacher's, exhaustively presented and criticized by Wilfried Brandt, *Der Heilige Geist und die Kirche bei Schleiermacher* (Zurich: Zwingli, 1968).

2 1 Cor. 11:27. The point, if developed, would make the *locus* on the sacraments.

3 On the following history of the *filioque* ("and from the Son") controversy, see Dietrich Ritschl, "The History of the Filioque Controversy," in *Conflicts about the Holy Spirit*, ed. Hans Küng and Jürgen Moltmann (New York: Seabury Press, 1979), pp. 3–14; on the Eastern tradition, see Werner Jaeger, *Gregor von Nyssa's Lehre vom Heiligen Geist*

(Leiden: E. J. Brill, 1966), pp. 122–53; in Augustine, who initiated the Western tradition, see esp. *On the Trinity*, xv, 17, 27–29.

4   If this point is not apparent, note the alternative below.

5   The standard history of the formative years of the struggle is Hans von Campenhausen, *Ecclesiastical Authority and Spiritual Power in the Church of the First Three Centuries*, trans. J. Baker (London: A. & C. Black, 1969). For a more complete statement of the author's analysis, see Robert W. Jenson, *Visible Words* (Philadelphia: Fortress Press, 1978), pp. 188–97. The clash of charisma and office goes back to the church's very beginning, if the interpretation of Matt. 7:22–23 and 23:8–10 offered by Käsemann is correct; Ernst Kasemann, "Die Anfänge christlicher Theologie," *ZThK* 57 (1960): 163–71.

6   On the following, see Jenson, *Visible Words*, pp. 197ff.

7   On the following history, see Bernhard Poschman, *Busse und Letzte Ölung*, vol. 4, fasc. 3 of *HDG*.

8   W. H. C. Frend, *The Donatist Church* (Oxford: At the Clarendon Press, 1971).

9   Esp. Augustine, *On Baptism against the Donatists*. See James Breckenridge, "Augustine and the Donatists," *Foundation* 19 (1976): 69–77.

10 The charismatic claims for the official ministry appear as soon as the latter itself appears; Ignatius, *To the Smyrneans*, viii.

11 Roy J. Enquist, "Afrikaner Religion as a Model of Liberation Theology," *Dialog* 17 (1978): 207–11.

12 E.g., Robert McAfee Brown, *Theology in a New Key* (Philadelphia: Westminster Press, 1978).

13 Briefly, Walther Zimmerli, *Old Testament Theology in Outline*, trans. D. E. Green (Atlanta: John Knox Press, 1978), pp. 105ff.

14 Classically, Mircea Eliade, *Cosmos and History*, trans. W. R. Trask (New York: Harper & Row, 1959).

15 E.g., *The Thirty-Nine Articles of Religion*, VI: "Holy Scripture containeth all things necessary to salvation: so that whatsoever is not read therein, nor may be proved thereby, is not to be required of any man, that it should be believed as an article of the Faith . . . ;" *The Formula of Concord*, Solid Declaration, "On . . . the Norm," 3: the "prophetic and apostolic writings" are "the pure and limpid fountain of Israel and the sole true measure, by which all teachers and teachings are to be judged."

16 The title of Augustine's study of hermeneutics.

17 *Augsburg Confession*, V, 4. On the bases of Luther's opposition to enthusiasm and on its dogmatization in this confessional article, see Inge Lonning, "The Reformation and the Enthusiasts," in *Conflicts about the Holy Spirit*, pp. 3–14.

18 Robert L. Tuveson, *Millennium and Utopia* (Berkeley: University of California, 1949).

19 On the following, see Kurt Aland, "Bemerkungen zum Montanismus und zur frühchristlichen Eschatologie," in *Kirchengeschichtliche Entwürfe* (Gütersloh: Gerd Mohn, 1960), pp. 105–48; here the Montanist oracles are edited and collected. See also Douglas Powell, "Tertullian and the Cataphrygians," *VigChr* 29 (1975): 33–54; Jaroslav Pelikan, *The Christian Tradition: A History of the Development of Doctrine*, vol. 1, *The Emergence of the Catholic Tradition (100–600)* (Chicago: University of Chicago Press, 1971), pp. 98ff., 106ff.

20 In Aland, "Bemerkungen," p. 114.

21 Ibid.

22 Ibid., pp. 132–33.

23 Hans von Campenhausen, *Die Entstehung der christlichen Bibel* (Tübingen: J. C. B. Mohr [Paul Siebeck], 1968), pp. 236–70.

24 Jean-Jacques Rousseau, *The Social Contract*; see esp., ii, 3.

25 See Ralph E. Stavins, "Political Ethics," in *Religion and the Dilemma of Nationhood*, ed. Sydney E. Ahlstrom (Minneapolis: Lutheran Church in America, 1976), pp. 30–42.

26 Perry Miller, *The New England Mind* (Cambridge, Mass.: Harvard University Press, 1939–53).

27 On the history, see Sydney E. Ahlstrom, *A Religious History of the American People* (New Haven: Yale University Press, 1972), pp. 385–428, 637–47, 749–804, 842–94.

28 On the history, see Walter Hollenweger, *Enthusiastisches Christentum* (Zurich: Zollikon, 1969).

29 William Savarin, *Tongues of Men and Angels* (New York: Macmillan Co., 1972).

30 See, still, Hans Jonas, *Gnosis und spätantiker Geist*, 2d ed., 2 vols. (Göttingen: Vandenhoeck and Ruprecht, 1954), vol. I, pp. 178–90, 199–214, 243–83.

31 See Jenson, *Visible Words*, pp. 126–43.

32 Every few years somebody rediscovers the gnostics and proclaims them the "real" Christians. Anybody who wants to be a gnostic may, and there is no way to register "Christian" as a trademark. But someone who cannot tell that the New Testament documents one faith and, for example, the interesting Nag Hammadi texts another, is clearly not to be trusted out alone in the world.

33 On this paragraph, see Hans-Jochen Jaschke, *Der Heilige Geist im Bekenntnis der Kirche* (Münster: Aschendorff, 1976), pp. 181–86, 277–82, 299–303.

34 Irenaeus, *Demonstration of the Apostolic Preaching*, vii, xvii, 1.

35 The Greek tradition itself did not call its upper ontological level *pneuma*; H. Kleinknecht, in *TDNT*, s.v.

36 Aquinas, *Summa Theologica*, i, 36, 1.

37 On the whole history of scholastic difficulty at this point, through Luther's radical innovations, see Hartmut Hilgenfeld, *Mittelalterlich-traditionelle Elemente in Luthers Abendmahlsschriften* (Zurich: Theologischer Verlag, 1971), pp. 183–232.

38 Martin Luther, *Confession of the Lord's Supper* (1528), WA 26:352.

Chapter 4: Cosmic Spirit

1 This identification may have been facilitated by the general fluidity of Theophilus' distinction between the Logos and the Spirit; e.g., *To Autolycus*, 1, 7; ii, 22.

2 There apparently is Jewish tradition behind this. The identification of Wisdom and Spirit persists even through Tertullian, Eustathius of Antioch, and Origen. See Georg Kretschmar, *Studien zur frühchristlichen Trinitätstheologie* (Tübingen: J. C. B. Mohr [Paul Siebeck], 1956), pp. 40–61.

3 Irenaeus, *Against All Heresies*, iv, vii, 4.

4 Hans-Jochen Jaschke, *Der Heilige Geist im Bekenntnis der Kirche* (Münster: Aschendorff, 1976), pp. 257–59.

5 Ibid., pp. 261ff.

6 Irenaeus, *Demonstration of the Apostolic Preaching*, 5.

7 Ibid., 97.

8 On Hegel in general, see Charles Taylor, *Hegel* (Cambridge: At the University Press, 1975).

9 Aristotelian fragment 46, 1483a, 24–28: "*ho theos e nous estin e epekeina ti tou nou*." The motionlessness of Mind *is* its deity; see Aristotle, *Metaphysics*, xiii, 7–9.

10 Especially on the following, see Georg W. F. Hegel, *Phenomenology of Mind* ("mind" is a bad translation of "Geist"), trans. J. Baillie, 2d ed. (London: George Allen & Unwin, 1931); *Lectures on the Philosophy of History*, trans. J. Sibree (London: H. G. Bohn, 1861), introd.

11 The writer's insistence is on "but also in that which is to come," but we note that "not only in this age, but" is also there.

12 On the profound ambiguity of Hegel's system at all such points, see, e.g., Hans Küng, *Menschwerdung Gottes* (Freiburg: Herder Verlag, 1970).

13 On this paragraph, see Robert W. Jenson, "The Kingdom of America's God," in *Religion and the Dilemma of Nationhood*, ed. Sydney E. Ahlstrom (Minneapolis: Lutheran Church in America, 1976), pp. 6–14.

14 E.g., Lewis S. Ford, *The Lure of God* (Philadelphia: Fortress Press, 1978), pp. 29–44, 99–112; G. Palmer Pardington III, "The Holy Ghost Is Dead—the Holy Spirit Lives," in *Religious Experience and Process Theology*, ed. Harry J. Cargas and Bernard Lee (New York: Paulist Press, 1976), pp. 121–38.

15 For the author's principle objections to process-theology, see his review of John Cobb's *Christ in a Pluralistic Age*, in *Interp.* 31 (1977): 307–11.

16 For a precise statement at the heart of the matter, see Hans Reichenbach, *Philosophic Foundations of Quantum Mechanics* (Berkeley: University of California, 1944), pp. 1–44.

17 E.g., Pierre Teilhard de Chardin, *The Future of Man*, trans. N. Denny (New York: Harper & Row, 1964).

18 Text in *Prex Eucharistica*, ed. A. Hänggi and J. Pahl (Freiburg: University of Freiburg, 1968), pp. 82–100.

19 Classically by Immanuel Kant, *Critique of Judgment*.

20 For the following, see, on our particular concern, Serge Boulgakof, *Le Paraclet*, trans. from the Russian by C. Andrioni (Paris: Aubier, 1946), pp. 171–219; a general description, concentrating on our range of topics and with all possible documentation, is given by Charles Graves, *The Holy Spirit in the Theology of Sergius Bulgakov* (Geneva: World Council of Churches, 1972).

21 John Meyendorff, *A Study of Gregory Palamas*, trans. G. Lawrence (Leighton Buzzard, Eng.: Faith Press, 1964); Vladimir Lossky, *The Vision of God*, trans. A. Moorhouse (Clayton, Wis.: American Orthodox Press, 1963), pp. 124–37; Leon Zander, "Die Weisheit Gottes im russischen Glauben und Denken," in *KuD* 2 (1956): 29–53.

22 On the following, Graves, *Holy Spirit*, pp. 7–29.

23 Boulgakof, *Le Paraclet*, p. 176.

24 Indeed, ibid., p. 179: "These masculine and feminine principles [from Gen. 1:27], where there is impressed the image of divine Wisdom, of prototypical humanity, are the translation into created language of the distinction and unity of the Logos and the Holy Spirit, in Wisdom."

25 Ernst Benz, "Sophia-Visionen des Westens," in *The Ecumenical World of Orthodox Civilization*, ed. Andrew Blane (The Hague: Mouton, 1974), pp. 121–38.

26 Zander, "Die Weisheit Gottes."

27 Wagner's ideal.

28 Karl Barth, *Die protestantische Theologie im 19. Jahrhundert*, 2d ed. (Zurich: Zollikon, 1952), pp. 411–12.